CALAMITY KATE ™

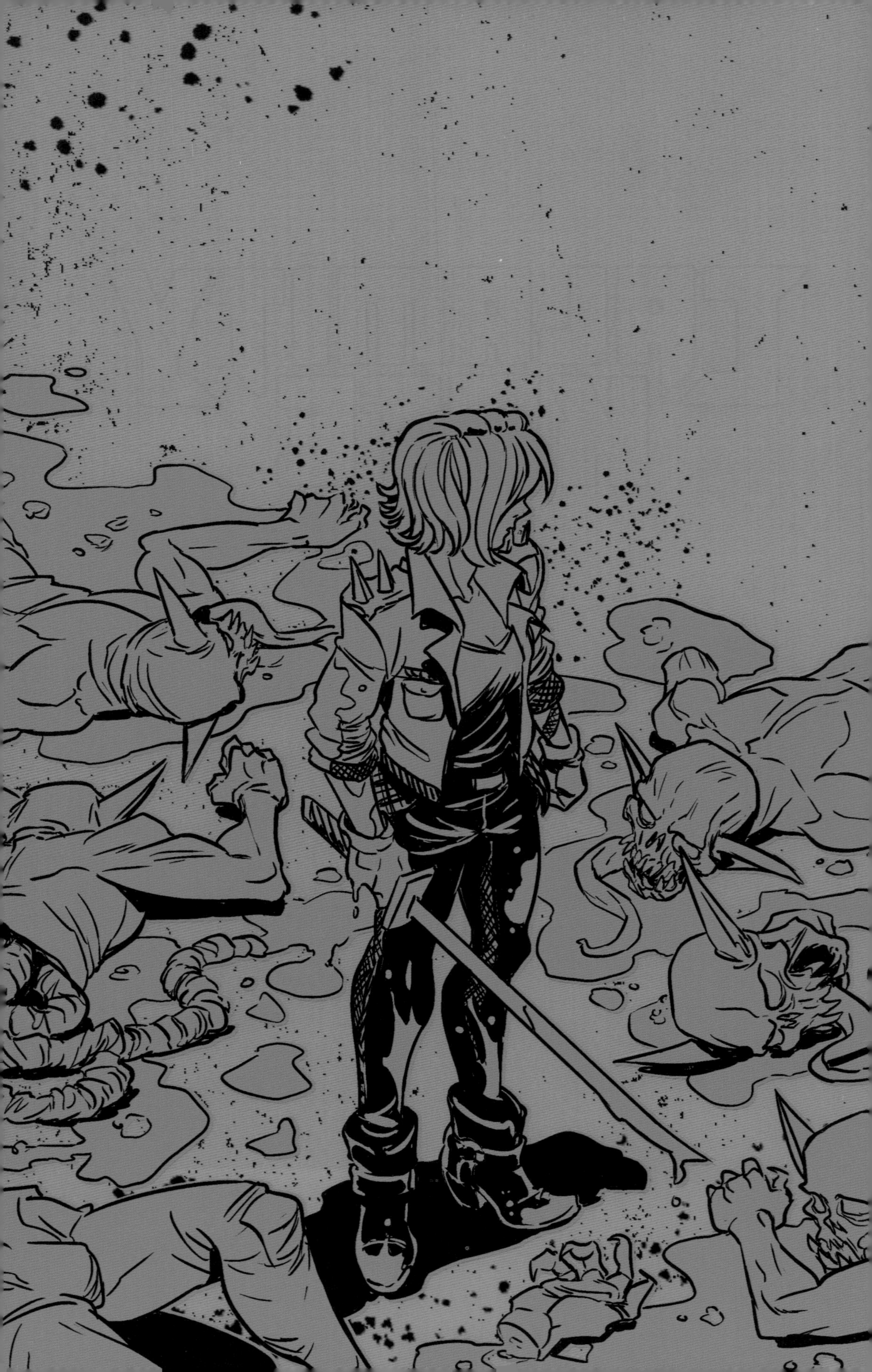

CALAMITY KATE

WRITTEN BY **MAGDALENE VISAGGIO**

ART BY **CORIN HOWELL**

COLORS BY **VALENTINA PINTO**

LETTERS BY **ZAKK SAAM**

CHAPTER BREAKS BY
**CORIN HOWELL, TANA FORD,
JAMES STOKOE, JENN ST-ONGE,** AND
BECKY CLOONAN

CALAMITY KATE CREATED BY
MAGDALENE VISAGGIO AND **CORIN HOWELL**

DARK HORSE BOOKS

PUBLISHER **MIKE RICHARDSON**
EDITOR **DANIEL CHABON**
ASSISTANT EDITORS **CHUCK HOWITT** AND **BRETT ISRAEL**
DESIGNER **BRENNAN THOME**
DIGITAL ART TECHNICIAN **JOSIE CHRISTENSEN**

COLLECTS ISSUES #1–#4 OF THE DARK HORSE COMICS SERIES *CALAMITY KATE*

Library of Congress Cataloging-in-Publication Data

Names: Visaggio, Magdalene, writer, cover artist. | Howell, Corin, artist. |
  Pinto, Valentina, 1987- colourist. | Saam, Zakk, letterer.
Title: Calamity Kate / written by Magdalene Visaggio ; art by Corin Howell ;
  colors by Valentina Pinto ; letters by Zakk Saam ; cover by Corin Howell
  with Valentina Pinto.
Description: First edition. | Milwaukie, OR : Dark Horse Books, 2019. |
  "Calamity Kate created by Magdalene Vissagio and Corin Howell" | "Collects
  issues #1-#4 of the Dark Horse Comics series Calamity Kate"
Identifiers: LCCN 2019018988 | ISBN 9781506711881 (paperback)
Subjects: LCSH: Comic books, strips, etc. | BISAC: COMICS & GRAPHIC NOVELS /
  Fantasy.
Classification: LCC PN6728.C3353 V57 2019 | DDC 741.5/973--dc23
LC record available at https://lccn.loc.gov/2019018988

PUBLISHED BY
DARK HORSE BOOKS
A DIVISION OF DARK HORSE COMICS LLC
10956 SE MAIN STREET
MILWAUKIE, OR 97222

DARKHORSE.COM

TO FIND A COMICS SHOP IN YOUR AREA, VISIT COMICSHOPLOCATOR.COM

FIRST EDITION: OCTOBER 2019
978-1-50671-188-1

1 3 5 7 9 10 8 6 4 2
PRINTED IN CHINA

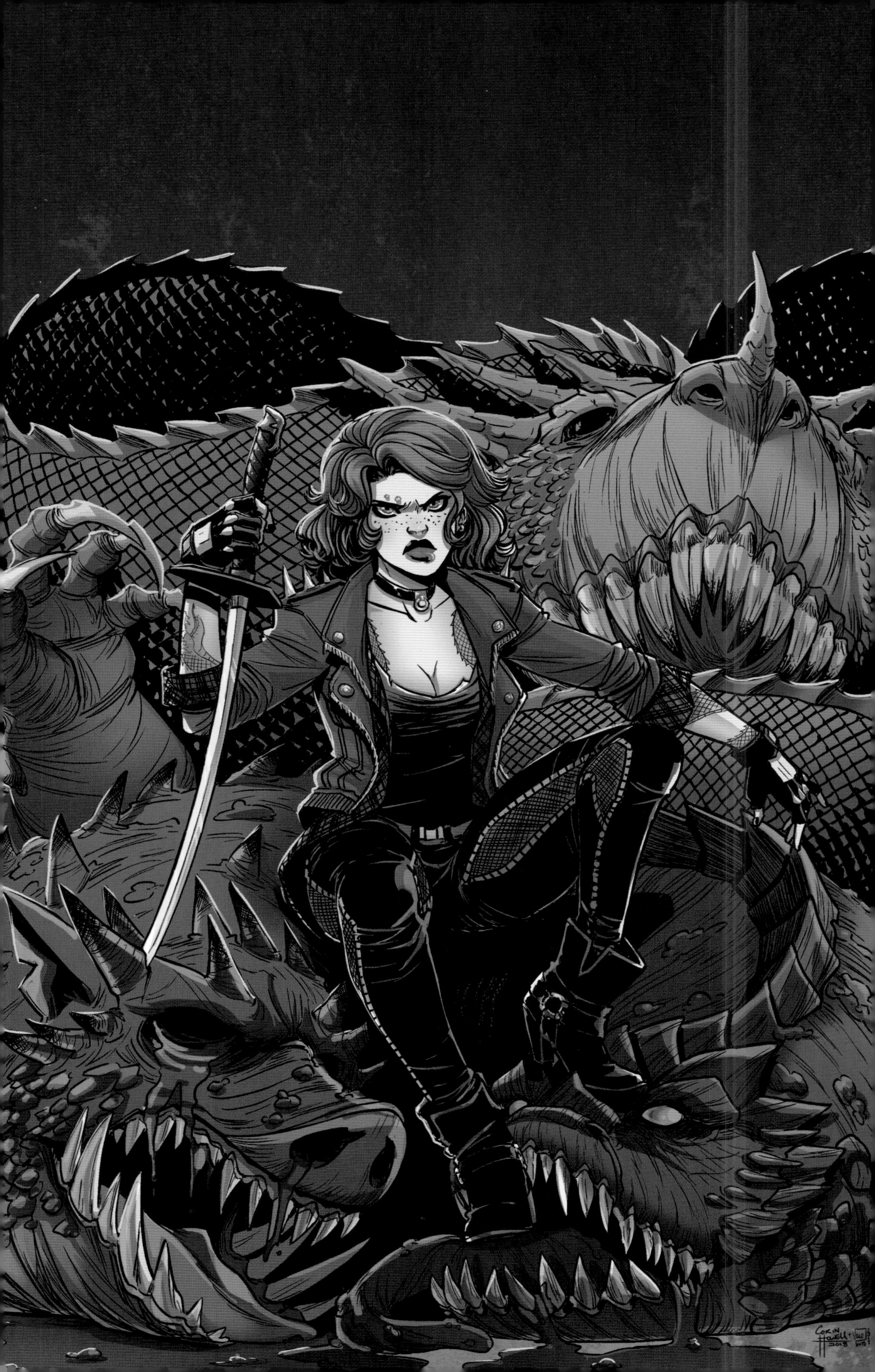

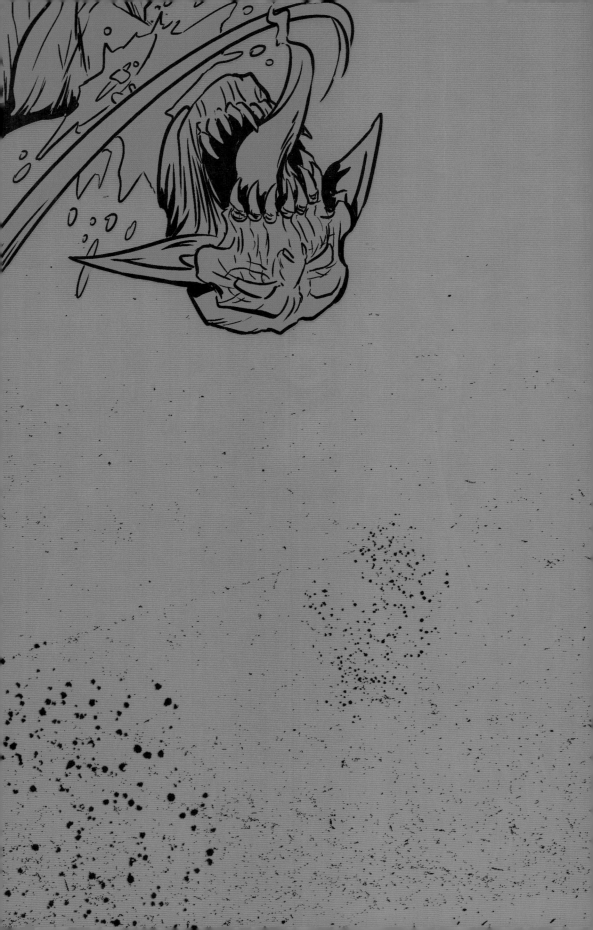

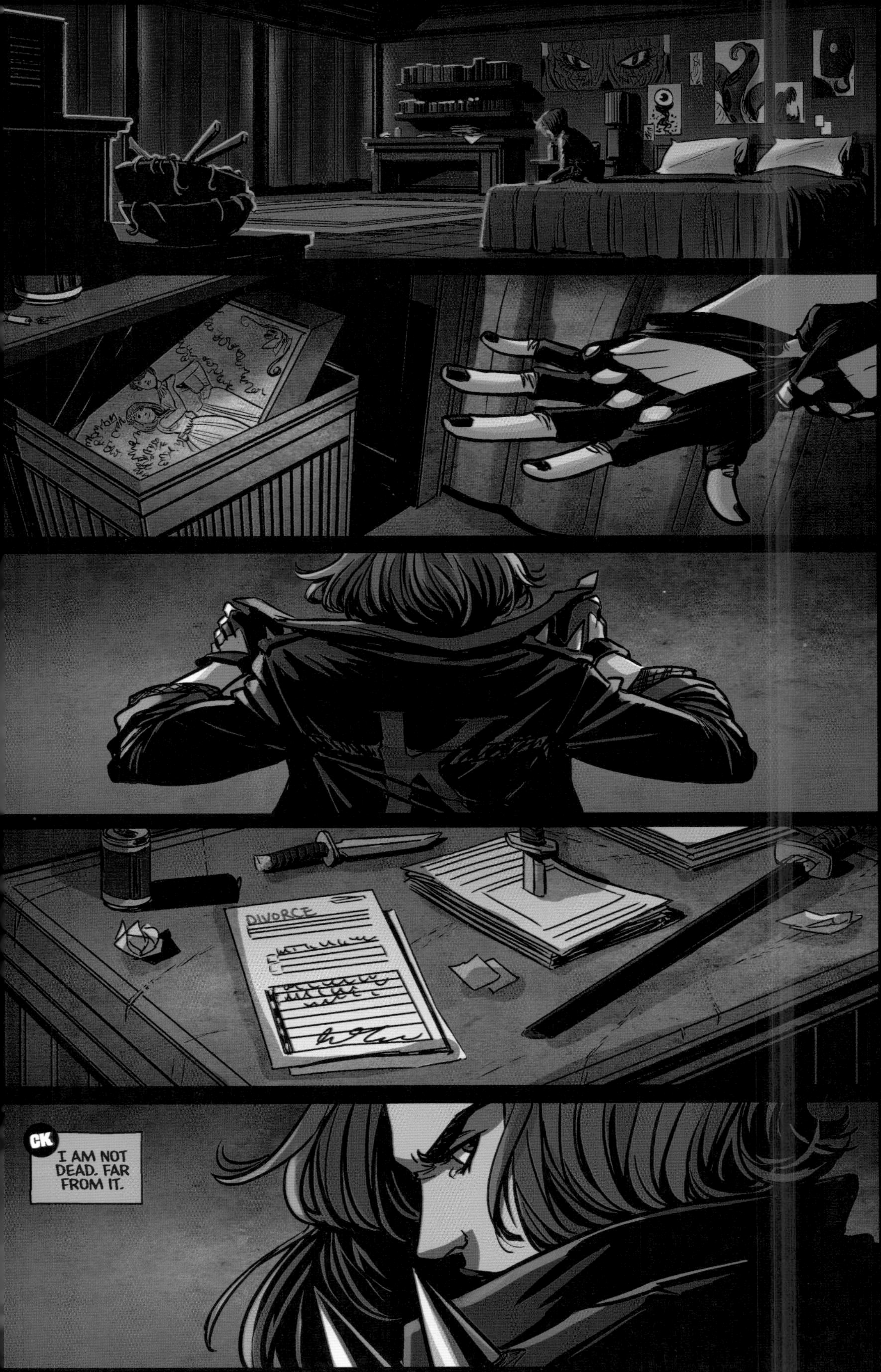
CK
I AM NOT DEAD. FAR FROM IT.
DIVORCE

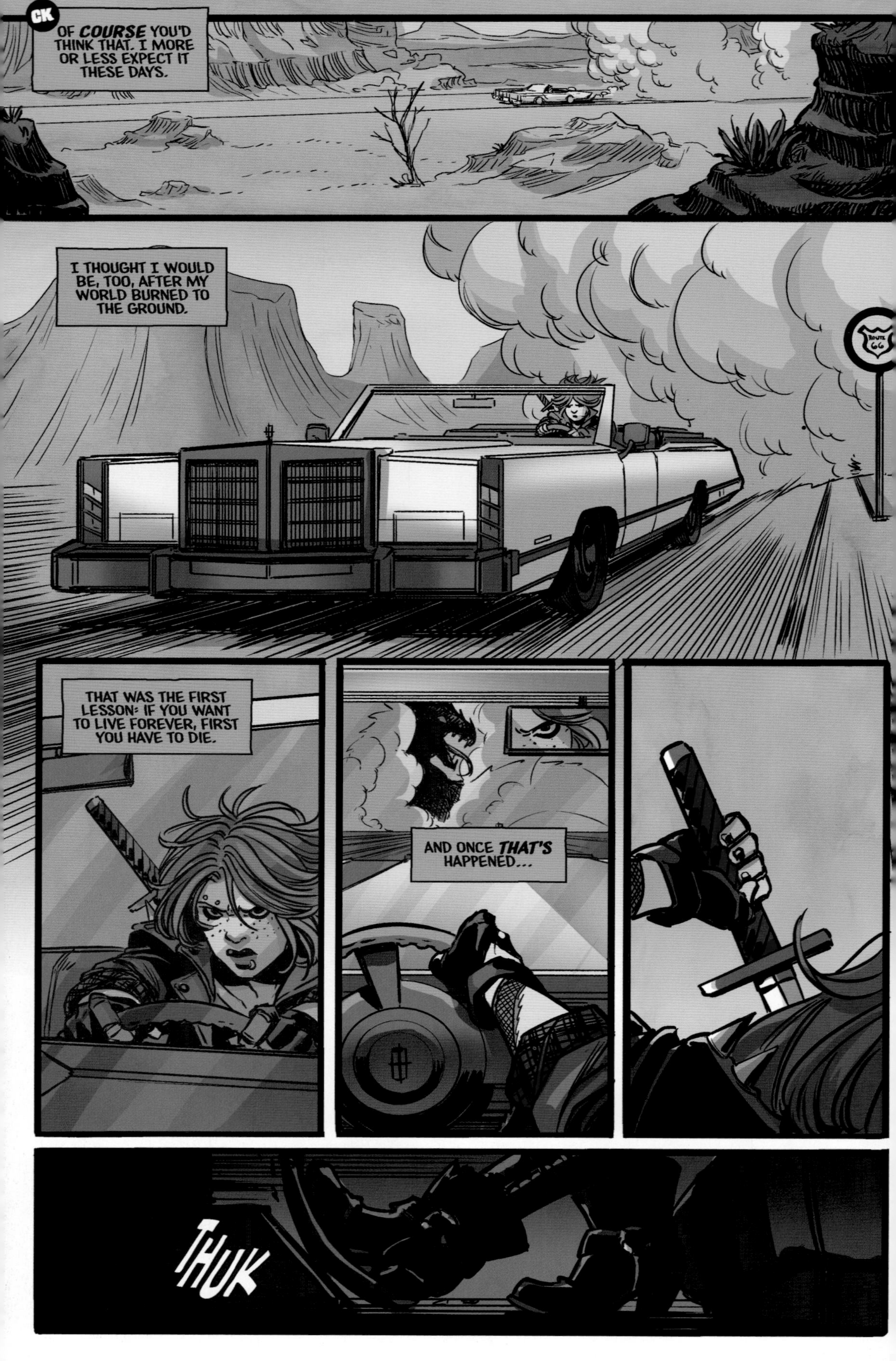
CK
OF COURSE YOU'D THINK THAT. I MORE OR LESS EXPECT IT THESE DAYS.
I THOUGHT I WOULD BE, TOO, AFTER MY WORLD BURNED TO THE GROUND.
ROUTE 66
THAT WAS THE FIRST LESSON: IF YOU WANT TO LIVE FOREVER, FIRST YOU HAVE TO DIE.
AND ONCE THAT'S HAPPENED...
THUK

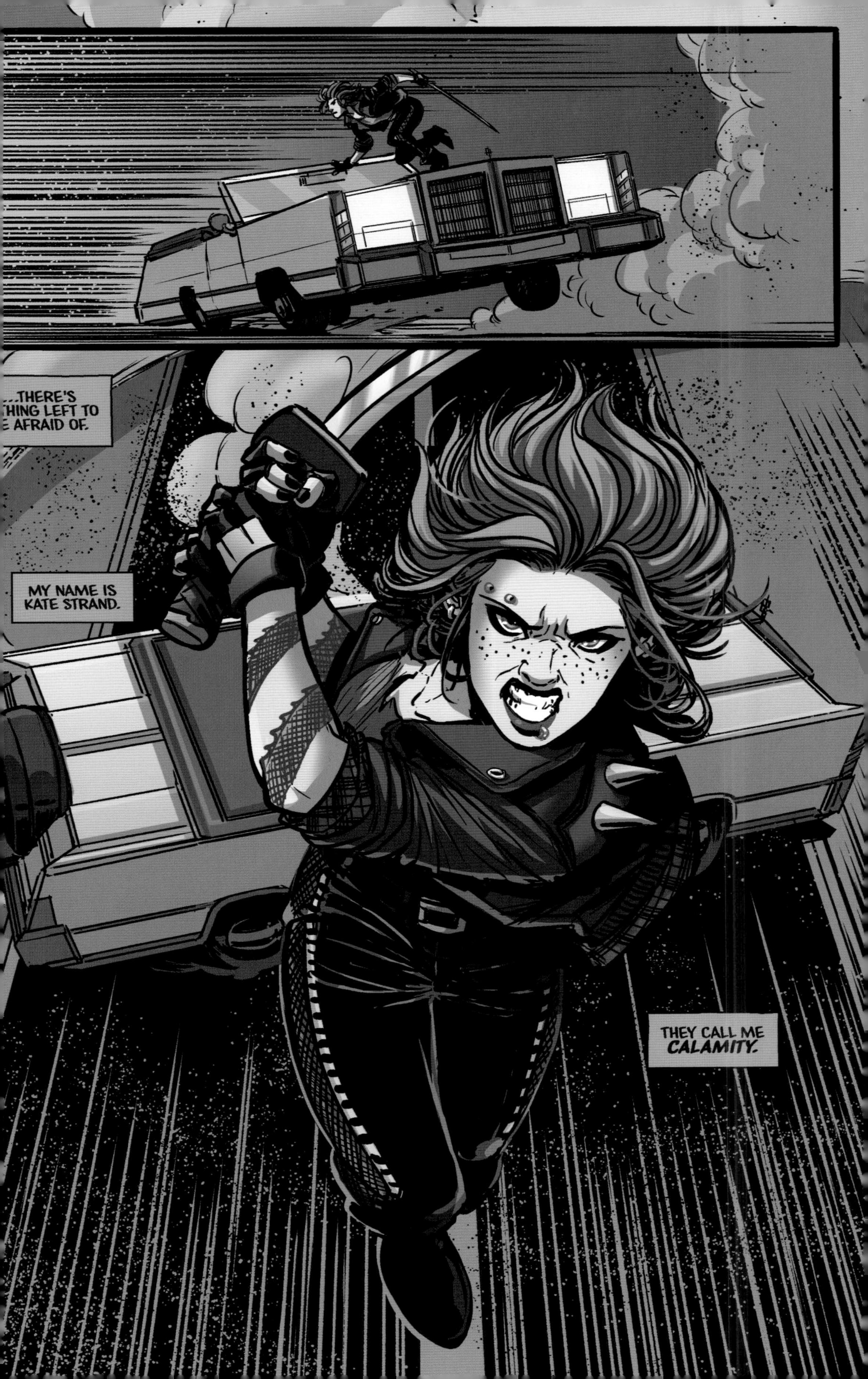
...THERE'S
THING LEFT TO
E AFRAID OF.
MY NAME IS KATE STRAND.
THEY CALL ME CALAMITY.

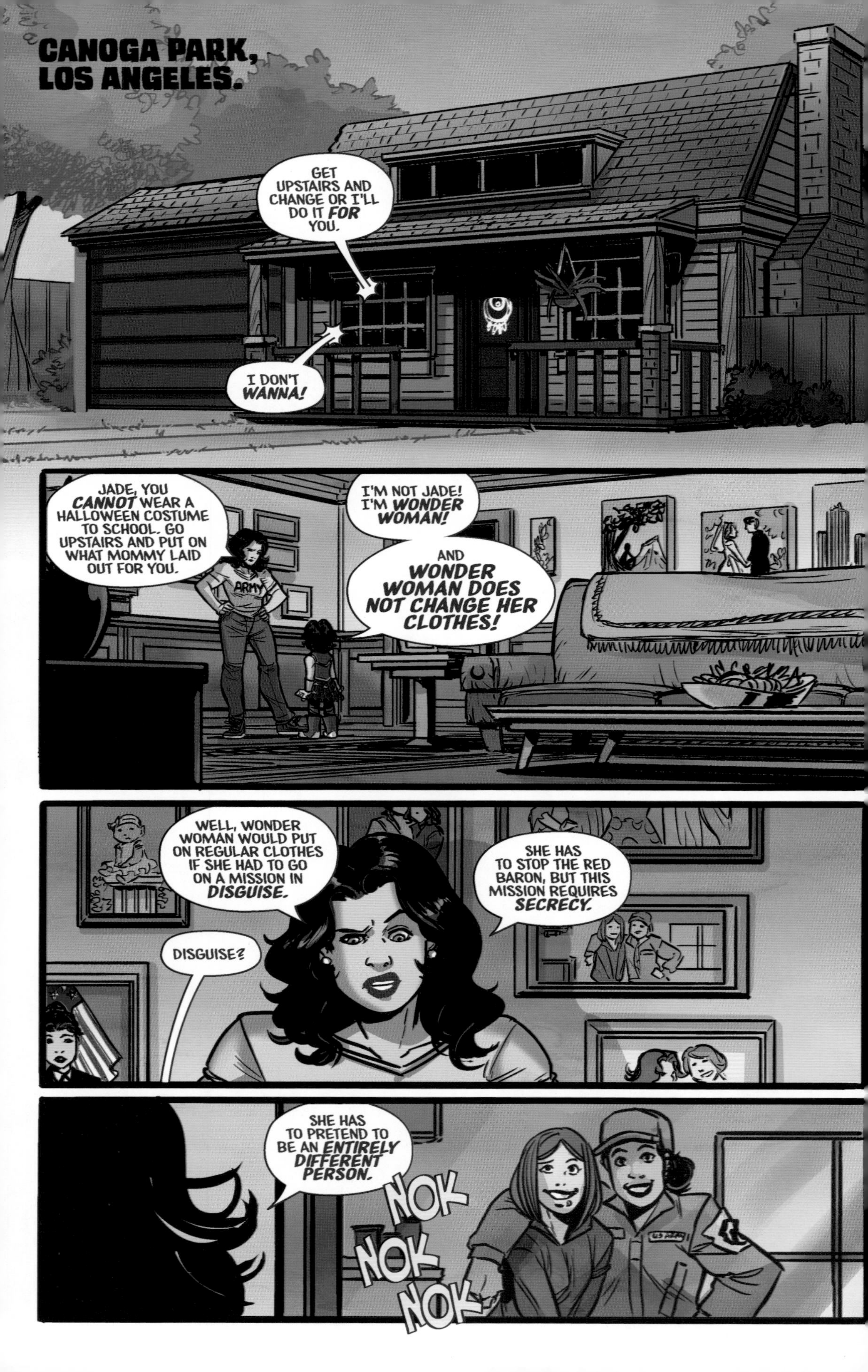
CANOGA PARK, LOS ANGELES.
GET UPSTAIRS AND CHANGE OR I'LL DO IT FOR YOU.
I DON'T WANNA!
JADE, YOU CANNOT WEAR A HALLOWEEN COSTUME TO SCHOOL. GO UPSTAIRS AND PUT ON WHAT MOMMY LAID OUT FOR YOU.
I'M NOT JADE! I'M WONDER WOMAN!
AND WONDER WOMAN DOES NOT CHANGE HER CLOTHES!
WELL, WONDER WOMAN WOULD PUT ON REGULAR CLOTHES IF SHE HAD TO GO ON A MISSION IN DISGUISE.
DISGUISE?
SHE HAS TO STOP THE RED BARON, BUT THIS MISSION REQUIRES SECRECY.
SHE HAS TO PRETEND TO BE AN ENTIRELY DIFFERENT PERSON.
NOK
NOK
NOK

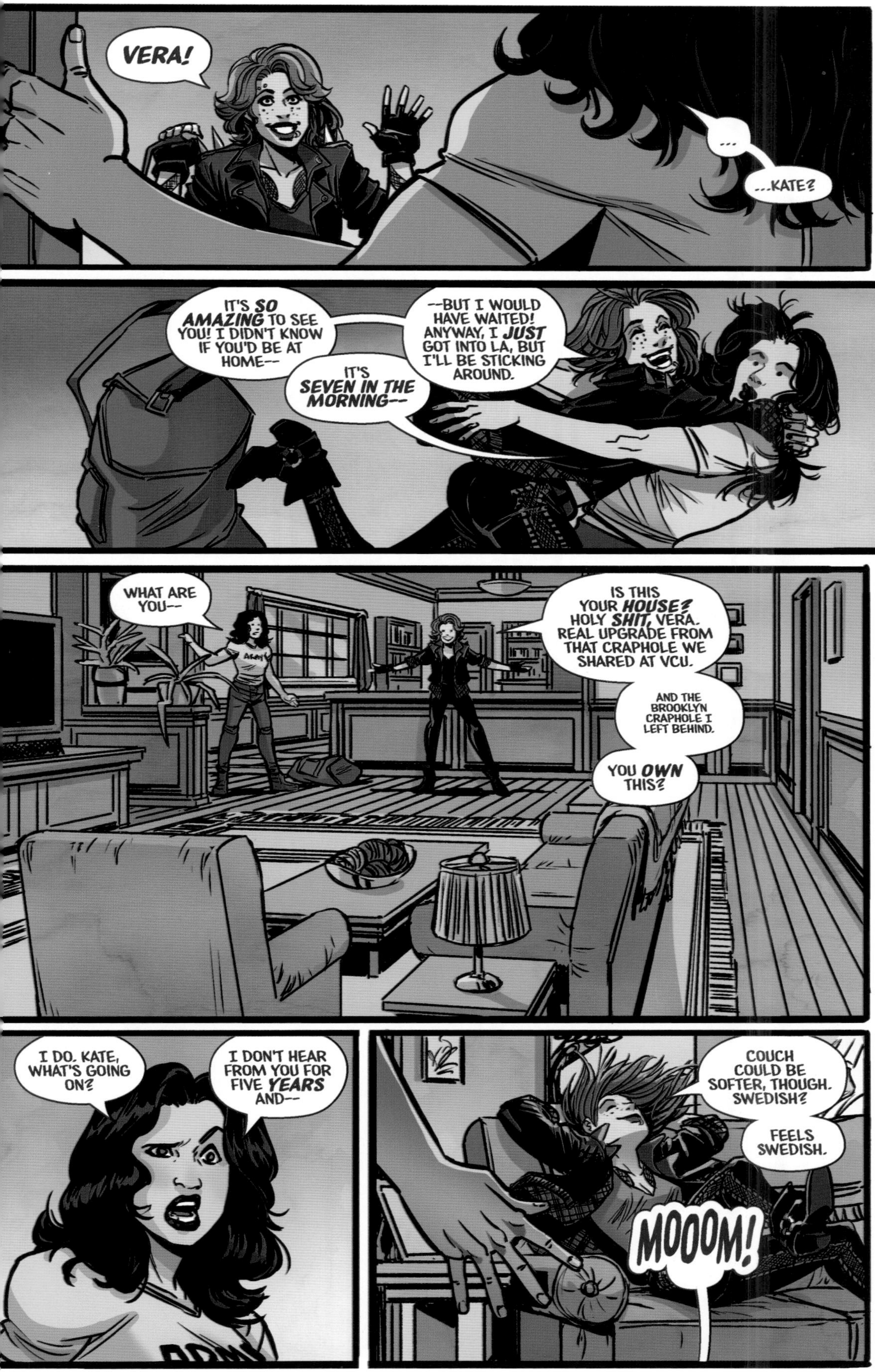
VERA!
...
...KATE?
IT'S SO AMAZING TO SEE YOU! I DIDN'T KNOW IF YOU'D BE AT HOME--
IT'S SEVEN IN THE MORNING--
--BUT I WOULD HAVE WAITED! ANYWAY, I JUST GOT INTO LA, BUT I'LL BE STICKING AROUND.
WHAT ARE YOU--
IS THIS YOUR HOUSE? HOLY SHIT, VERA. REAL UPGRADE FROM THAT CRAPHOLE WE SHARED AT VCU.
AND THE BROOKLYN CRAPHOLE I LEFT BEHIND.
YOU OWN THIS?
I DO. KATE, WHAT'S GOING ON?
I DON'T HEAR FROM YOU FOR FIVE YEARS AND--
COUCH COULD BE SOFTER, THOUGH. SWEDISH?
FEELS SWEDISH.
MOOOM!

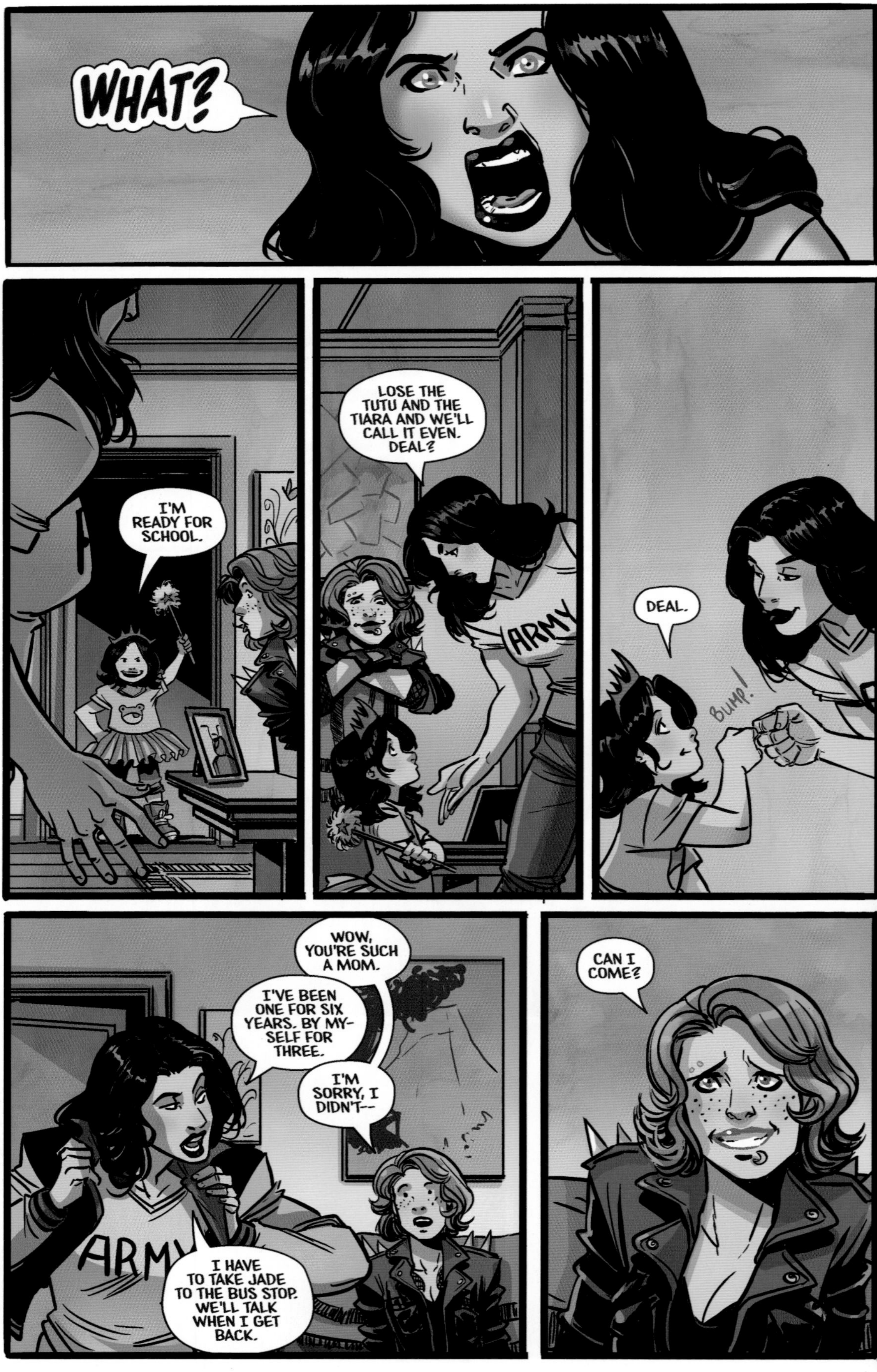
WHAT?
I'M READY FOR SCHOOL.
LOSE THE TUTU AND THE TIARA AND WE'LL CALL IT EVEN. DEAL?
ARMY
DEAL.
BUMP!
WOW, YOU'RE SUCH A MOM.
I'VE BEEN ONE FOR SIX YEARS. BY MY-SELF FOR THREE.
I'M SORRY, I DIDN'T--
ARMY
I HAVE TO TAKE JADE TO THE BUS STOP. WE'LL TALK WHEN I GET BACK.
CAN I COME?

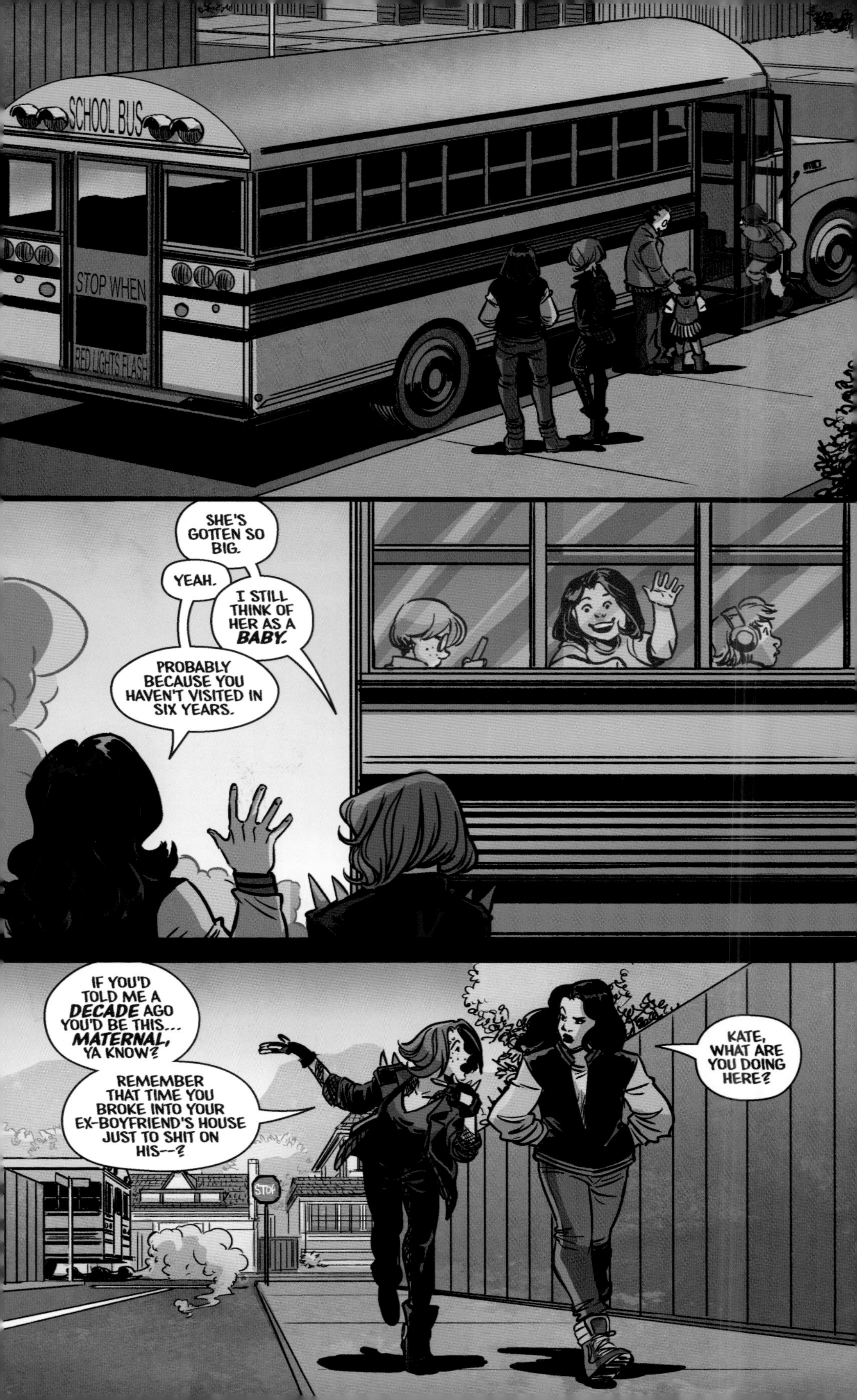
SCHOOL BUS
STOP WHEN
RED LIGHTS FLASH
SHE'S GOTTEN SO BIG.
YEAH.
I STILL THINK OF HER AS A BABY.
PROBABLY BECAUSE YOU HAVEN'T VISITED IN SIX YEARS.
IF YOU'D TOLD ME A DECADE AGO YOU'D BE THIS... MATERNAL, YA KNOW?
REMEMBER THAT TIME YOU BROKE INTO YOUR EX-BOYFRIEND'S HOUSE JUST TO SHIT ON HIS--?
KATE, WHAT ARE YOU DOING HERE?
STOP

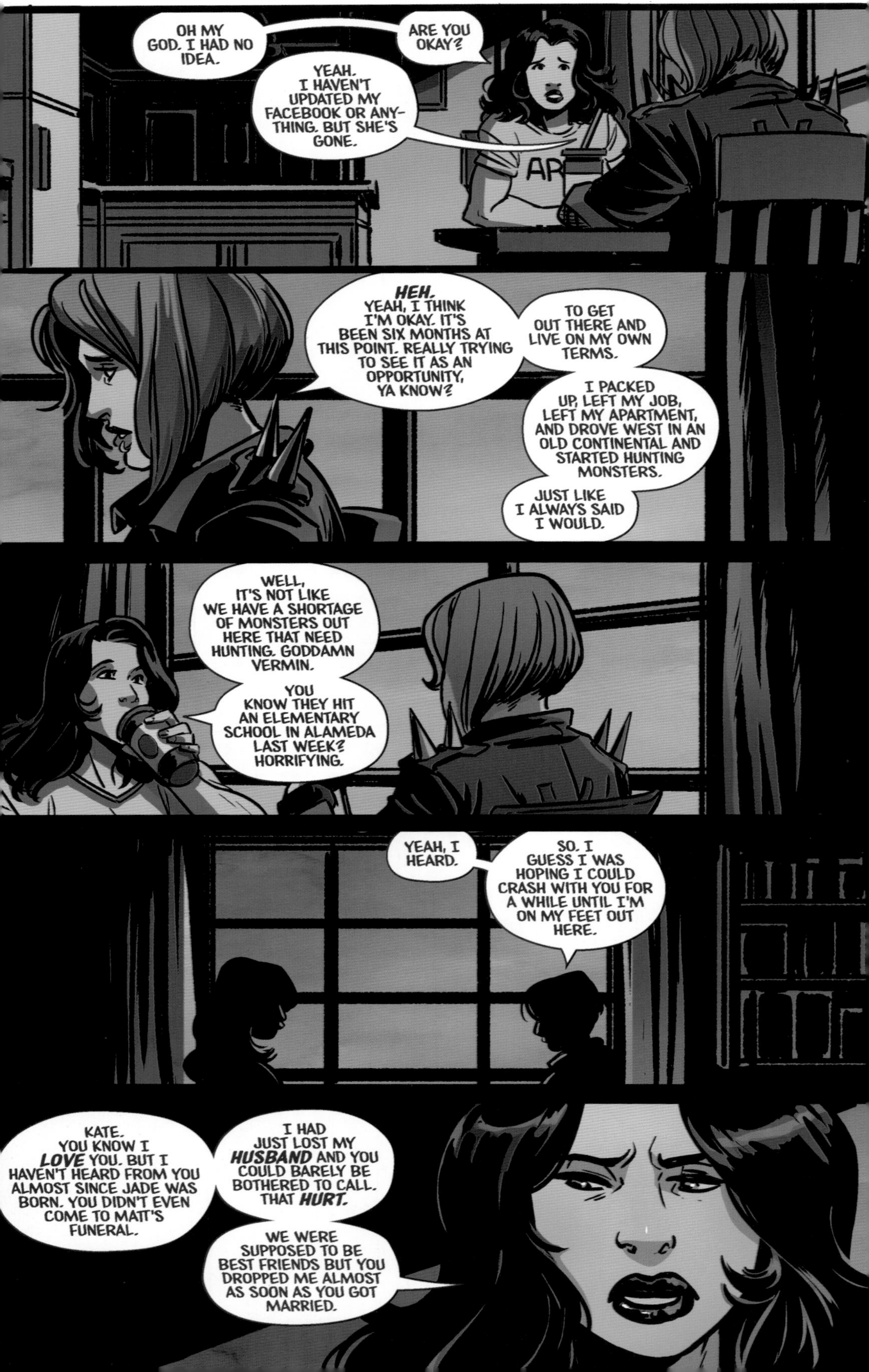

OH MY GOD. I HAD NO IDEA.
ARE YOU OKAY?
YEAH. I HAVEN'T UPDATED MY FACEBOOK OR ANY-THING. BUT SHE'S GONE.
AR
HEH. YEAH, I THINK I'M OKAY. IT'S BEEN SIX MONTHS AT THIS POINT. REALLY TRYING TO SEE IT AS AN OPPORTUNITY, YA KNOW?
TO GET OUT THERE AND LIVE ON MY OWN TERMS.
I PACKED UP, LEFT MY JOB, LEFT MY APARTMENT, AND DROVE WEST IN AN OLD CONTINENTAL AND STARTED HUNTING MONSTERS.
JUST LIKE I ALWAYS SAID I WOULD.
WELL, IT'S NOT LIKE WE HAVE A SHORTAGE OF MONSTERS OUT HERE THAT NEED HUNTING. GODDAMN VERMIN.
YOU KNOW THEY HIT AN ELEMENTARY SCHOOL IN ALAMEDA LAST WEEK? HORRIFYING.
YEAH, I HEARD.
SO, I GUESS I WAS HOPING I COULD CRASH WITH YOU FOR A WHILE UNTIL I'M ON MY FEET OUT HERE.
KATE. YOU KNOW I LOVE YOU. BUT I HAVEN'T HEARD FROM YOU ALMOST SINCE JADE WAS BORN. YOU DIDN'T EVEN COME TO MATT'S FUNERAL.
I HAD JUST LOST MY HUSBAND AND YOU COULD BARELY BE BOTHERED TO CALL. THAT HURT.
WE WERE SUPPOSED TO BE BEST FRIENDS BUT YOU DROPPED ME ALMOST AS SOON AS YOU GOT MARRIED.

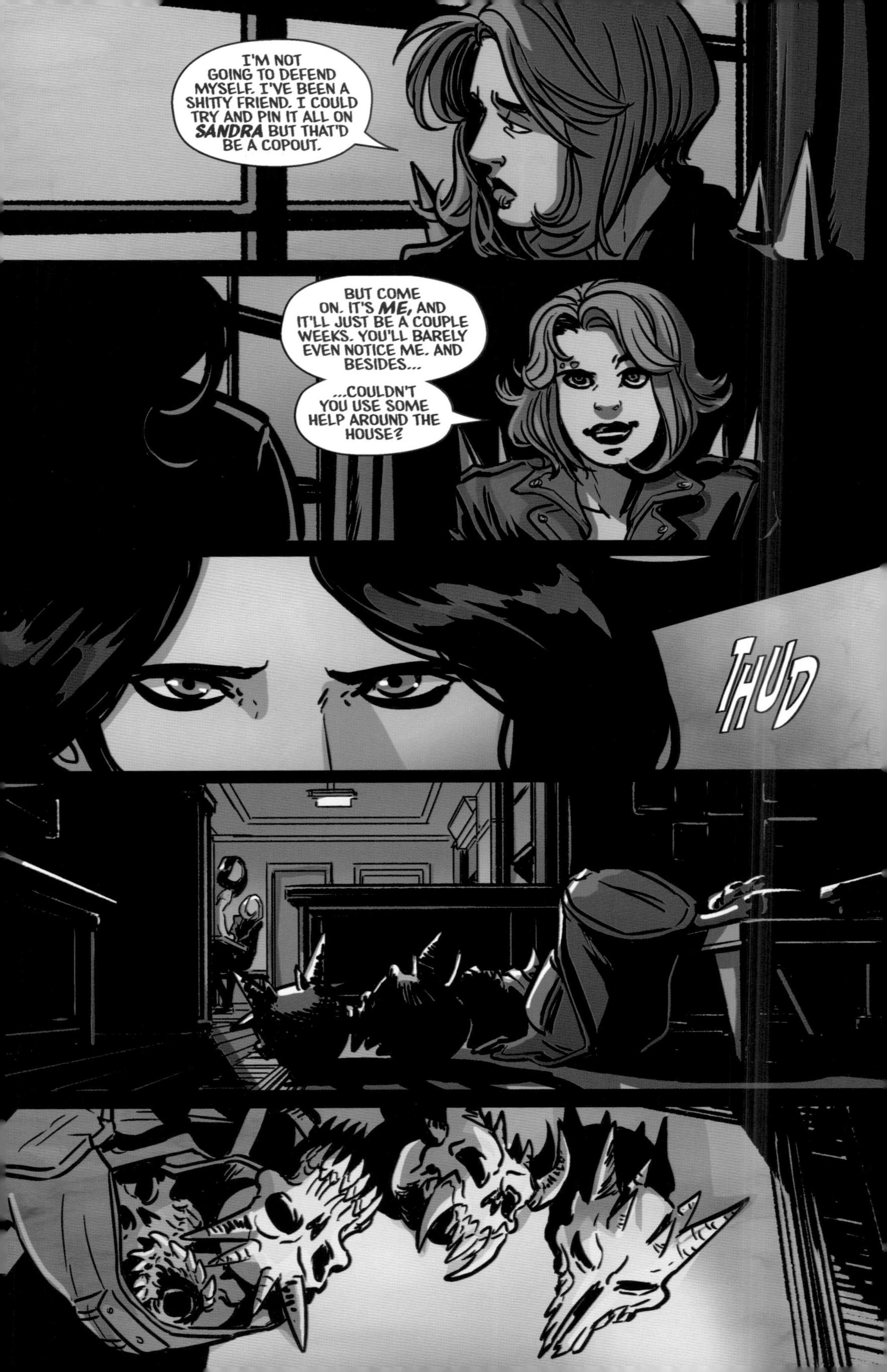
I'M NOT GOING TO DEFEND MYSELF. I'VE BEEN A SHITTY FRIEND. I COULD TRY AND PIN IT ALL ON SANDRA BUT THAT'D BE A COPOUT.
BUT COME ON. IT'S ME, AND IT'LL JUST BE A COUPLE WEEKS. YOU'LL BARELY EVEN NOTICE ME. AND BESIDES...
...COULDN'T YOU USE SOME HELP AROUND THE HOUSE?
THUD

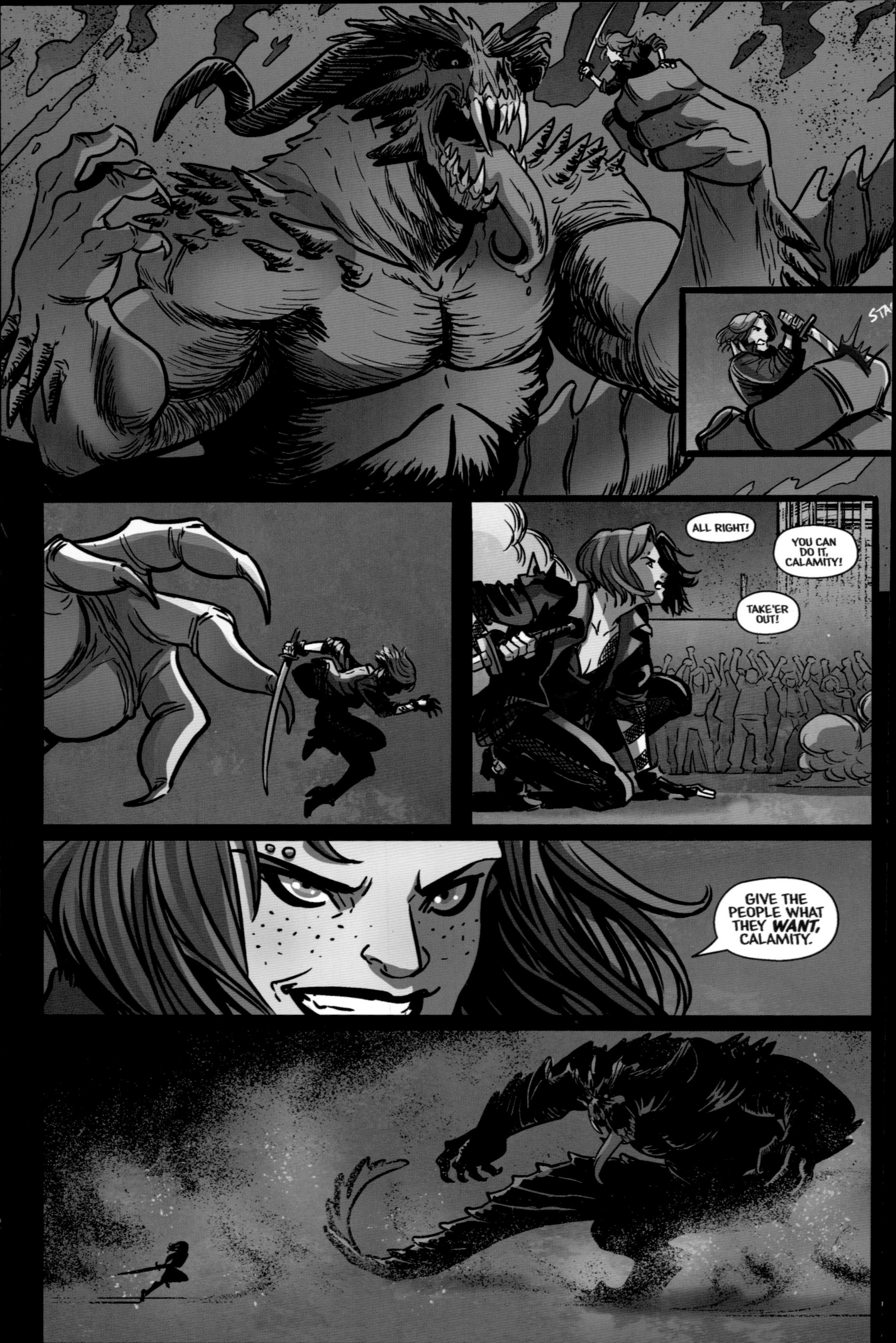
ALL RIGHT!
YOU CAN DO IT, CALAMITY!
TAKE'ER OUT!
GIVE THE PEOPLE WHAT THEY *WANT,* CALAMITY.

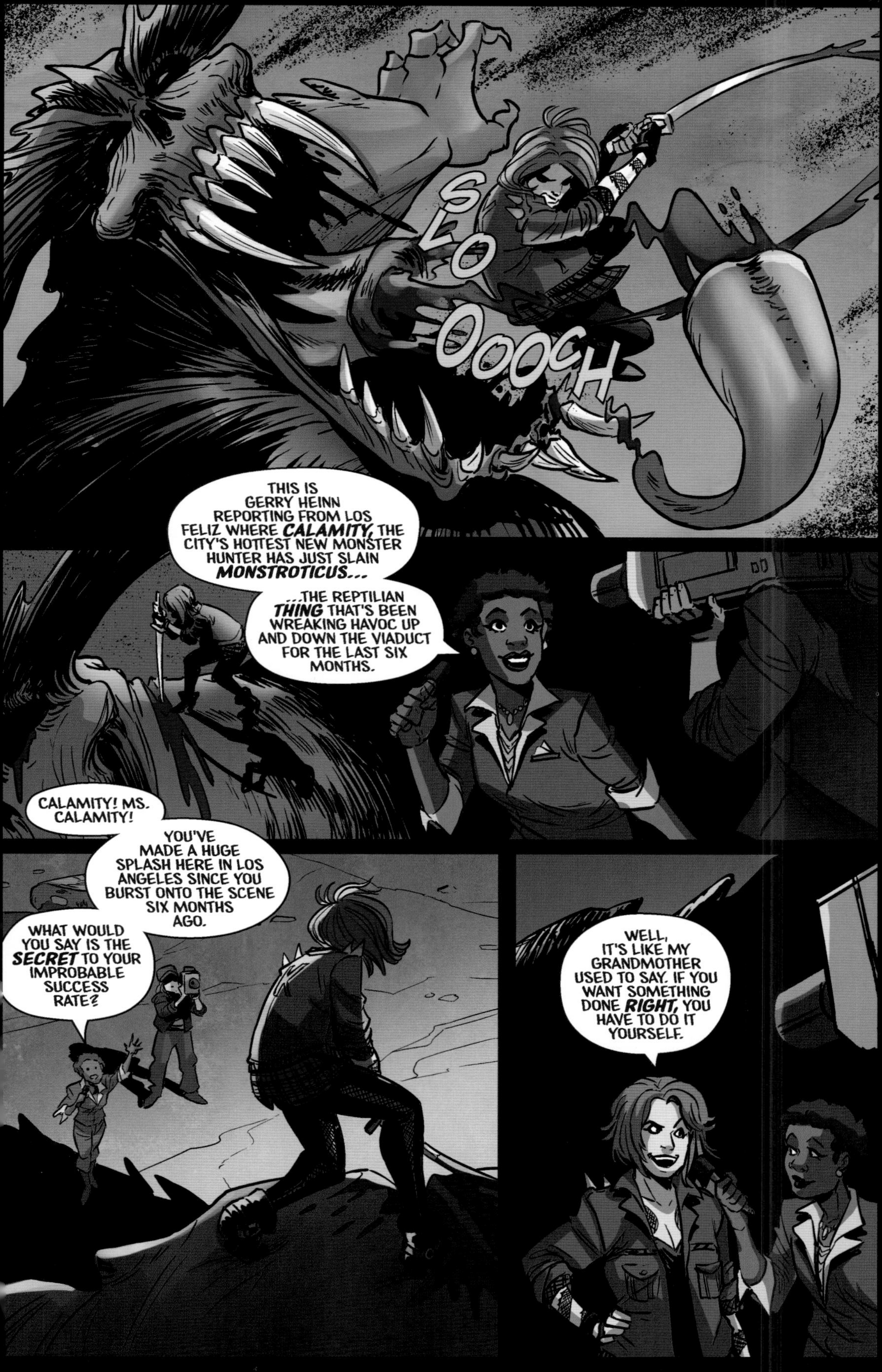

SLOOOOCH
THIS IS GERRY HEINN REPORTING FROM LOS FELIZ WHERE CALAMITY, THE CITY'S HOTTEST NEW MONSTER HUNTER HAS JUST SLAIN MONSTROTICUS...
...THE REPTILIAN THING THAT'S BEEN WREAKING HAVOC UP AND DOWN THE VIADUCT FOR THE LAST SIX MONTHS.
CALAMITY! MS. CALAMITY!
YOU'VE MADE A HUGE SPLASH HERE IN LOS ANGELES SINCE YOU BURST ONTO THE SCENE SIX MONTHS AGO.
WHAT WOULD YOU SAY IS THE SECRET TO YOUR IMPROBABLE SUCCESS RATE?
WELL, IT'S LIKE MY GRANDMOTHER USED TO SAY. IF YOU WANT SOMETHING DONE RIGHT, YOU HAVE TO DO IT YOURSELF.

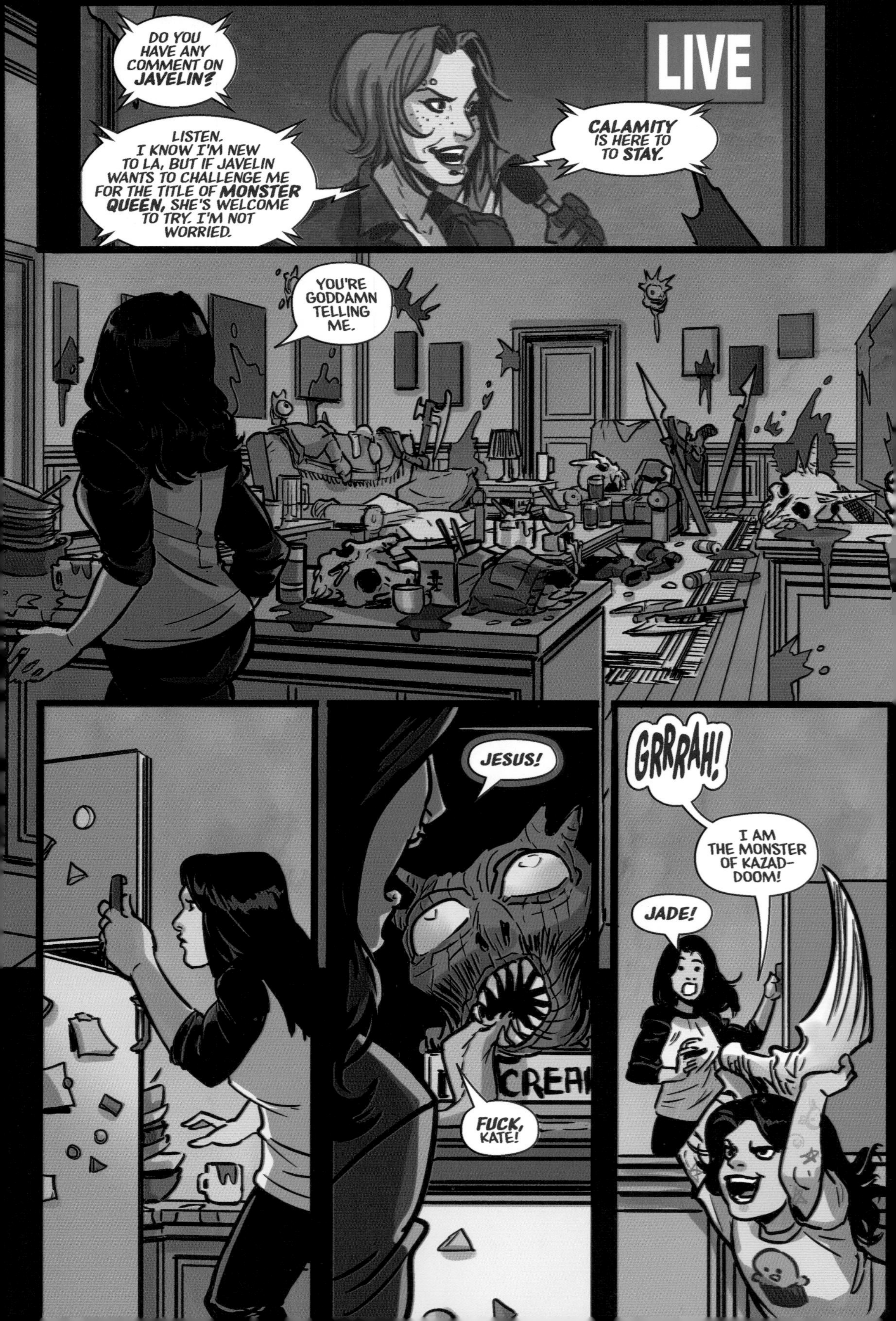

DO YOU HAVE ANY COMMENT ON JAVELIN?
LIVE
LISTEN. I KNOW I'M NEW TO LA, BUT IF JAVELIN WANTS TO CHALLENGE ME FOR THE TITLE OF MONSTER QUEEN, SHE'S WELCOME TO TRY. I'M NOT WORRIED.
CALAMITY IS HERE TO TO STAY.
YOU'RE GODDAMN TELLING ME.
JESUS!
CREAM
FUCK, KATE!
GRRRAH!
I AM THE MONSTER OF KAZAD-DOOM!
JADE!

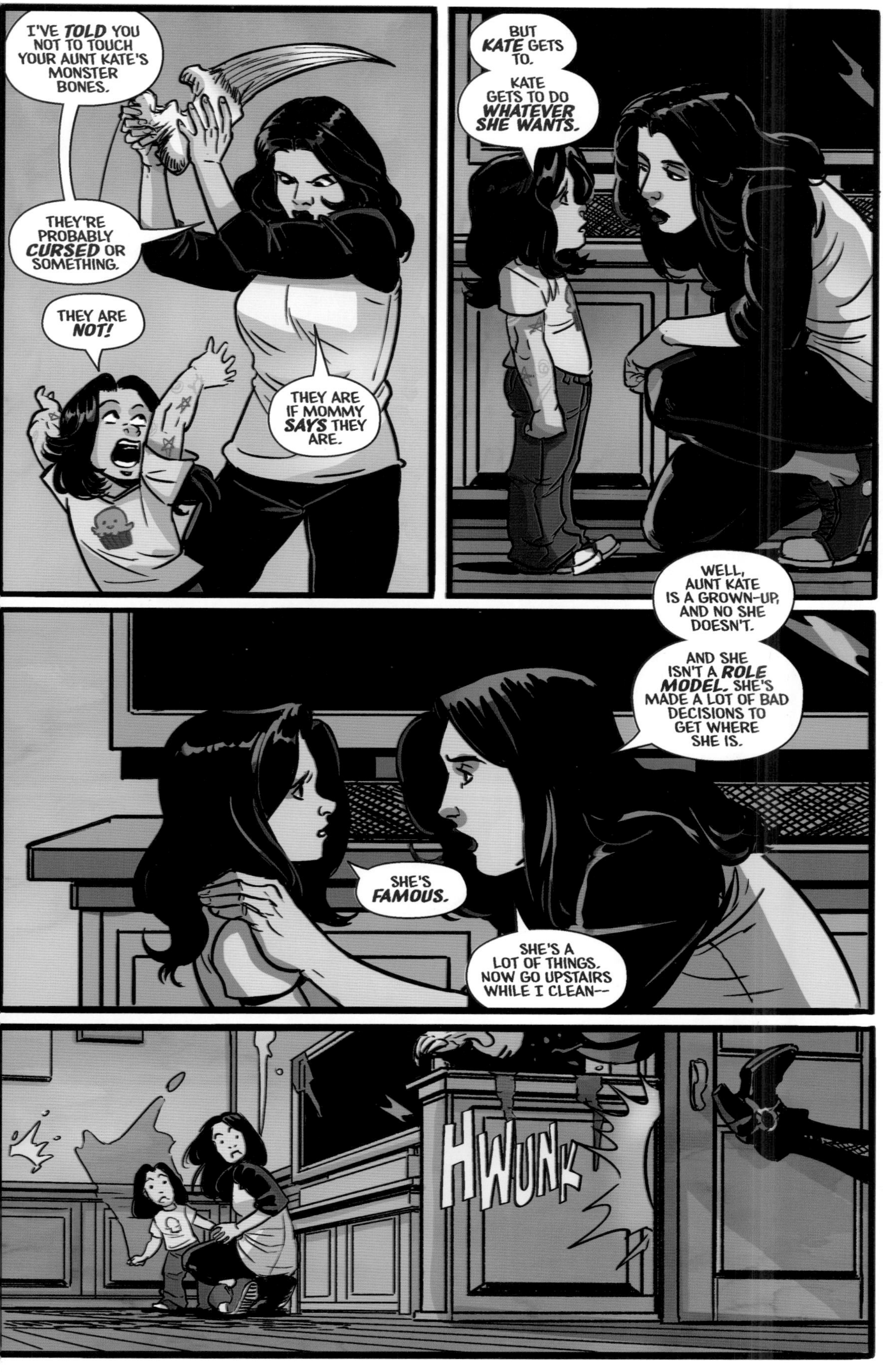
I'VE TOLD YOU NOT TO TOUCH YOUR AUNT KATE'S MONSTER BONES.
THEY'RE PROBABLY CURSED OR SOMETHING.
THEY ARE NOT!
THEY ARE IF MOMMY SAYS THEY ARE.
BUT KATE GETS TO.
KATE GETS TO DO WHATEVER SHE WANTS.
WELL, AUNT KATE IS A GROWN-UP, AND NO SHE DOESN'T.
AND SHE ISN'T A ROLE MODEL. SHE'S MADE A LOT OF BAD DECISIONS TO GET WHERE SHE IS.
SHE'S FAMOUS.
SHE'S A LOT OF THINGS. NOW GO UPSTAIRS WHILE I CLEAN--
HWUNK

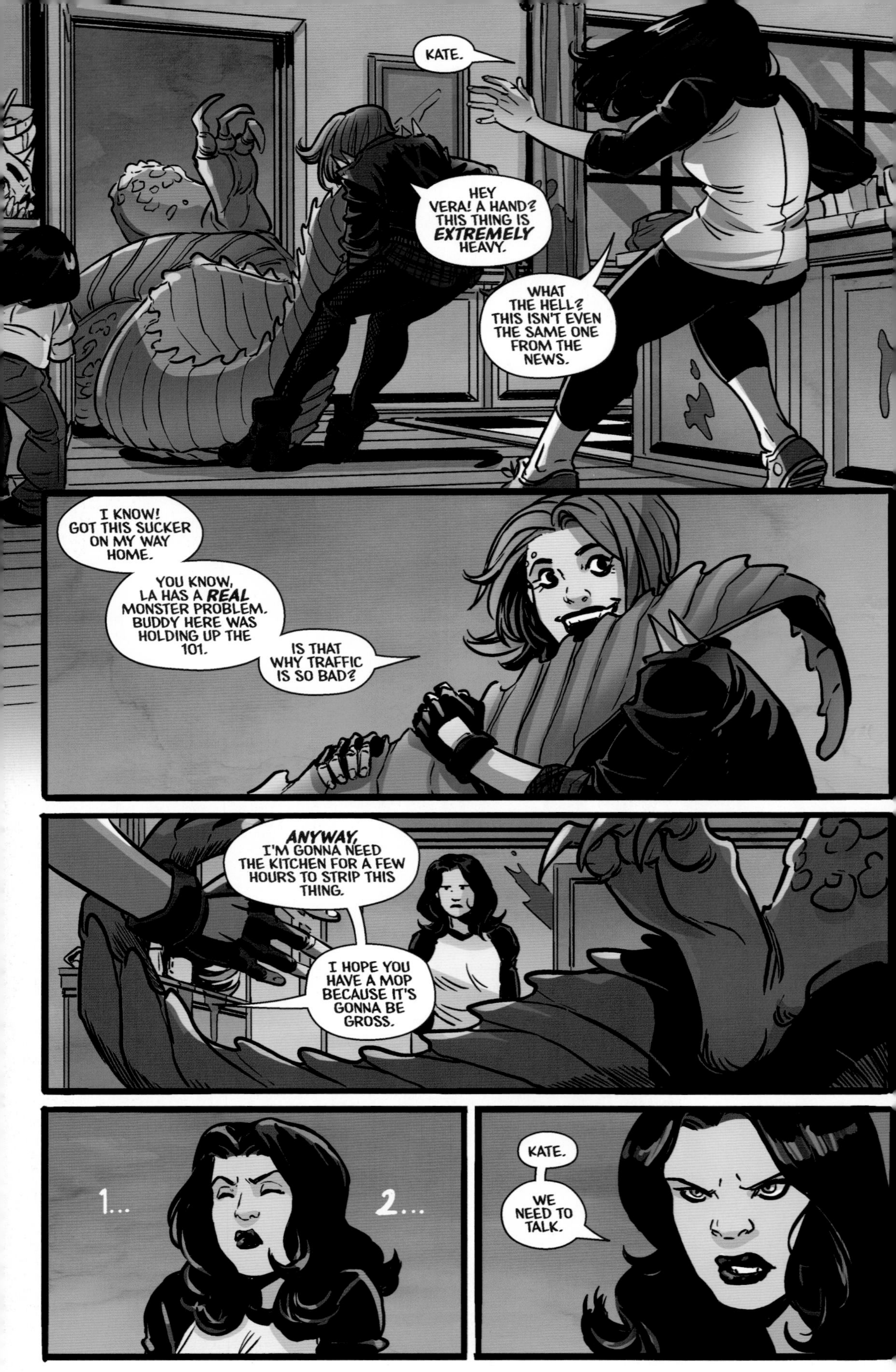
KATE.
HEY VERA! A HAND? THIS THING IS *EXTREMELY* HEAVY.
WHAT THE HELL? THIS ISN'T EVEN THE SAME ONE FROM THE NEWS.
I KNOW! GOT THIS SUCKER ON MY WAY HOME.
YOU KNOW, LA HAS A *REAL* MONSTER PROBLEM. BUDDY HERE WAS HOLDING UP THE 101.
IS THAT WHY TRAFFIC IS SO BAD?
ANYWAY, I'M GONNA NEED THE KITCHEN FOR A FEW HOURS TO STRIP THIS THING.
I HOPE YOU HAVE A MOP BECAUSE IT'S GONNA BE GROSS.
1...
2...
KATE.
WE NEED TO TALK.

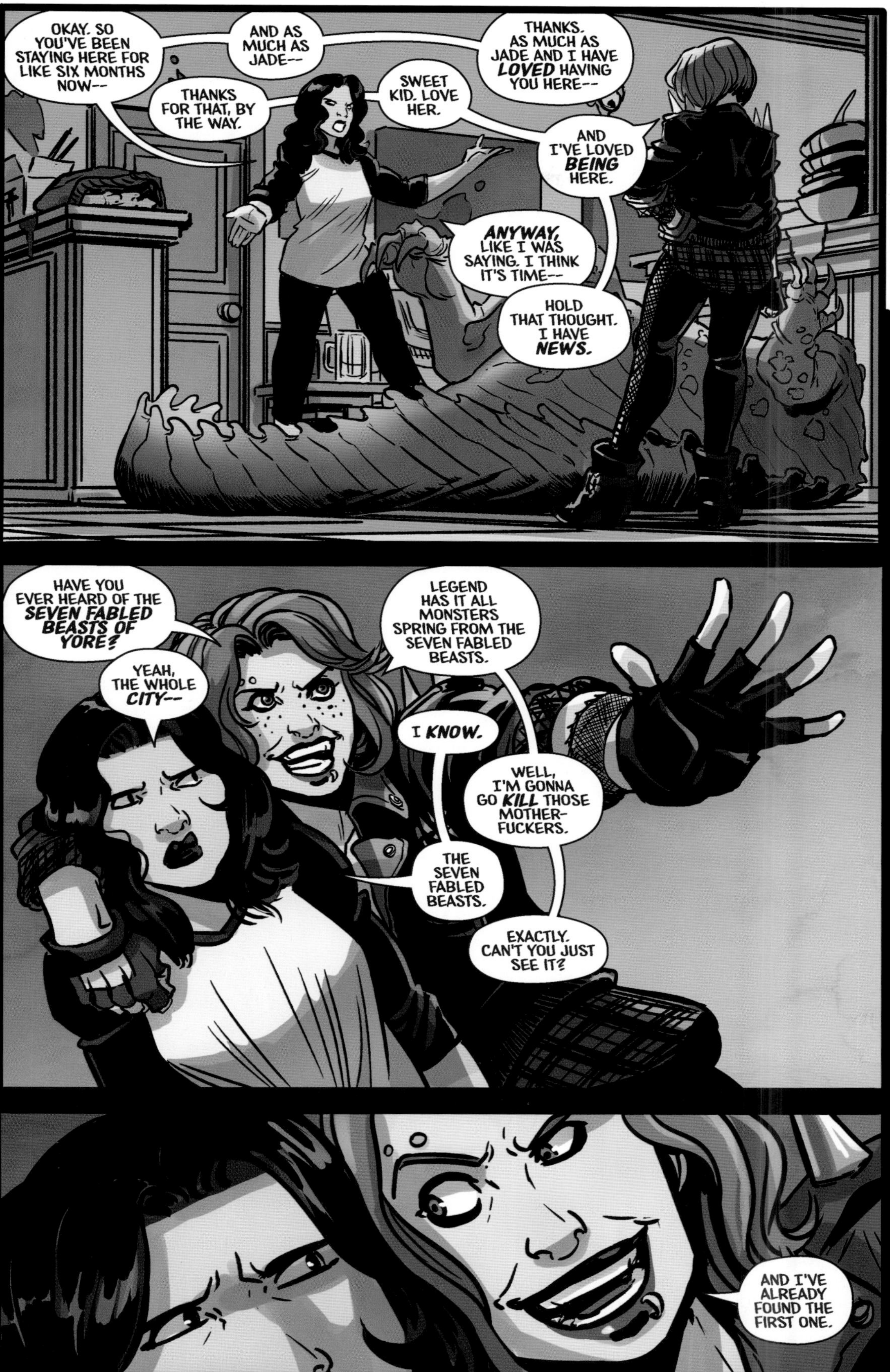
OKAY. SO YOU'VE BEEN STAYING HERE FOR LIKE SIX MONTHS NOW--
THANKS FOR THAT, BY THE WAY.
AND AS MUCH AS JADE--
SWEET KID. LOVE HER.
THANKS. AS MUCH AS JADE AND I HAVE LOVED HAVING YOU HERE--
AND I'VE LOVED BEING HERE.
ANYWAY, LIKE I WAS SAYING. I THINK IT'S TIME--
HOLD THAT THOUGHT. I HAVE NEWS.
HAVE YOU EVER HEARD OF THE SEVEN FABLED BEASTS OF YORE?
YEAH, THE WHOLE CITY--
LEGEND HAS IT ALL MONSTERS SPRING FROM THE SEVEN FABLED BEASTS.
I KNOW.
WELL, I'M GONNA GO KILL THOSE MOTHER-FUCKERS.
THE SEVEN FABLED BEASTS.
EXACTLY. CAN'T YOU JUST SEE IT?
AND I'VE ALREADY FOUND THE FIRST ONE.

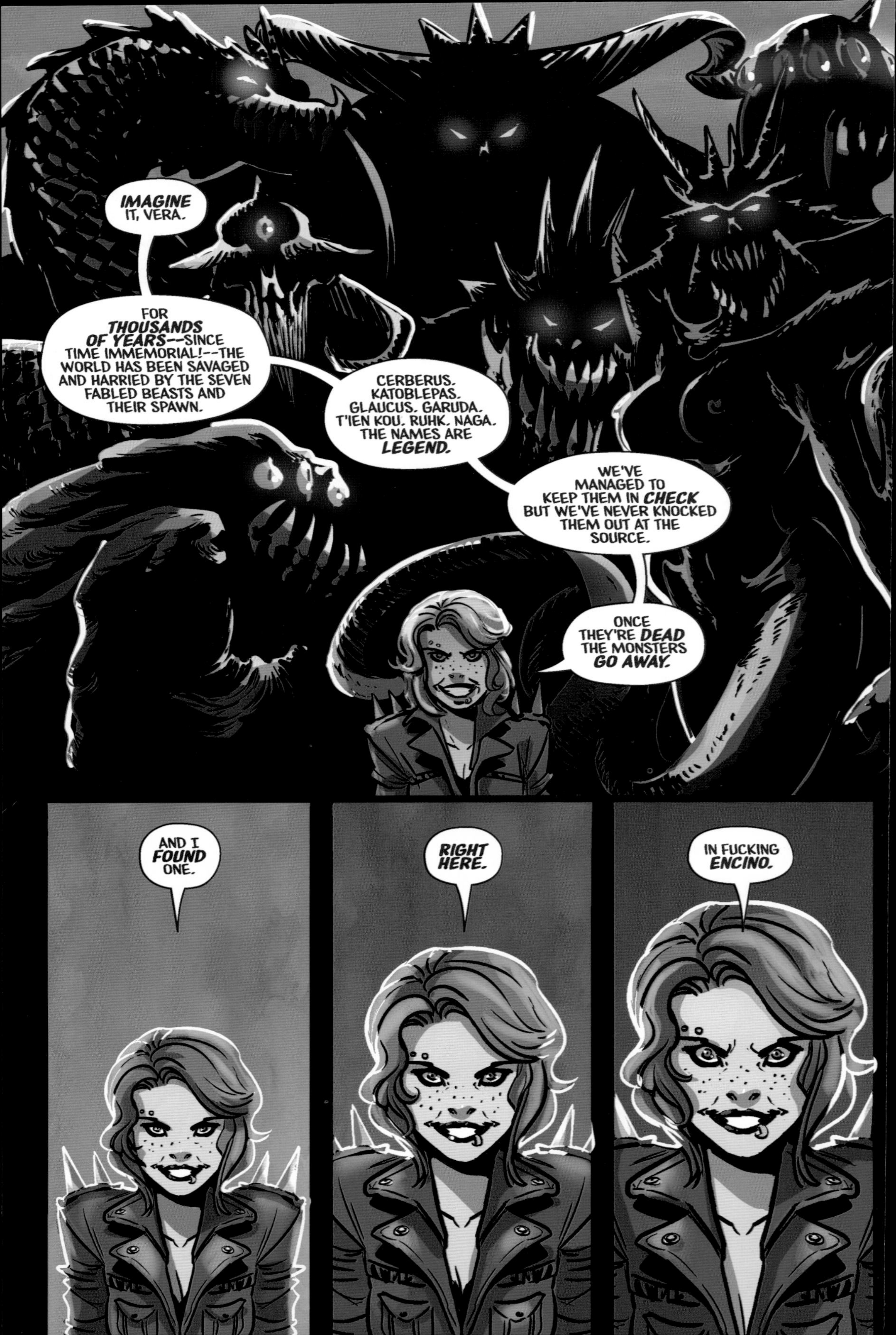
IMAGINE IT, VERA.
FOR THOUSANDS OF YEARS--SINCE TIME IMMEMORIAL!--THE WORLD HAS BEEN SAVAGED AND HARRIED BY THE SEVEN FABLED BEASTS AND THEIR SPAWN.
CERBERUS. KATOBLEPAS. GLAUCUS. GARUDA. T'IEN KOU. RUHK. NAGA. THE NAMES ARE LEGEND.
WE'VE MANAGED TO KEEP THEM IN CHECK BUT WE'VE NEVER KNOCKED THEM OUT AT THE SOURCE.
ONCE THEY'RE DEAD THE MONSTERS GO AWAY.
AND I FOUND ONE.
RIGHT HERE.
IN FUCKING ENCINO.

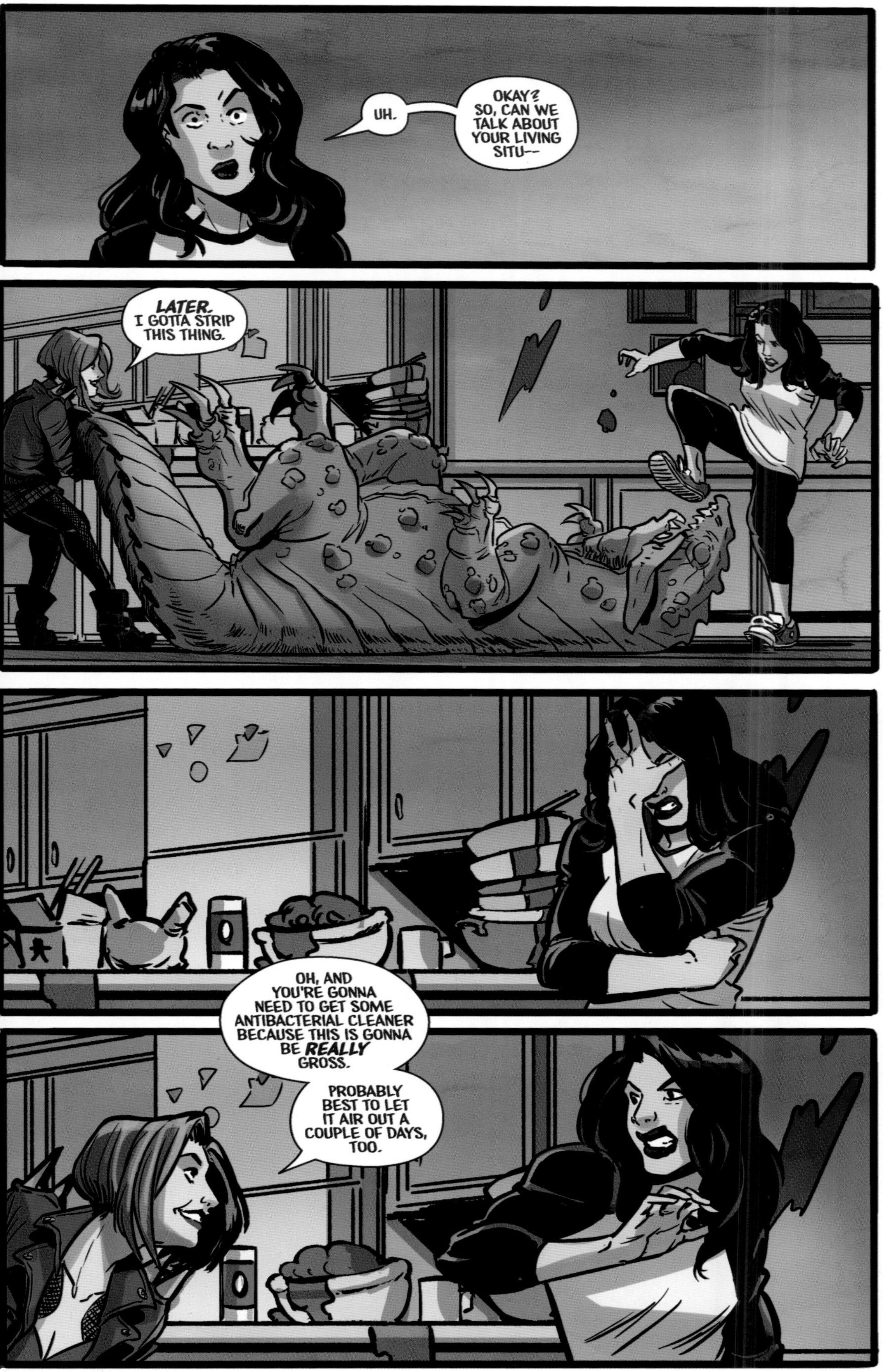
UH.
OKAY? SO, CAN WE TALK ABOUT YOUR LIVING SITU--
LATER. I GOTTA STRIP THIS THING.
OH, AND YOU'RE GONNA NEED TO GET SOME ANTIBACTERIAL CLEANER BECAUSE THIS IS GONNA BE REALLY GROSS.
PROBABLY BEST TO LET IT AIR OUT A COUPLE OF DAYS, TOO.

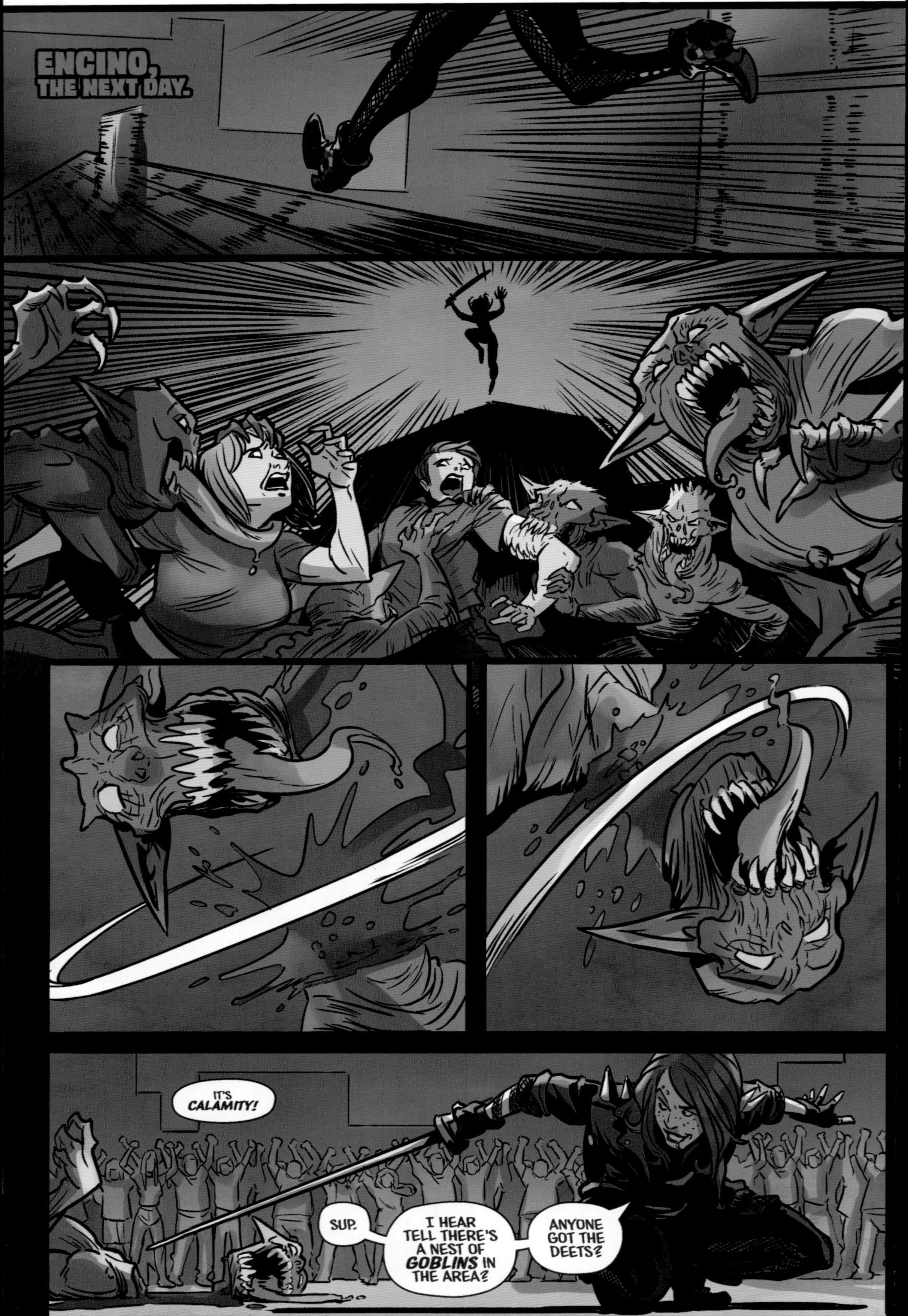
ENCINO, THE NEXT DAY.
IT'S CALAMITY!
SUP.
I HEAR TELL THERE'S A NEST OF GOBLINS IN THE AREA?
ANYONE GOT THE DEETS?

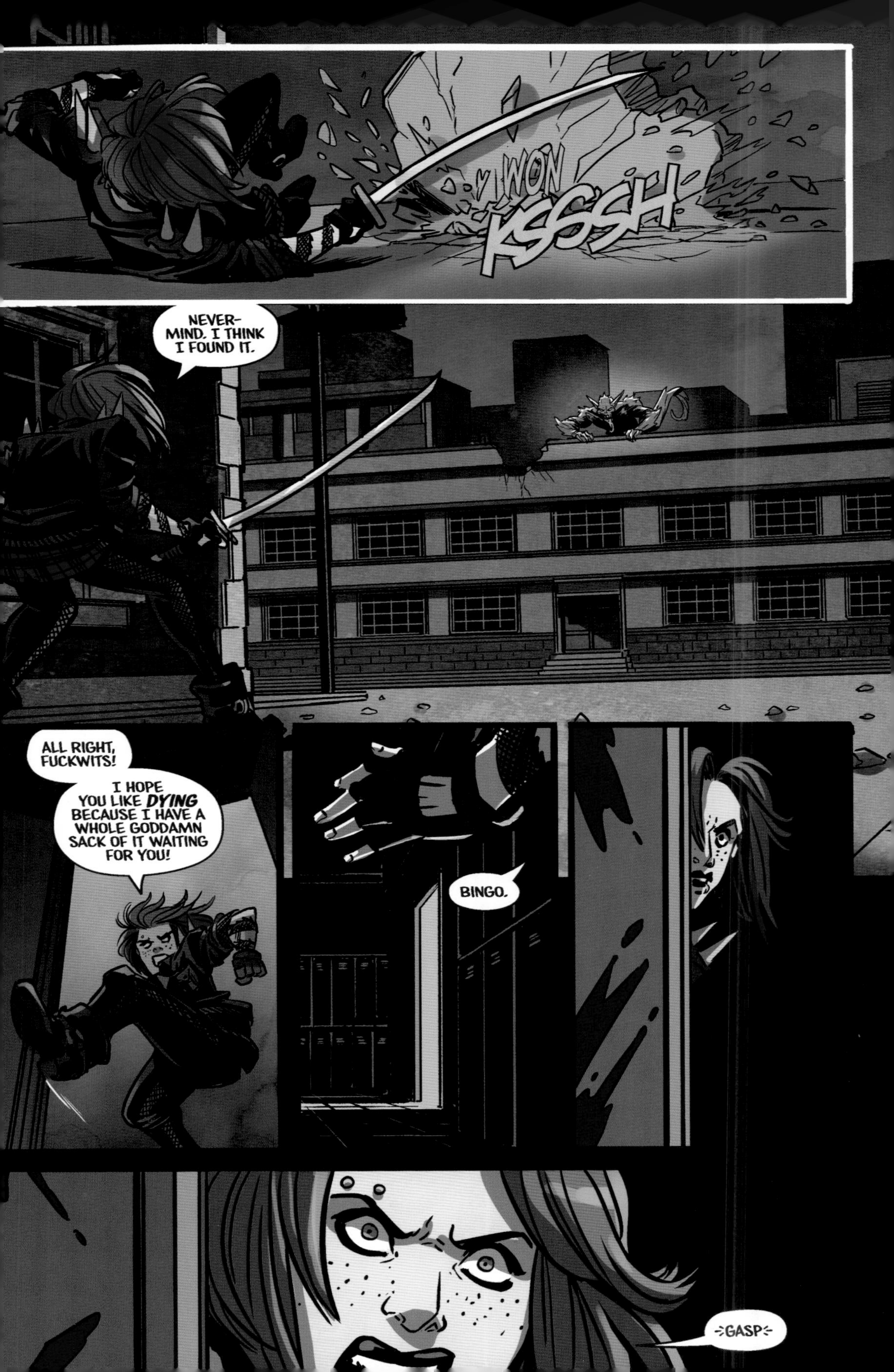
WON
KSSSH
NEVER-MIND. I THINK I FOUND IT.
ALL RIGHT, FUCKWITS!
I HOPE YOU LIKE *DYING* BECAUSE I HAVE A WHOLE GODDAMN SACK OF IT WAITING FOR YOU!
BINGO.
GASP

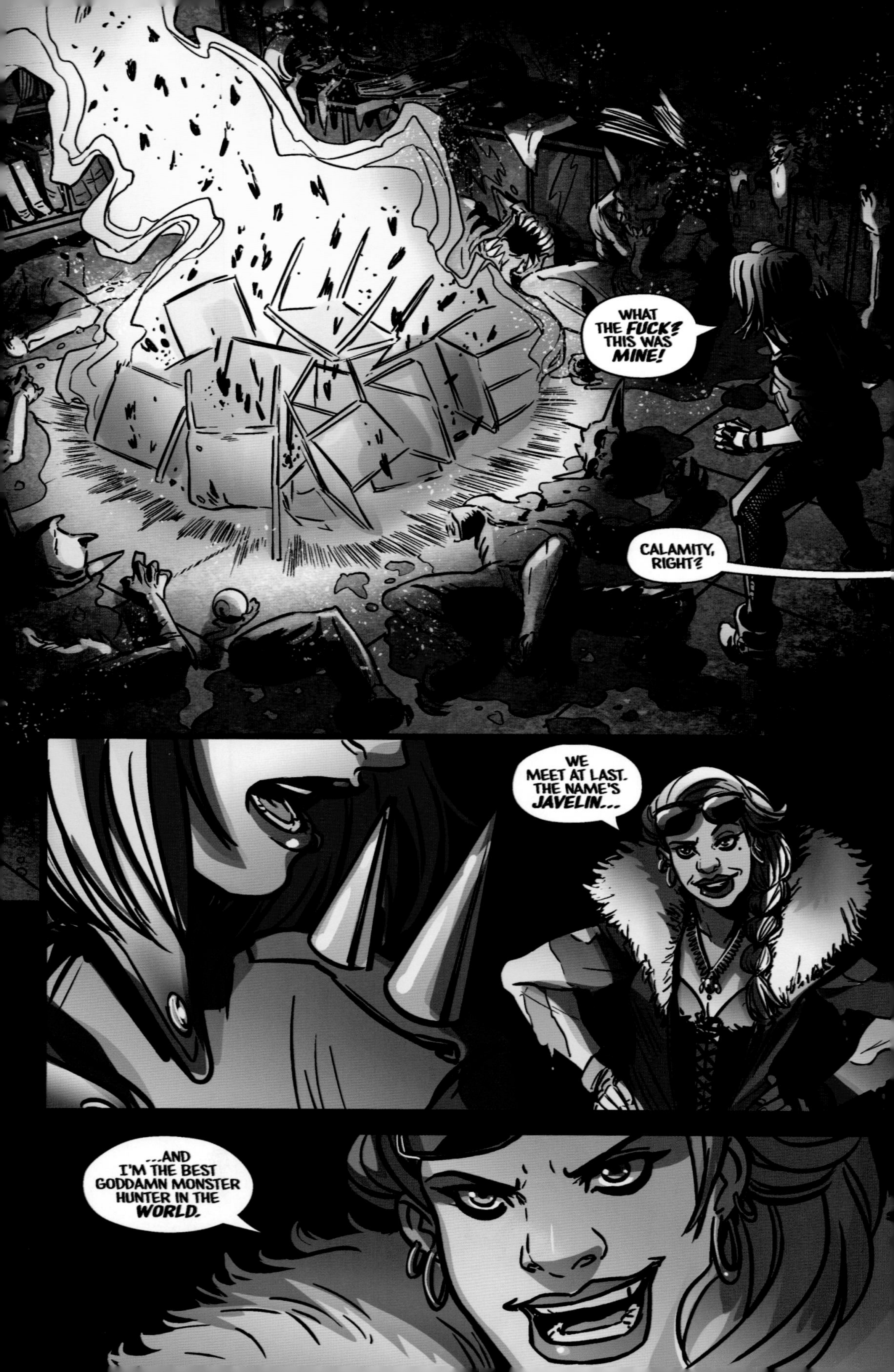
WHAT THE FUCK? THIS WAS MINE!
CALAMITY, RIGHT?
WE MEET AT LAST. THE NAME'S JAVELIN...
...AND I'M THE BEST GODDAMN MONSTER HUNTER IN THE WORLD.

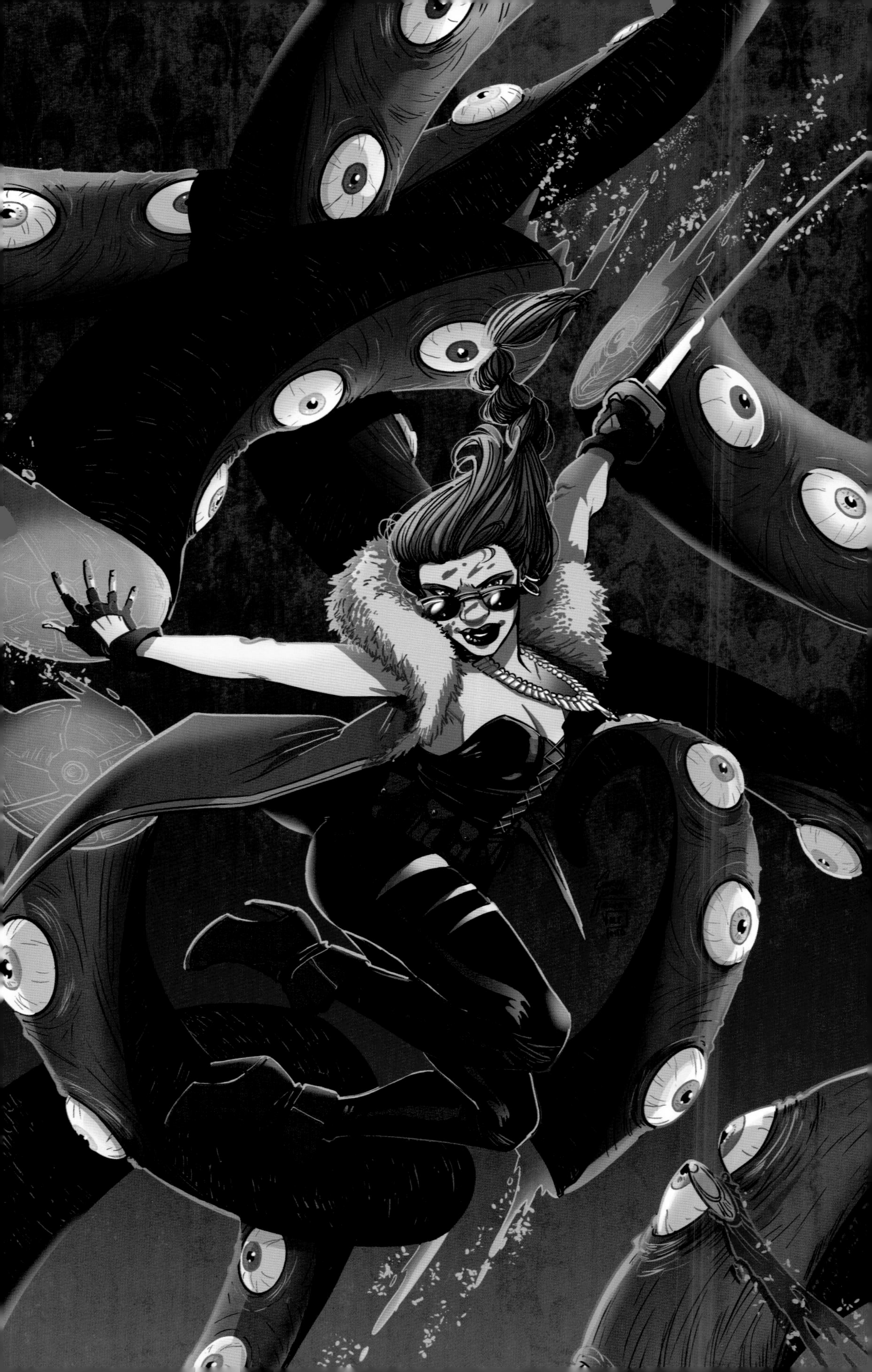

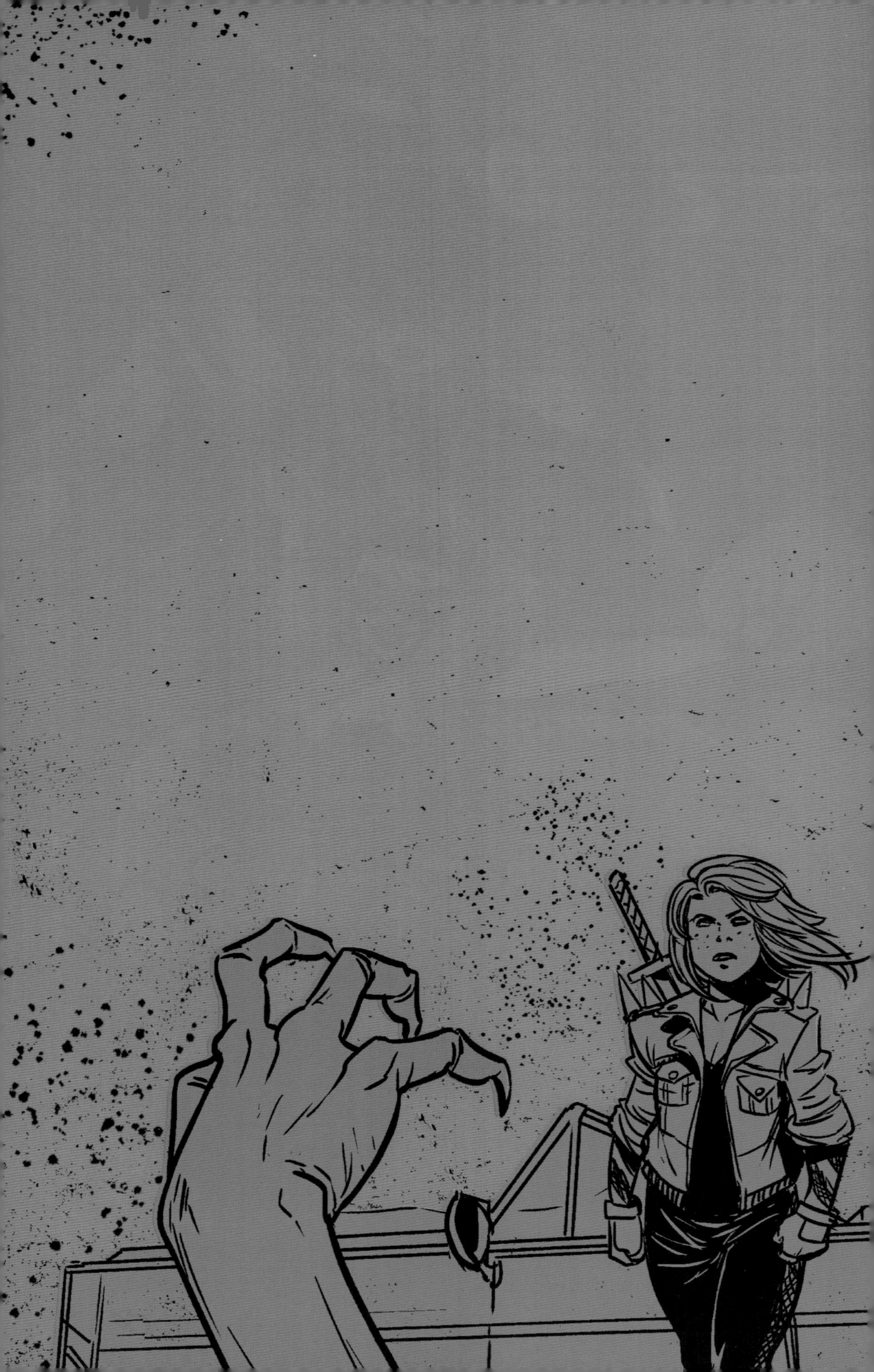

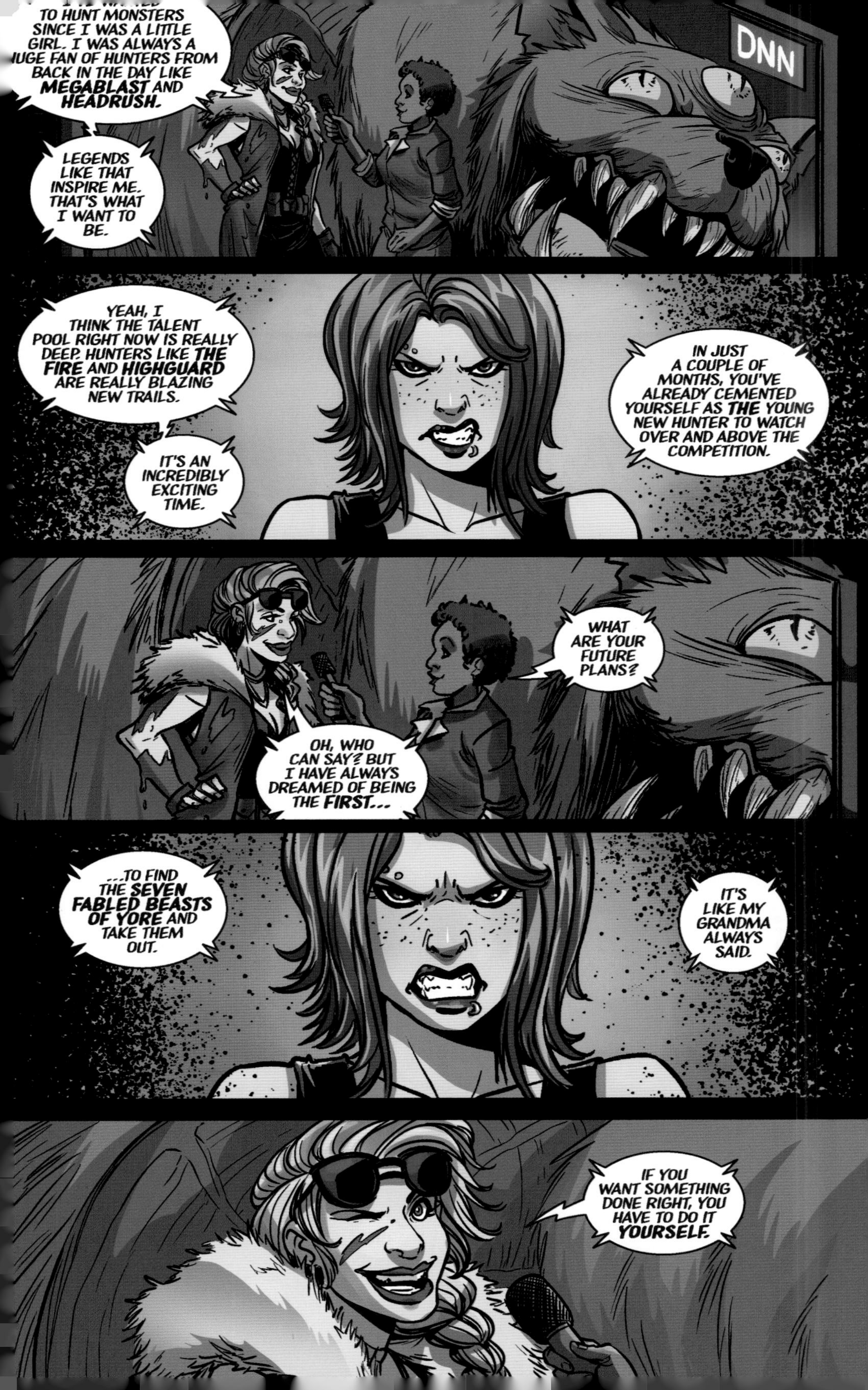
TO HUNT MONSTERS SINCE I WAS A LITTLE GIRL. I WAS ALWAYS A UGE FAN OF HUNTERS FROM BACK IN THE DAY LIKE MEGABLAST AND HEADRUSH.
LEGENDS LIKE THAT INSPIRE ME. THAT'S WHAT I WANT TO BE.
DNN
IN JUST A COUPLE OF MONTHS, YOU'VE ALREADY CEMENTED YOURSELF AS THE YOUNG NEW HUNTER TO WATCH OVER AND ABOVE THE COMPETITION.
YEAH, I THINK THE TALENT POOL RIGHT NOW IS REALLY DEEP. HUNTERS LIKE THE FIRE AND HIGHGUARD ARE REALLY BLAZING NEW TRAILS.
IT'S AN INCREDIBLY EXCITING TIME.
WHAT ARE YOUR FUTURE PLANS?
OH, WHO CAN SAY? BUT I HAVE ALWAYS DREAMED OF BEING THE FIRST...
...TO FIND THE SEVEN FABLED BEASTS OF YORE AND TAKE THEM OUT.
IT'S LIKE MY GRANDMA ALWAYS SAID.
IF YOU WANT SOMETHING DONE RIGHT, YOU HAVE TO DO IT YOURSELF.

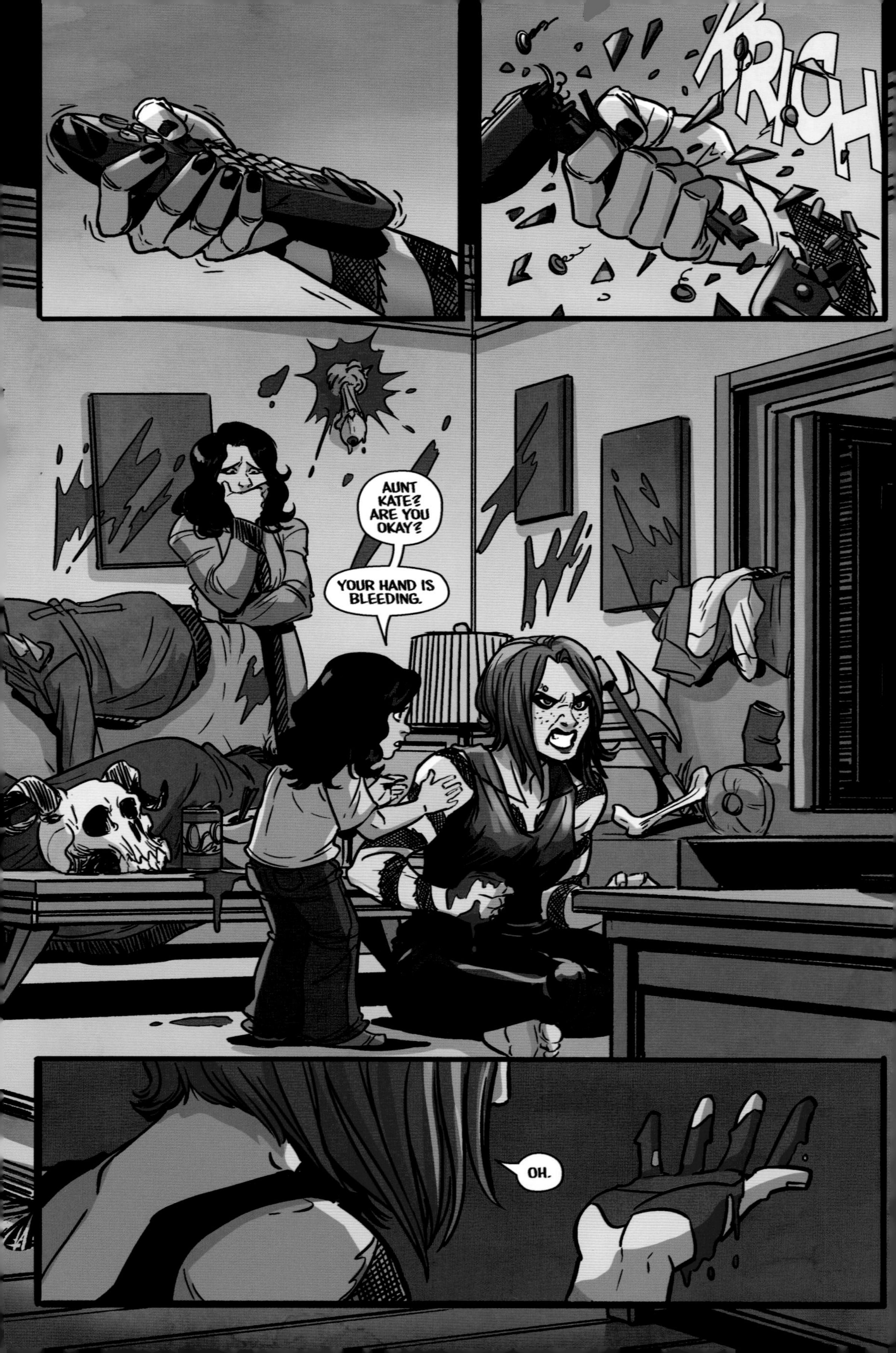

KRICH
AUNT KATE? ARE YOU OKAY?
YOUR HAND IS BLEEDING.
OH.

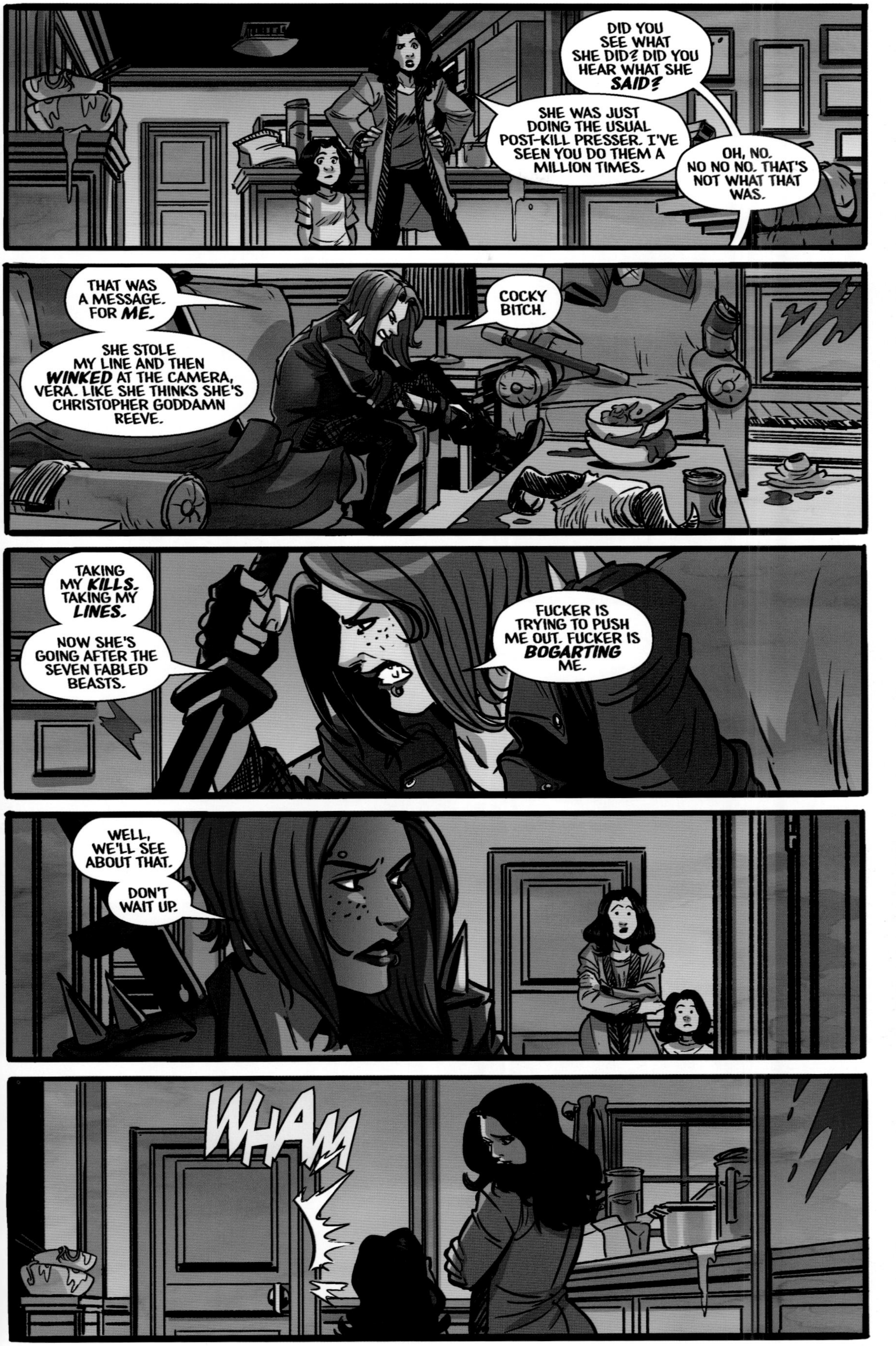
DID YOU SEE WHAT SHE DID? DID YOU HEAR WHAT SHE SAID?
SHE WAS JUST DOING THE USUAL POST-KILL PRESSER. I'VE SEEN YOU DO THEM A MILLION TIMES.
OH, NO. NO NO NO. THAT'S NOT WHAT THAT WAS.
THAT WAS A MESSAGE. FOR ME.
SHE STOLE MY LINE AND THEN WINKED AT THE CAMERA, VERA. LIKE SHE THINKS SHE'S CHRISTOPHER GODDAMN REEVE.
COCKY BITCH.
TAKING MY KILLS. TAKING MY LINES.
NOW SHE'S GOING AFTER THE SEVEN FABLED BEASTS.
FUCKER IS TRYING TO PUSH ME OUT. FUCKER IS BOGARTING ME.
WELL, WE'LL SEE ABOUT THAT.
DON'T WAIT UP.
WHAM

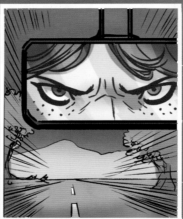

FWUNK

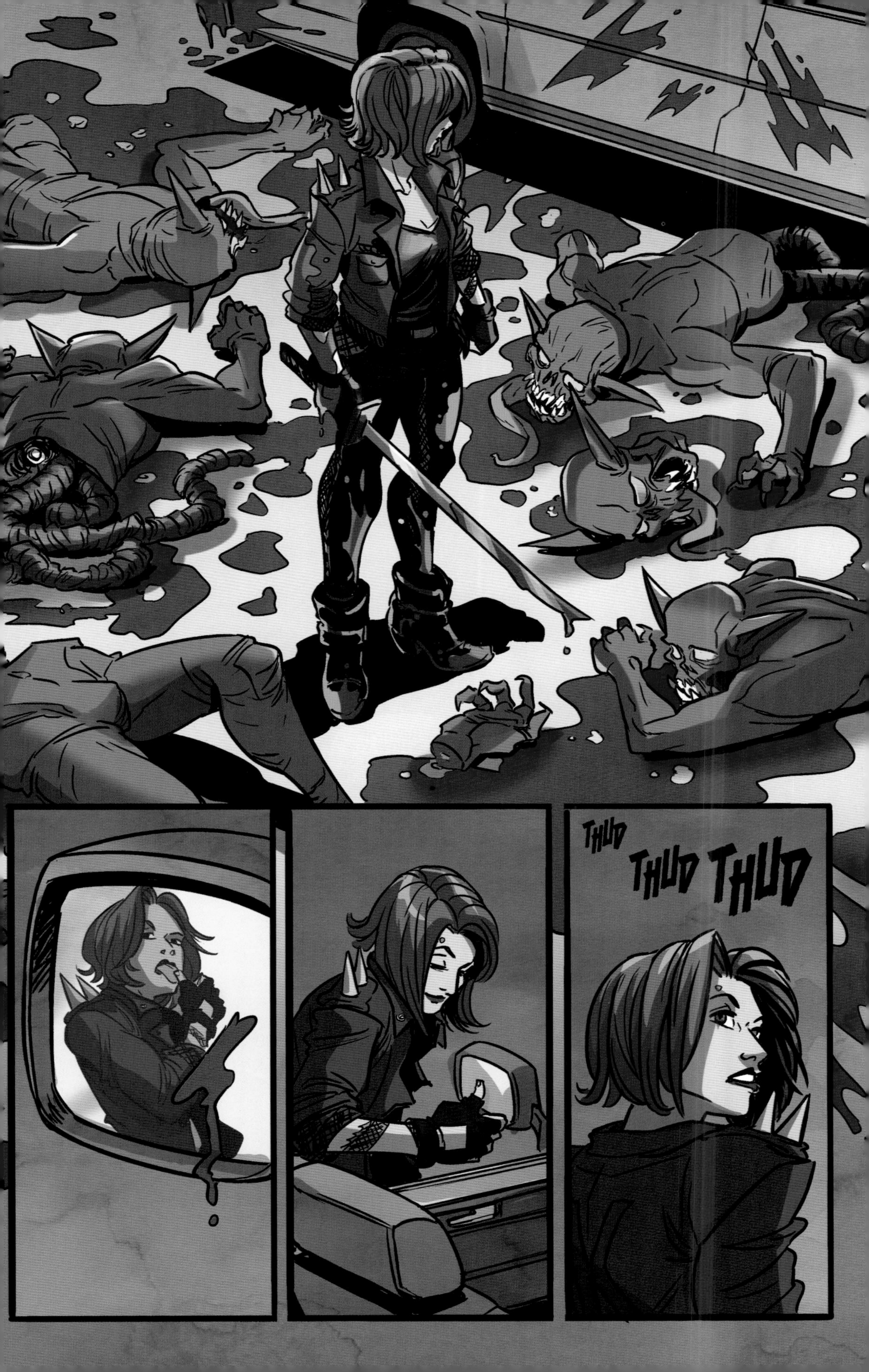
THUD
THUD THUD

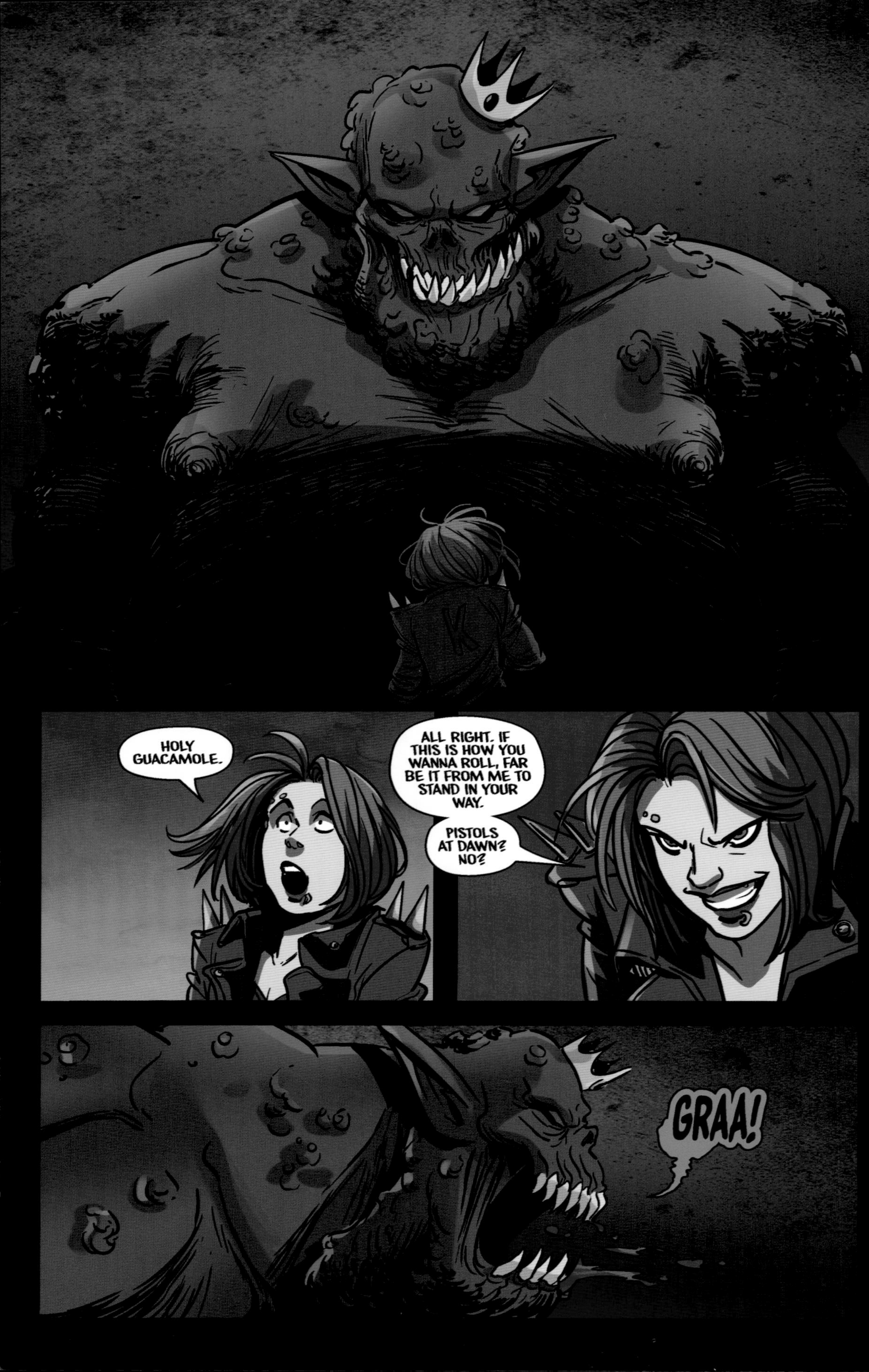
HOLY GUACAMOLE.
ALL RIGHT. IF THIS IS HOW YOU WANNA ROLL, FAR BE IT FROM ME TO STAND IN YOUR WAY.
PISTOLS AT DAWN? NO?
GRAA!

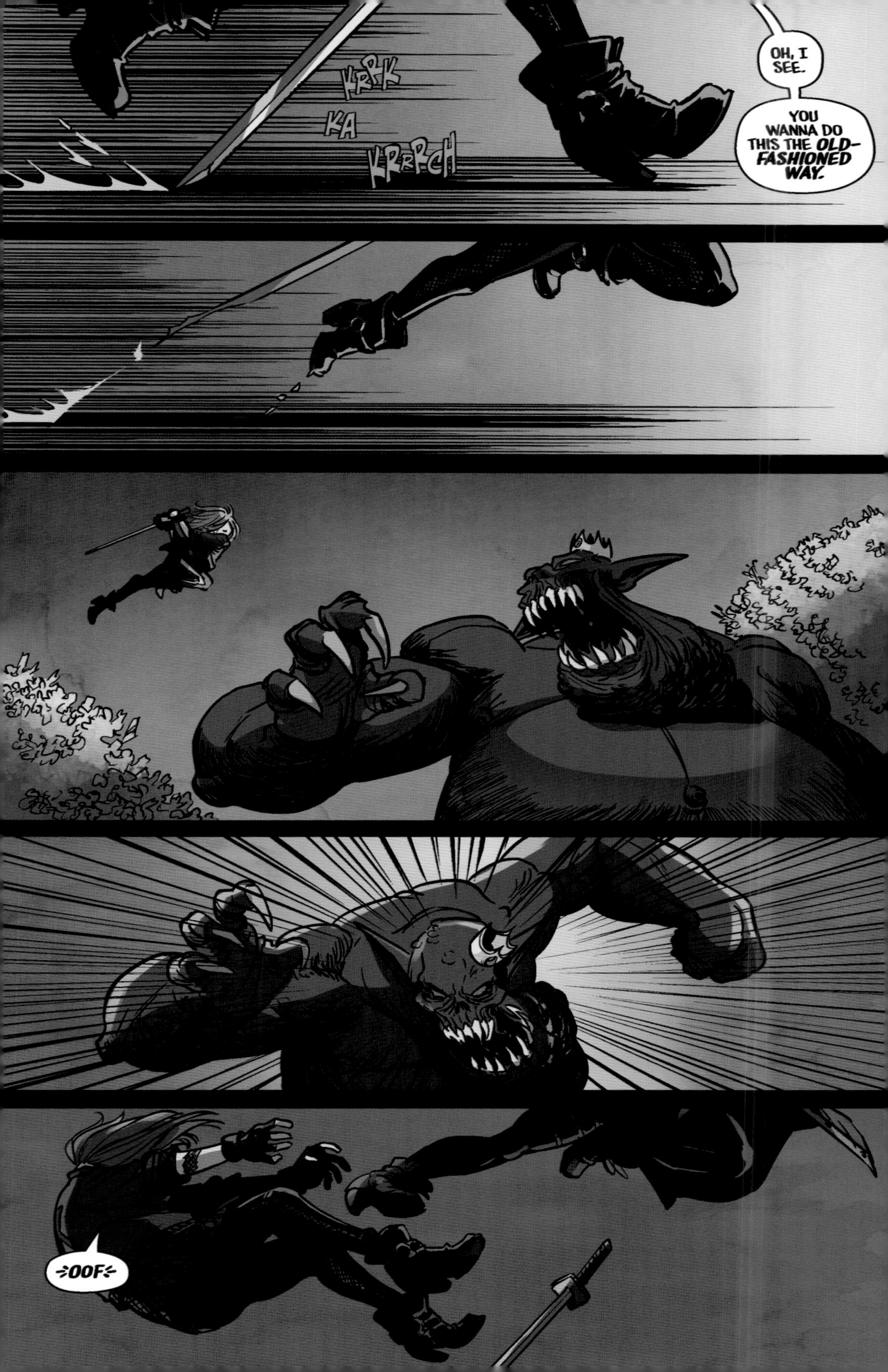

KRRK
KA
KRRRCH
OH, I SEE.
YOU WANNA DO THIS THE OLD-FASHIONED WAY.
OOF

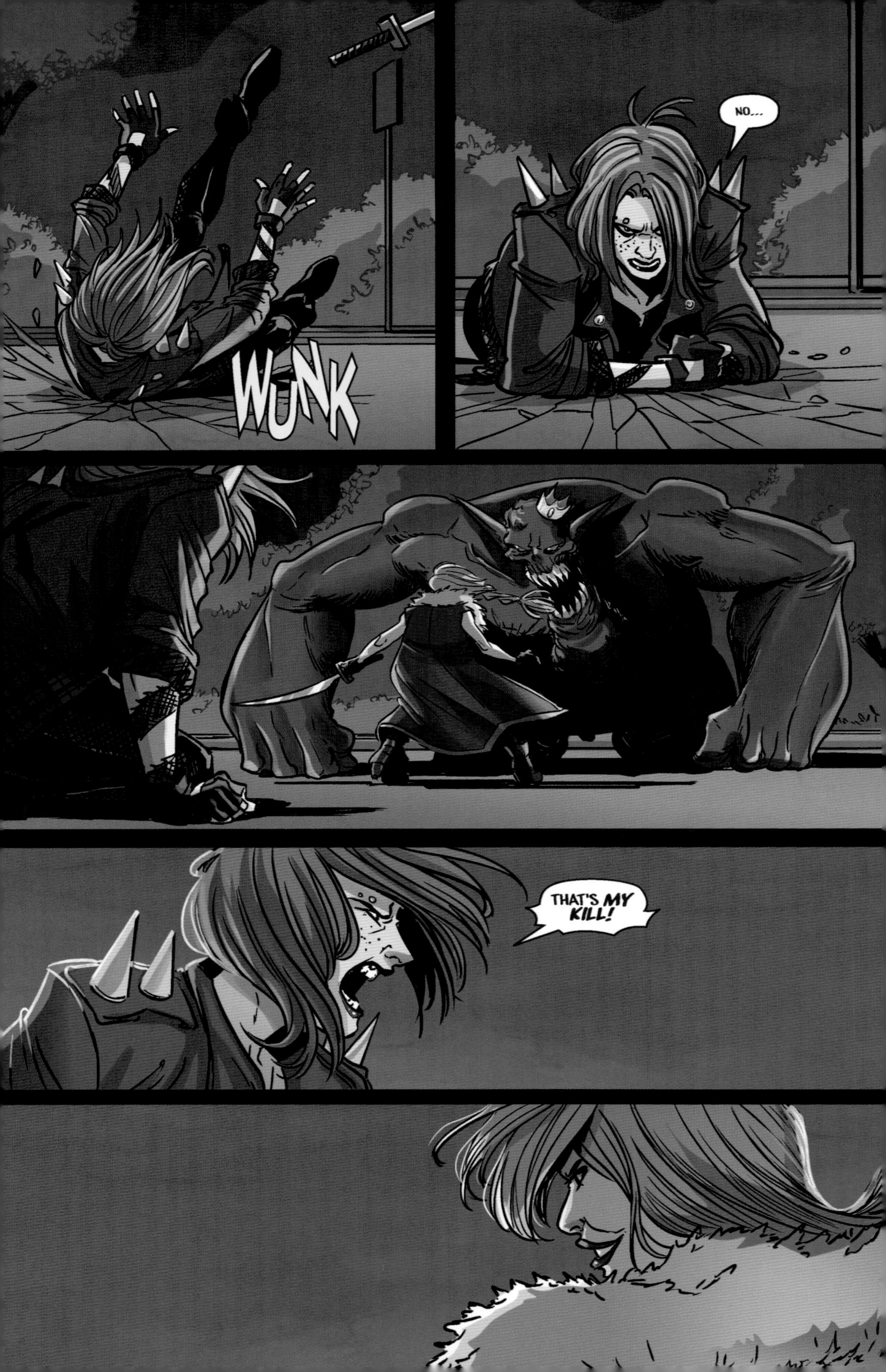
WUNK
NO...
THAT'S MY KILL!

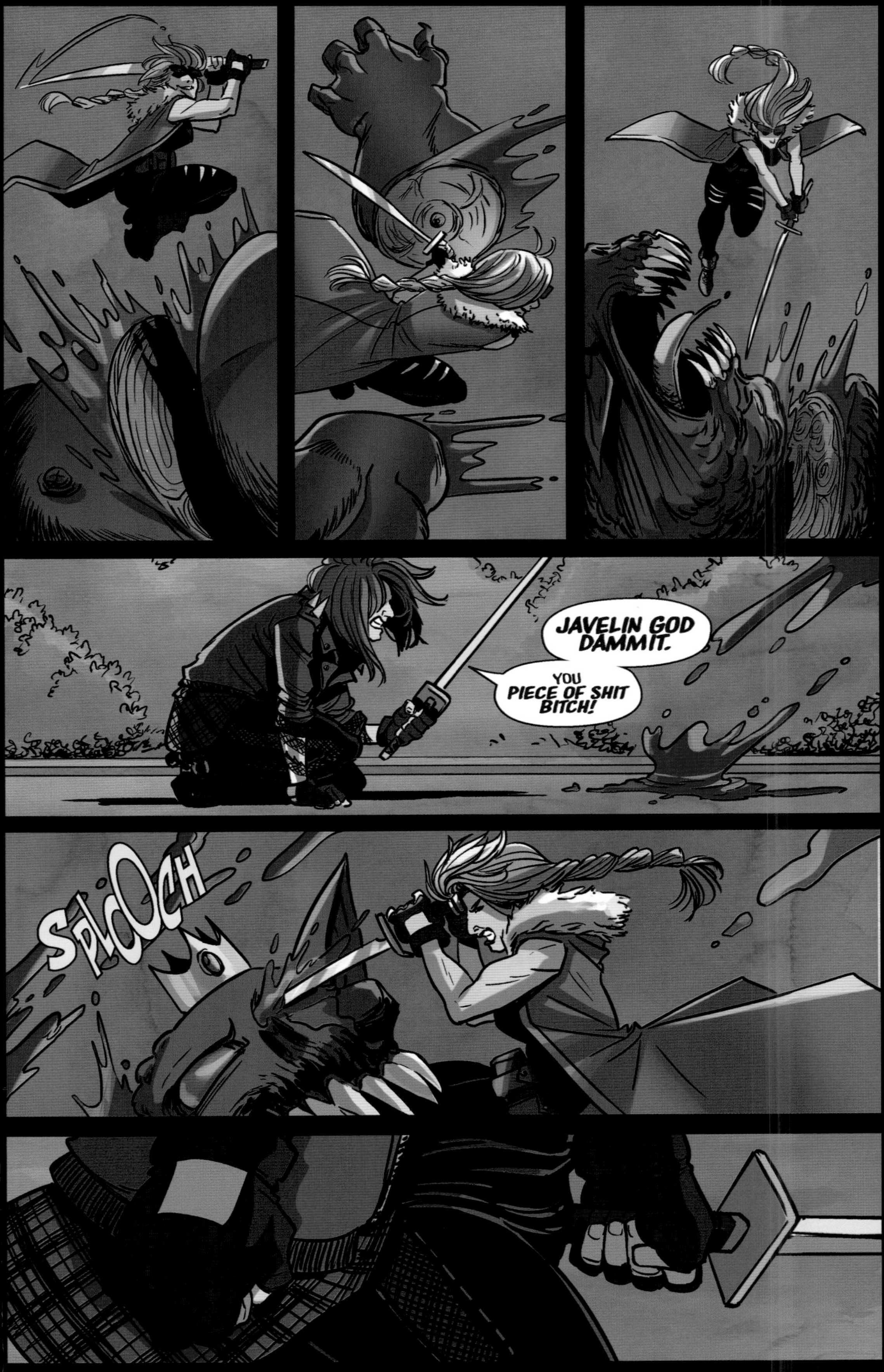
JAVELIN GOD DAMMIT.
YOU PIECE OF SHIT BITCH!
SPLOOCH

OVER, UNDER, AROUND THE TREE...
I KNOW THIS PART, MOM. IT DOESN'T WORK.
YES, IT DOES. YOU JUST HAVE TO REMEMBER WHAT ACTIONS GO WITH THE RHYME.
IF I KNEW THAT, I WOULDN'T NEED THE RHYME.
HONEY, YOU HAVE TO KNOW HOW TO DO THIS.
WHY? AUNT KATE'S BOOTS ZIP UP. CAN I WEAR THOSE?
EVEN AUNT KATE CAN TIE HER SHOES.
WELL, I'VE NEVER SEEN IT.
NOW THAT YOU MENTION IT, NEITHER HAVE I. LET'S TRY THIS AGAIN...
EVERYTHING SUCKS. CANCEL THE WORLD. NOTHING MATTERS.
WHAT HAPPENED?
I HOPE YOU'RE GOING TO CLEAN THAT UP--
JAVELIN HAPPENED. AS USUAL. IT'S LIKE SHE'S DEDICATED HER LIFE TO RUINING ME.
RUINING ME.

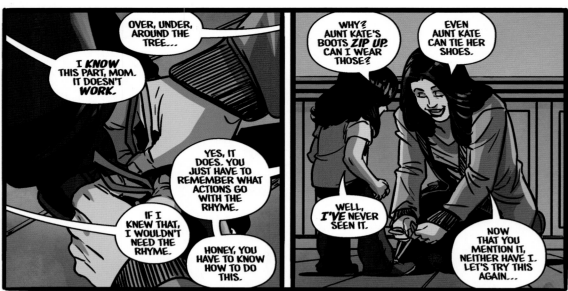

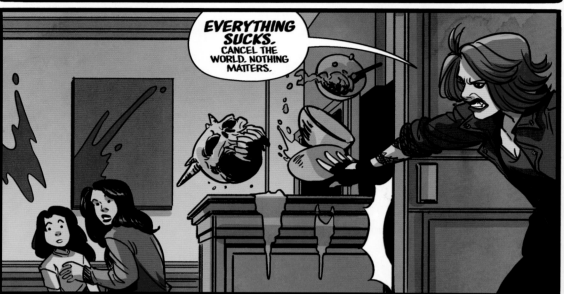

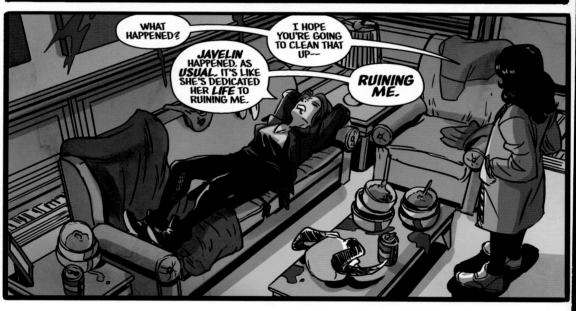

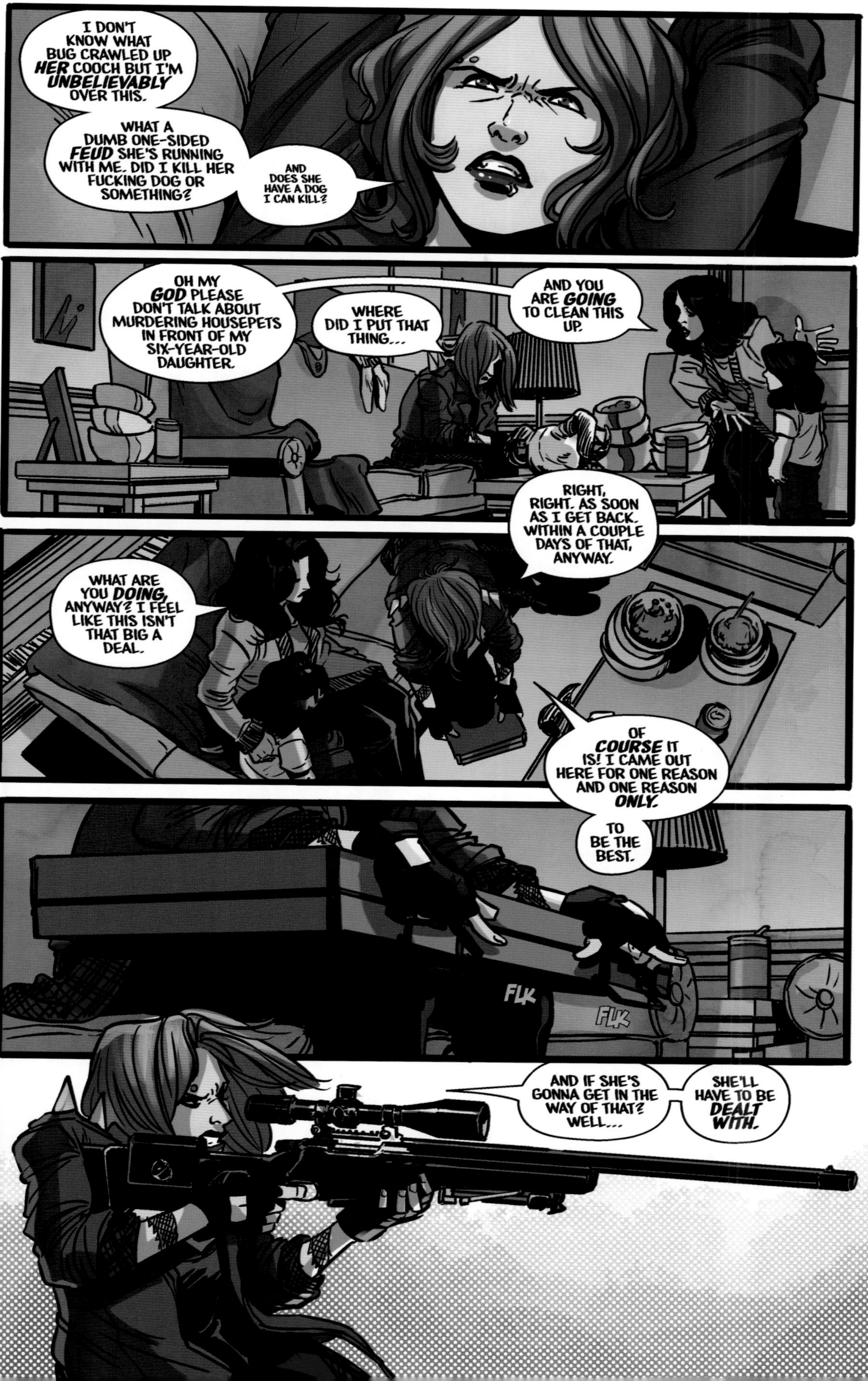

I DON'T KNOW WHAT BUG CRAWLED UP HER COOCH BUT I'M UNBELIEVABLY OVER THIS.
WHAT A DUMB ONE-SIDED FEUD SHE'S RUNNING WITH ME. DID I KILL HER FUCKING DOG OR SOMETHING?
AND DOES SHE HAVE A DOG I CAN KILL?
OH MY GOD PLEASE DON'T TALK ABOUT MURDERING HOUSEPETS IN FRONT OF MY SIX-YEAR-OLD DAUGHTER.
WHERE DID I PUT THAT THING...
AND YOU ARE GOING TO CLEAN THIS UP.
RIGHT, RIGHT. AS SOON AS I GET BACK. WITHIN A COUPLE DAYS OF THAT, ANYWAY.
WHAT ARE YOU DOING, ANYWAY? I FEEL LIKE THIS ISN'T THAT BIG A DEAL.
OF COURSE IT IS! I CAME OUT HERE FOR ONE REASON AND ONE REASON ONLY.
TO BE THE BEST.
FLK
FLK
AND IF SHE'S GONNA GET IN THE WAY OF THAT? WELL...
SHE'LL HAVE TO BE DEALT WITH.

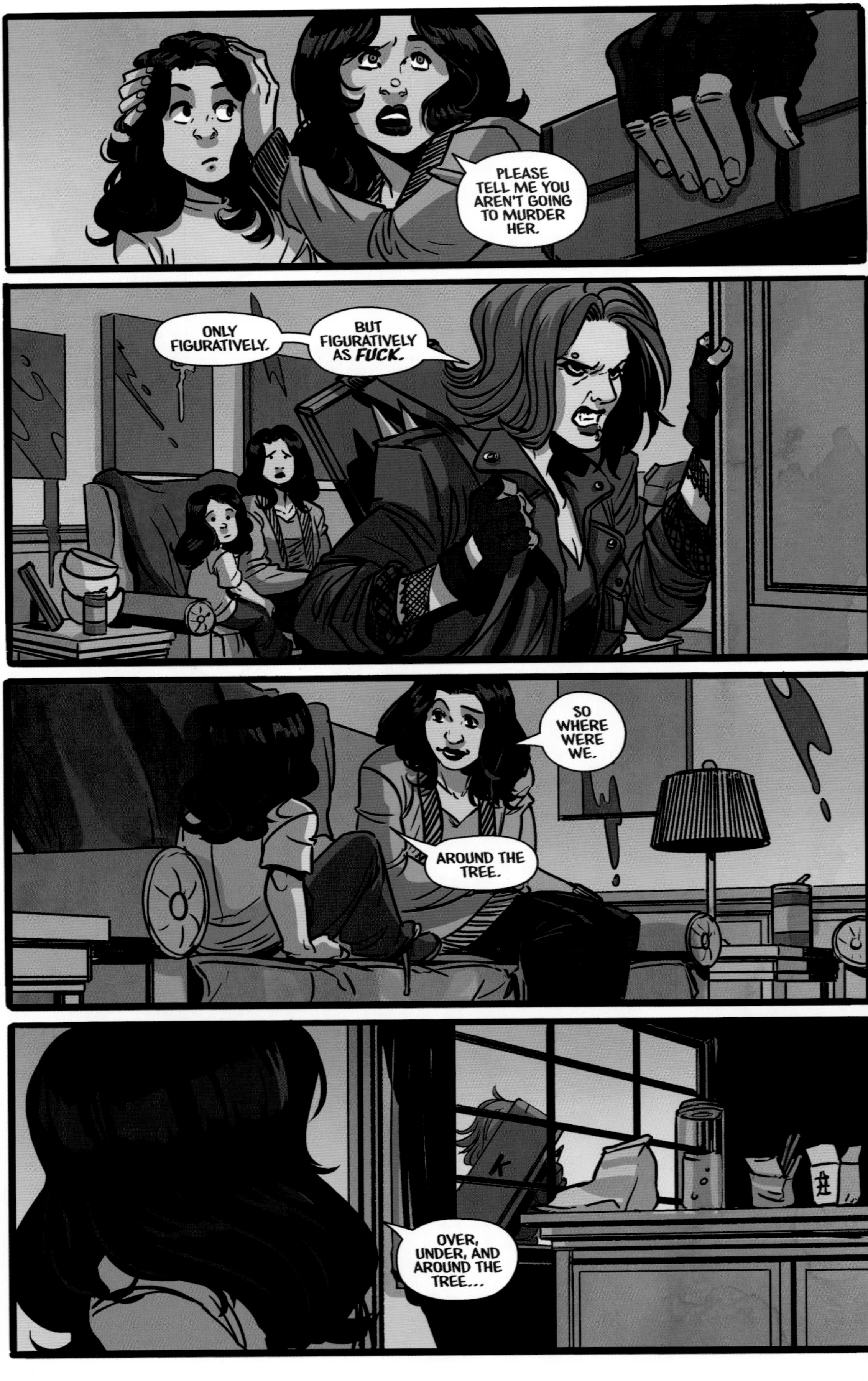
PLEASE TELL ME YOU AREN'T GOING TO MURDER HER.
ONLY FIGURATIVELY.
BUT FIGURATIVELY AS FUCK.
SO WHERE WERE WE.
AROUND THE TREE.
OVER, UNDER, AND AROUND THE TREE...

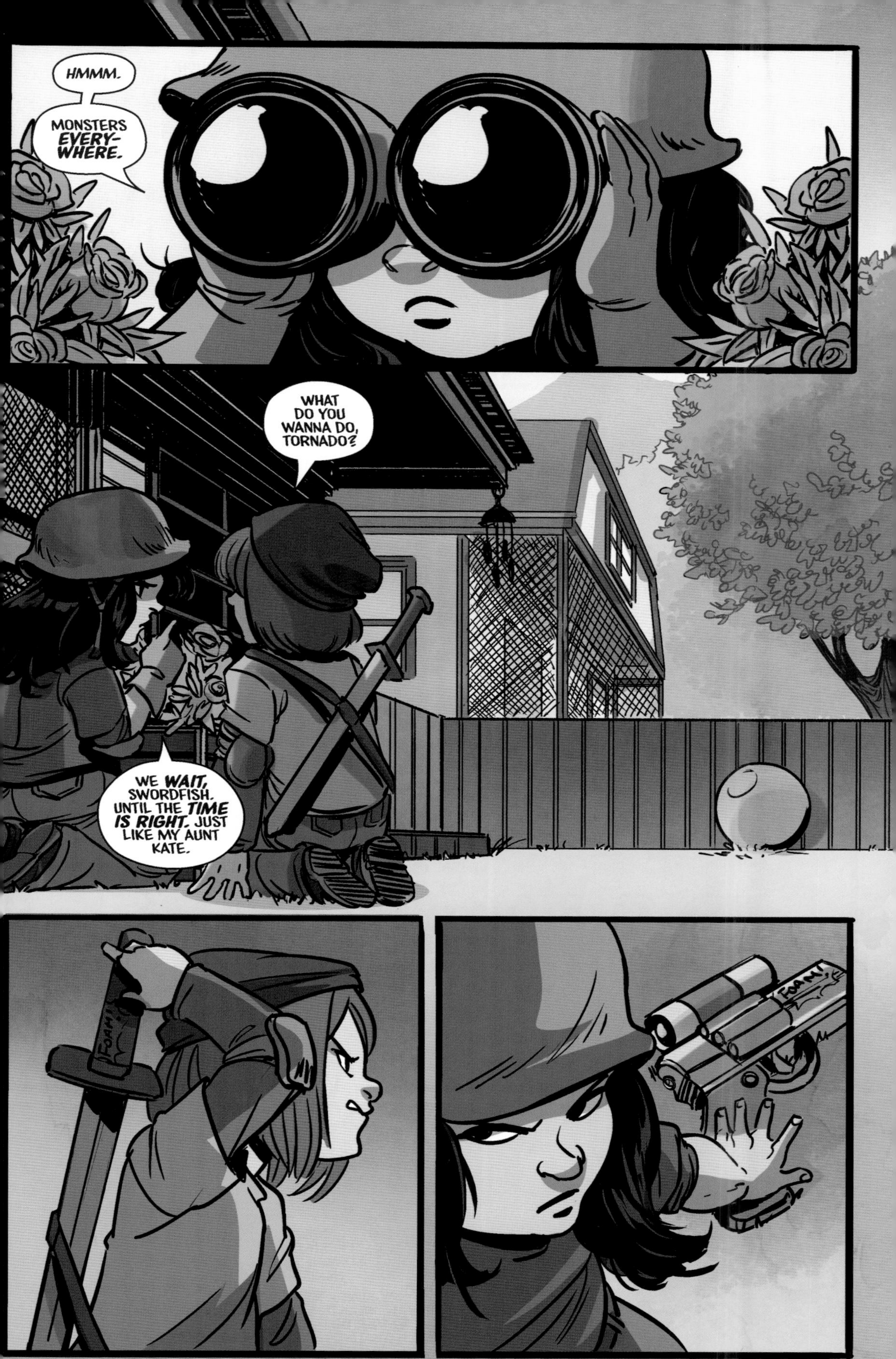
HMMM.
MONSTERS EVERY-WHERE.
WHAT DO YOU WANNA DO, TORNADO?
WE WAIT, SWORDFISH. UNTIL THE TIME IS RIGHT. JUST LIKE MY AUNT KATE.
FOAM!
FOAM!

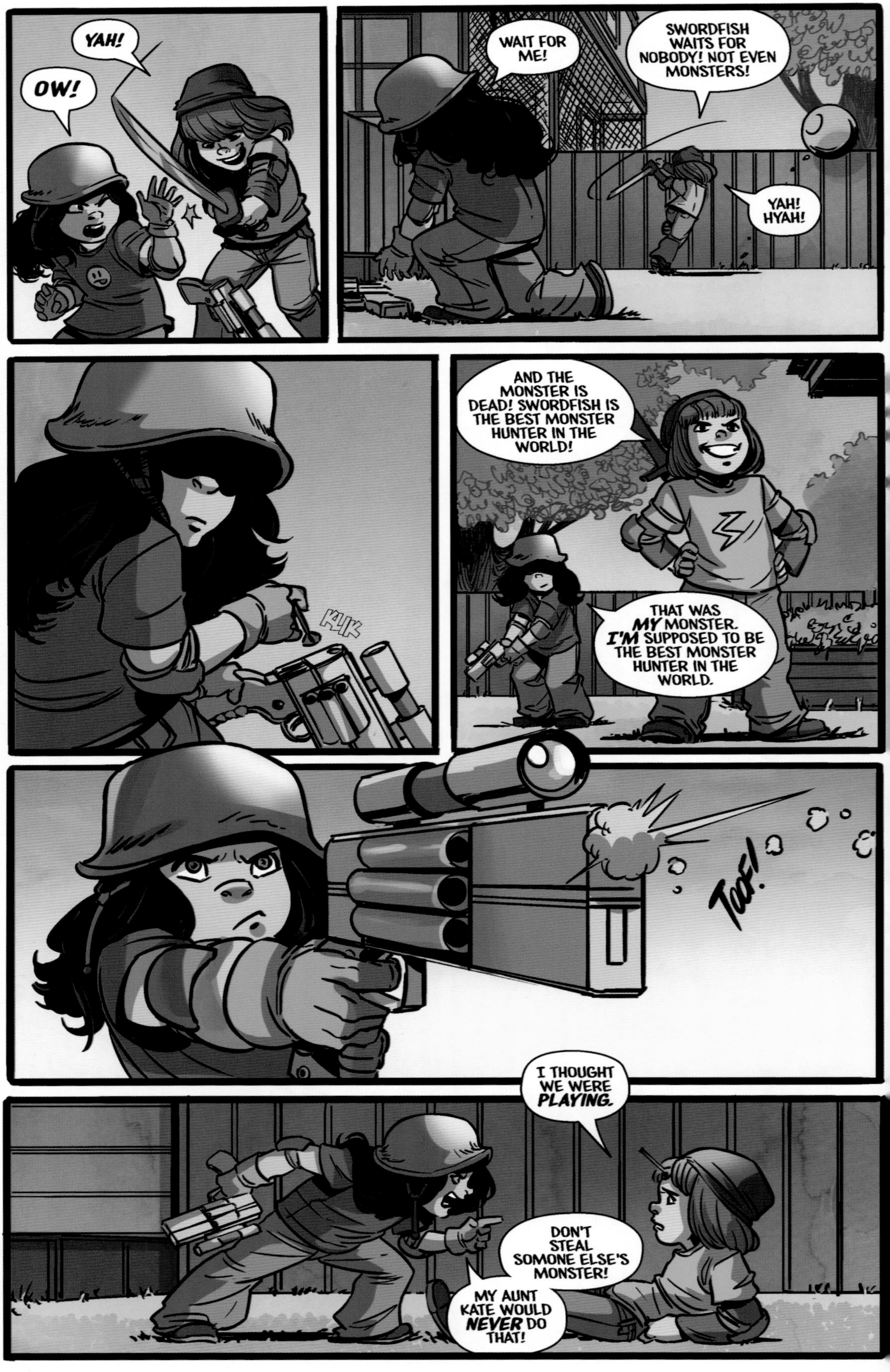
YAH!
OW!
WAIT FOR ME!
SWORDFISH WAITS FOR NOBODY! NOT EVEN MONSTERS!
YAH! HYAH!
KLIK
AND THE MONSTER IS DEAD! SWORDFISH IS THE BEST MONSTER HUNTER IN THE WORLD!
THAT WAS MY MONSTER. I'M SUPPOSED TO BE THE BEST MONSTER HUNTER IN THE WORLD.
TOOF!
I THOUGHT WE WERE PLAYING.
DON'T STEAL SOMONE ELSE'S MONSTER!
MY AUNT KATE WOULD NEVER DO THAT!

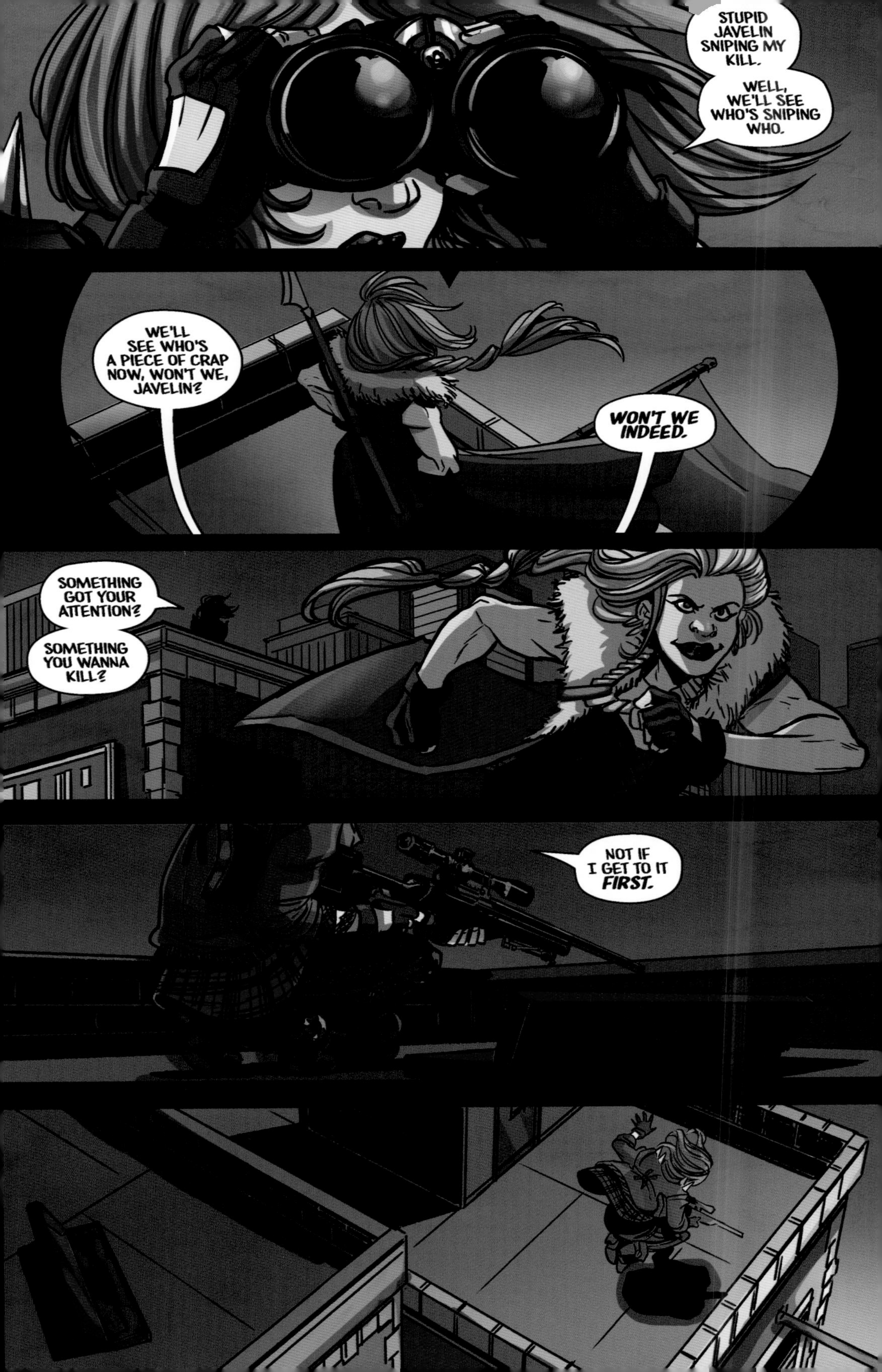

STUPID JAVELIN SNIPING MY KILL.
WELL, WE'LL SEE WHO'S SNIPING WHO.
WE'LL SEE WHO'S A PIECE OF CRAP NOW, WON'T WE, JAVELIN?
WON'T WE INDEED.
SOMETHING GOT YOUR ATTENTION?
SOMETHING YOU WANNA KILL?
NOT IF I GET TO IT FIRST.

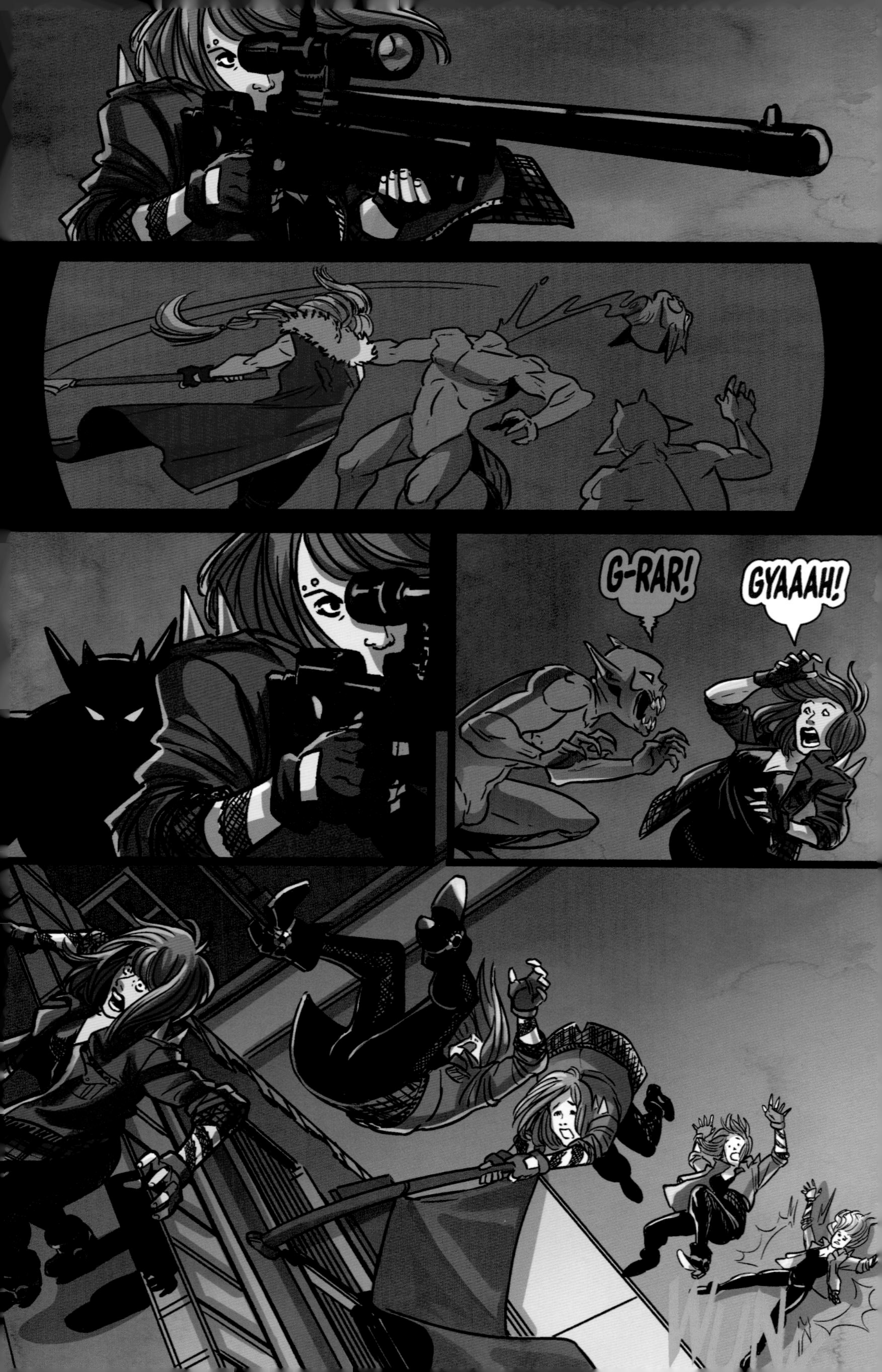
G-RAR!
GYAAAH!

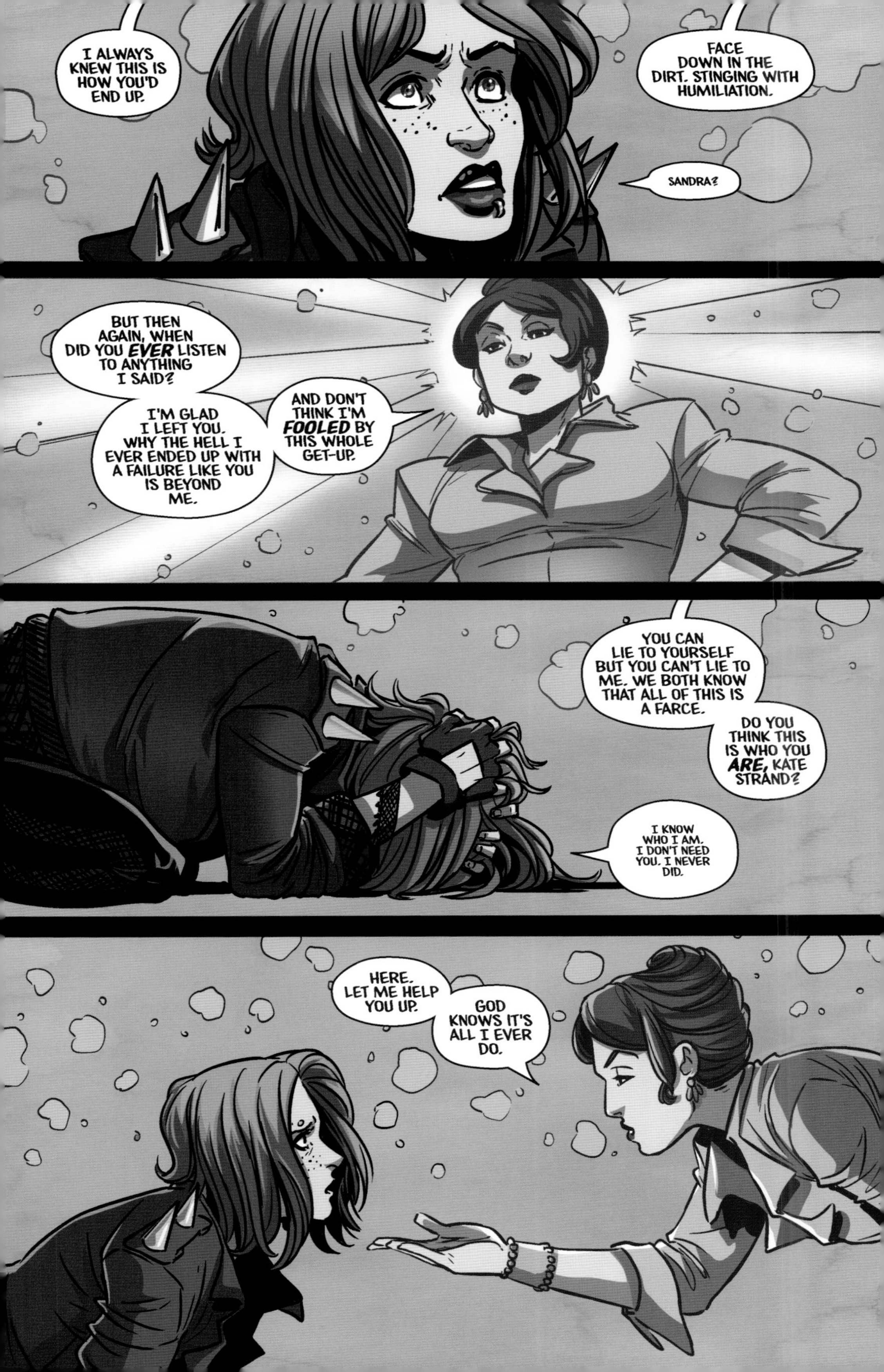
I ALWAYS KNEW THIS IS HOW YOU'D END UP.
FACE DOWN IN THE DIRT. STINGING WITH HUMILIATION.
SANDRA?
BUT THEN AGAIN, WHEN DID YOU EVER LISTEN TO ANYTHING I SAID?
I'M GLAD I LEFT YOU. WHY THE HELL I EVER ENDED UP WITH A FAILURE LIKE YOU IS BEYOND ME.
AND DON'T THINK I'M FOOLED BY THIS WHOLE GET-UP.
YOU CAN LIE TO YOURSELF BUT YOU CAN'T LIE TO ME. WE BOTH KNOW THAT ALL OF THIS IS A FARCE.
DO YOU THINK THIS IS WHO YOU ARE, KATE STRAND?
I KNOW WHO I AM. I DON'T NEED YOU. I NEVER DID.
HERE. LET ME HELP YOU UP.
GOD KNOWS IT'S ALL I EVER DO.

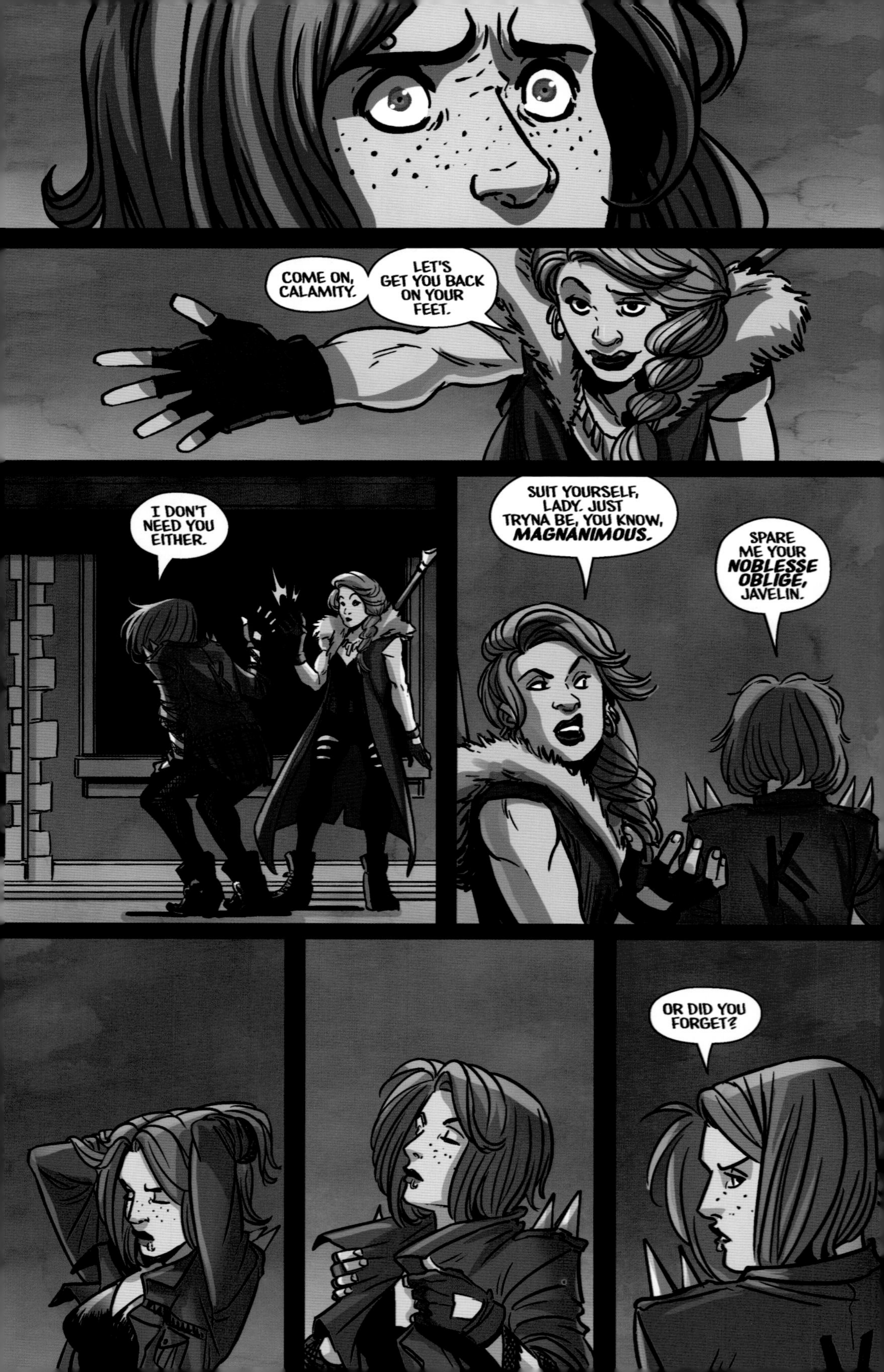

COME ON, CALAMITY.
LET'S GET YOU BACK ON YOUR FEET.
I DON'T NEED YOU EITHER.
SUIT YOURSELF, LADY. JUST TRYNA BE, YOU KNOW, MAGNANIMOUS.
SPARE ME YOUR NOBLESSE OBLIGE, JAVELIN.
OR DID YOU FORGET?

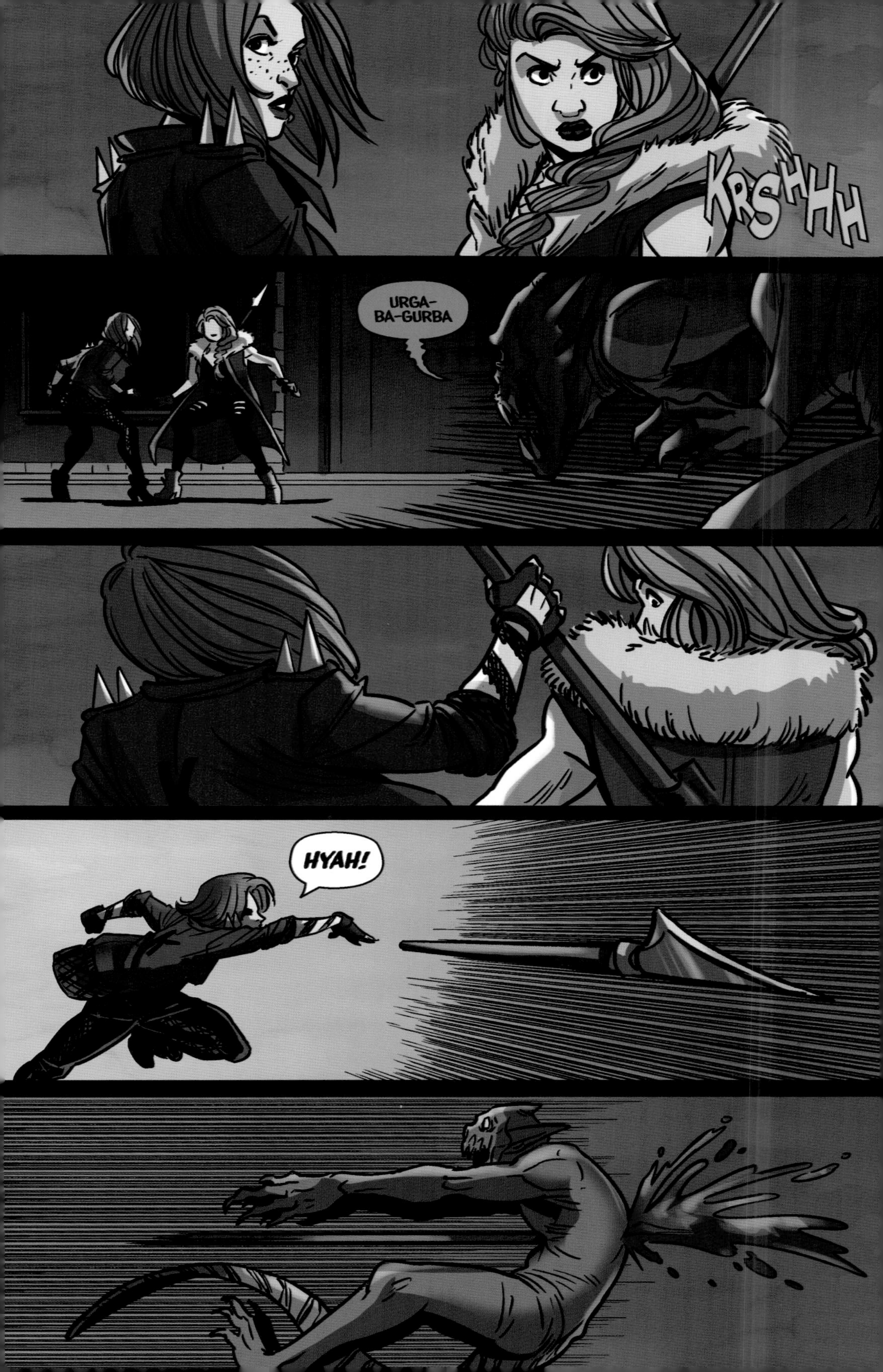
KRSHHH
URGA-BA-GURBA
HYAH!

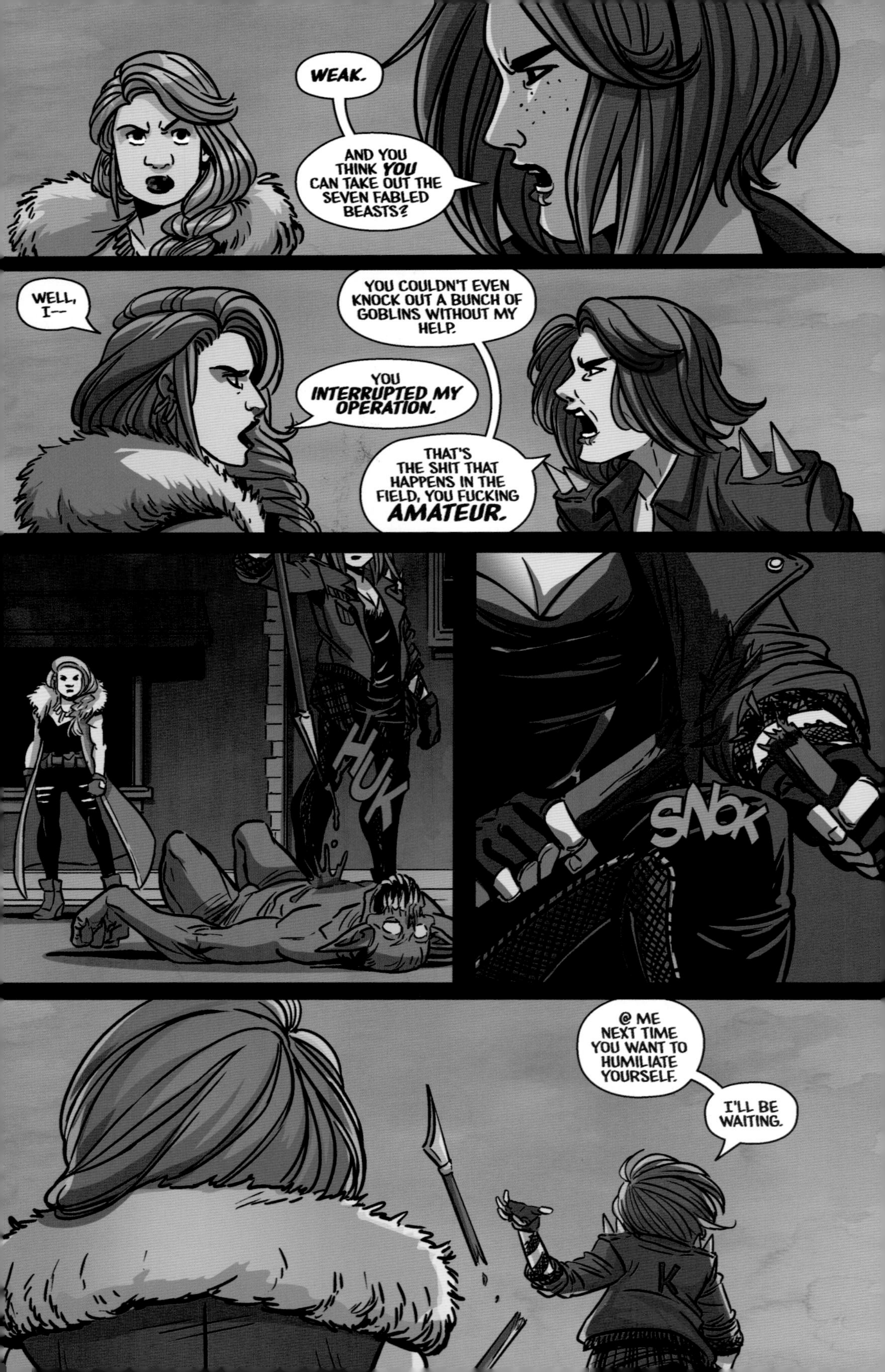
WEAK.
AND YOU THINK YOU CAN TAKE OUT THE SEVEN FABLED BEASTS?
WELL, I--
YOU COULDN'T EVEN KNOCK OUT A BUNCH OF GOBLINS WITHOUT MY HELP.
YOU INTERRUPTED MY OPERATION.
THAT'S THE SHIT THAT HAPPENS IN THE FIELD, YOU FUCKING AMATEUR.
HUK
SNOK
@ ME NEXT TIME YOU WANT TO HUMILIATE YOURSELF.
I'LL BE WAITING.

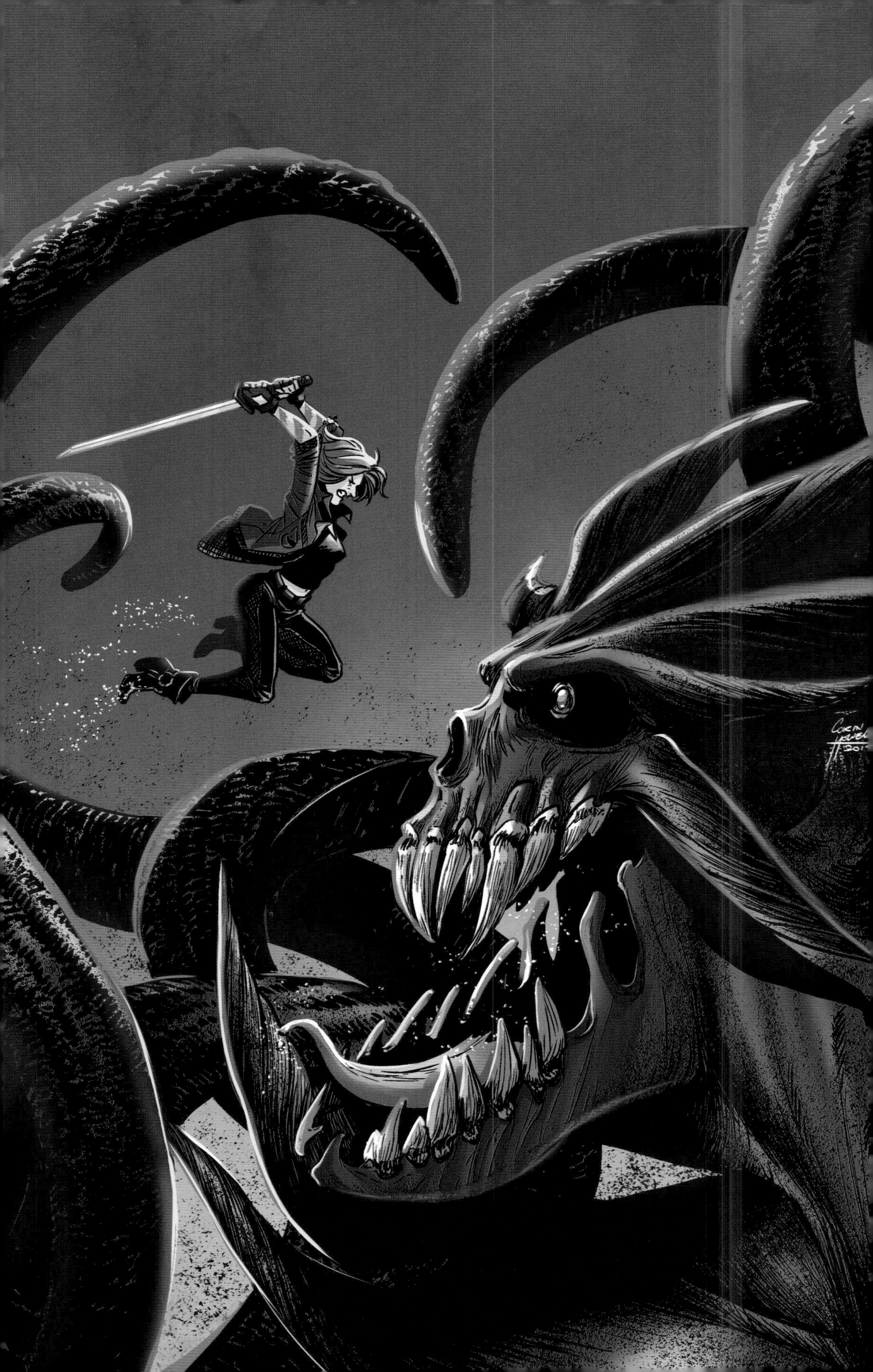

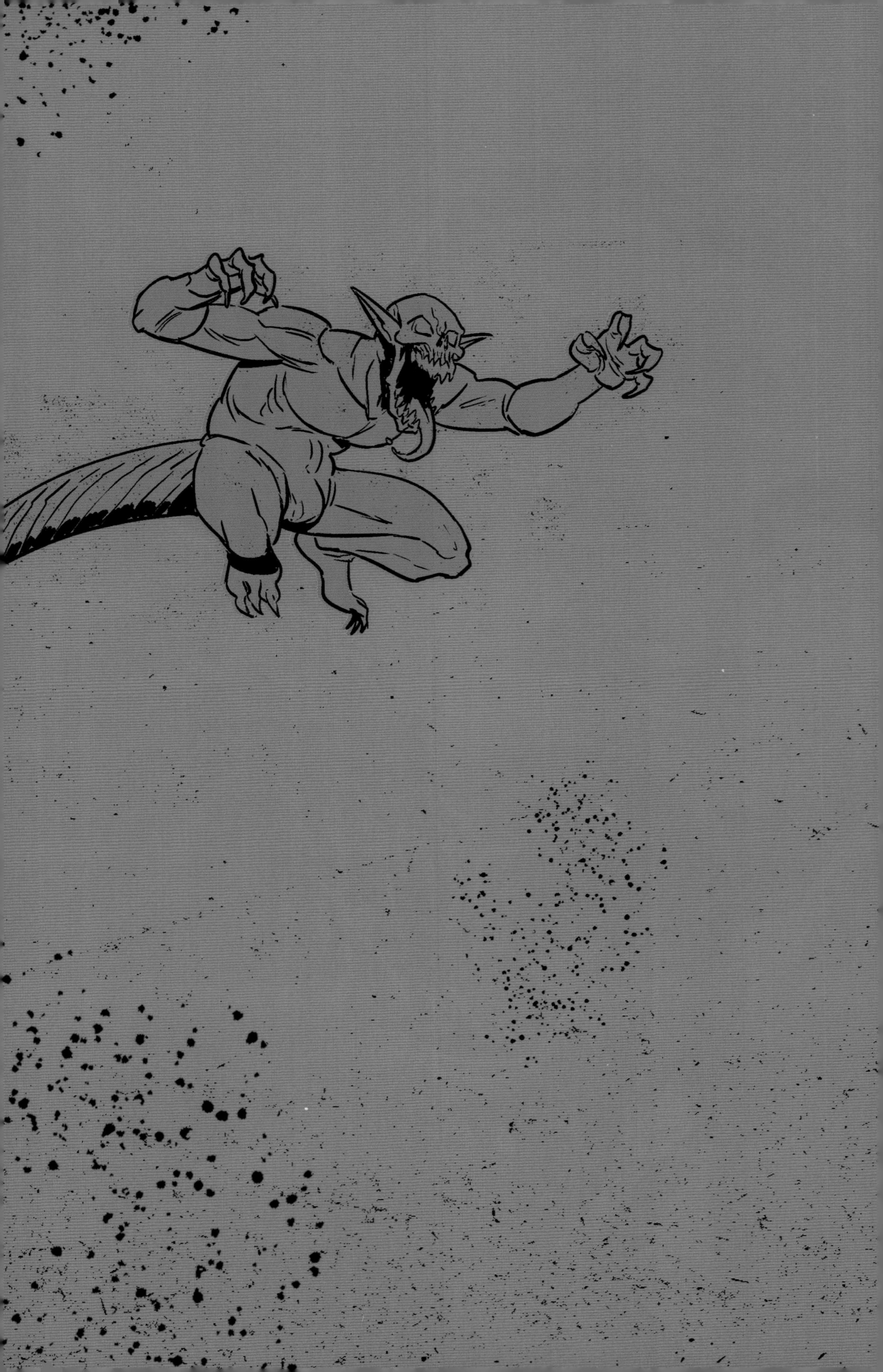

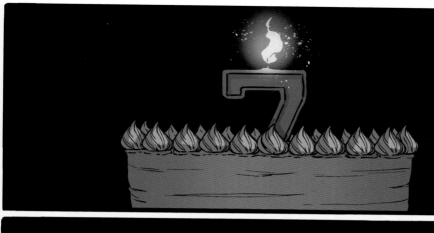

OKAY, SWEETIE! MAKE A WISH!

FIRST COMES THE *DESIRE.*

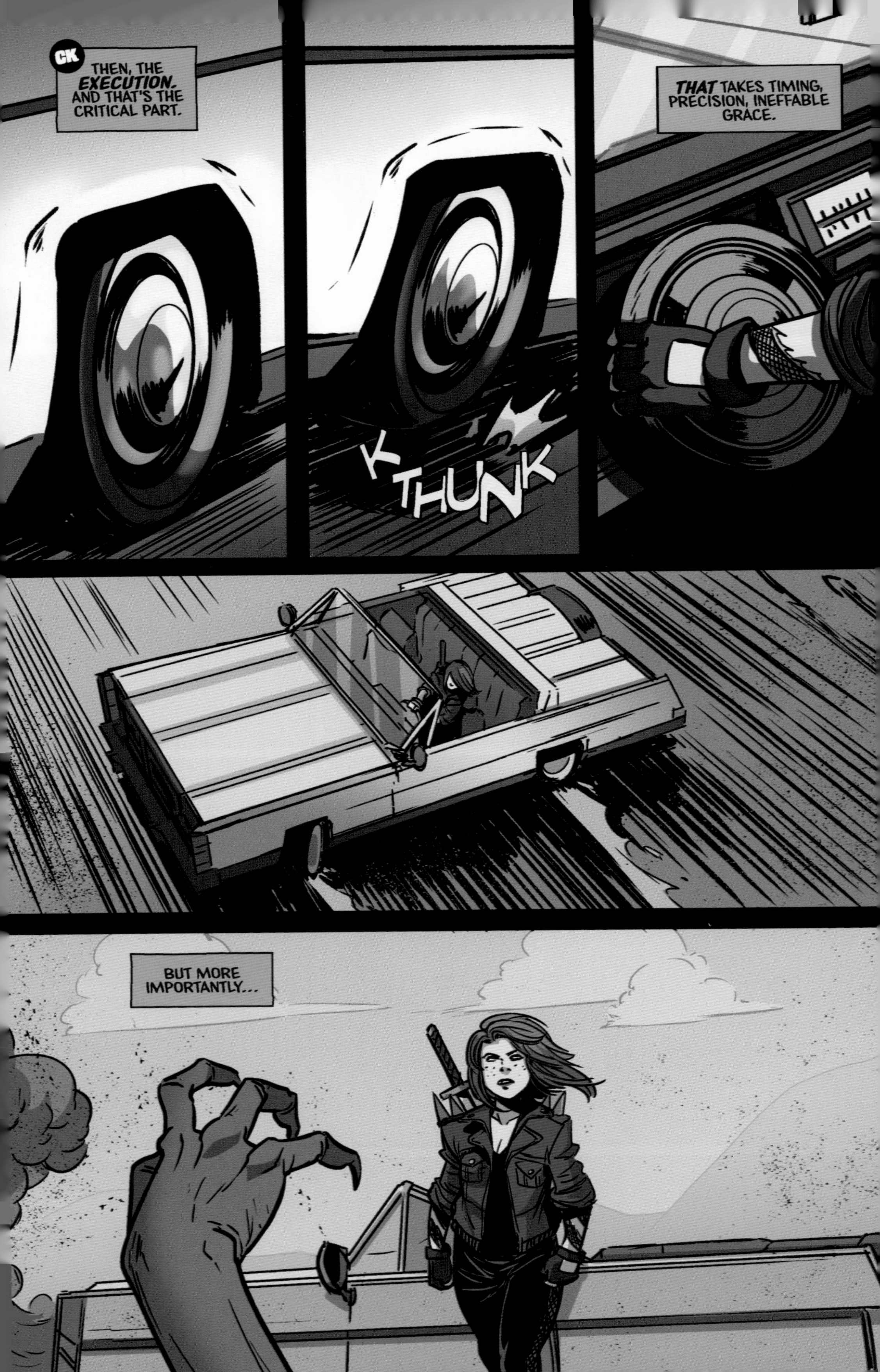
CK
THEN, THE EXECUTION. AND THAT'S THE CRITICAL PART.
KTHUNK
THAT TAKES TIMING, PRECISION, INEFFABLE GRACE.
BUT MORE IMPORTANTLY...

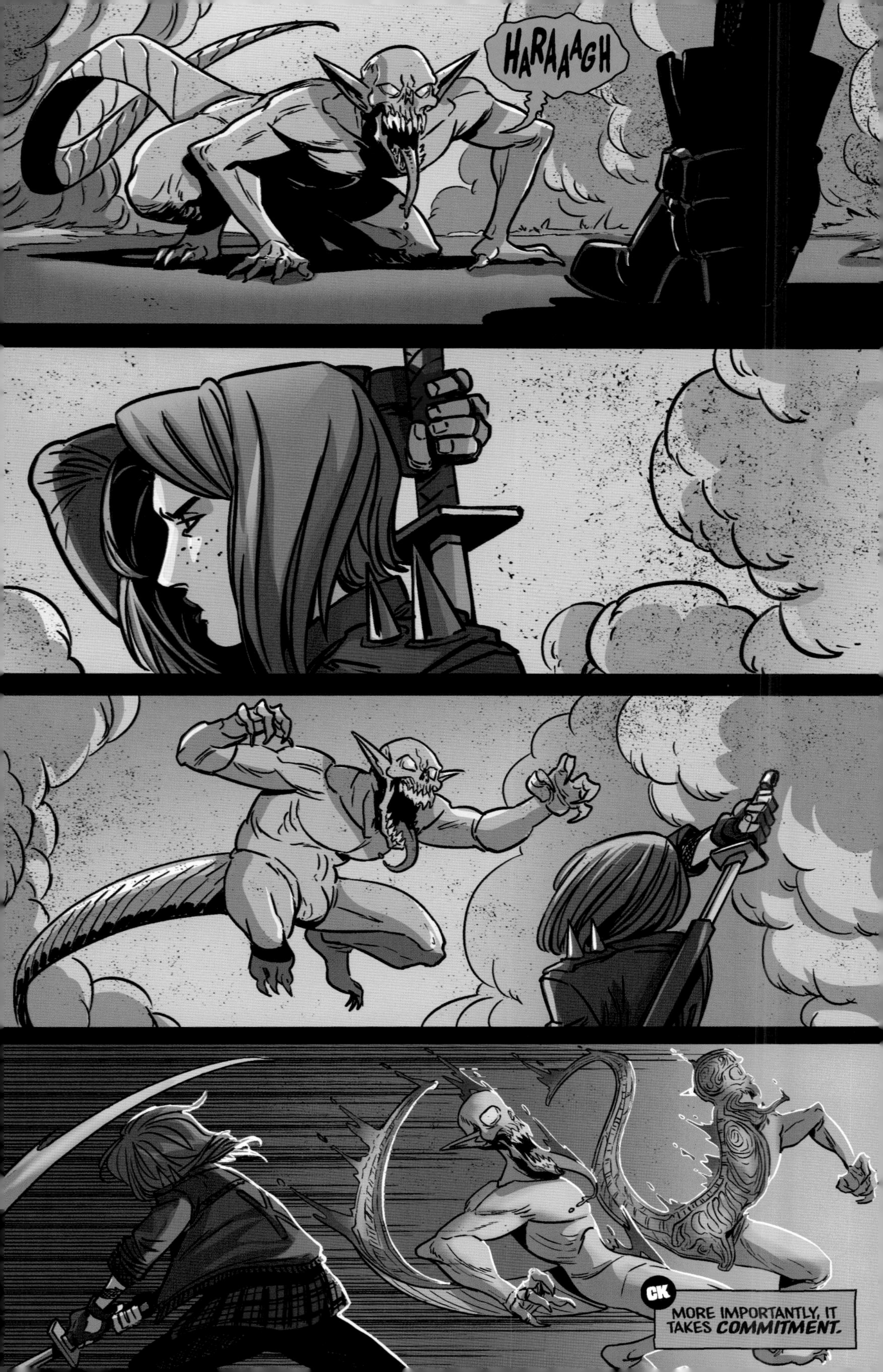
HARAAAGH
CK
MORE IMPORTANTLY, IT TAKES *COMMITMENT.*

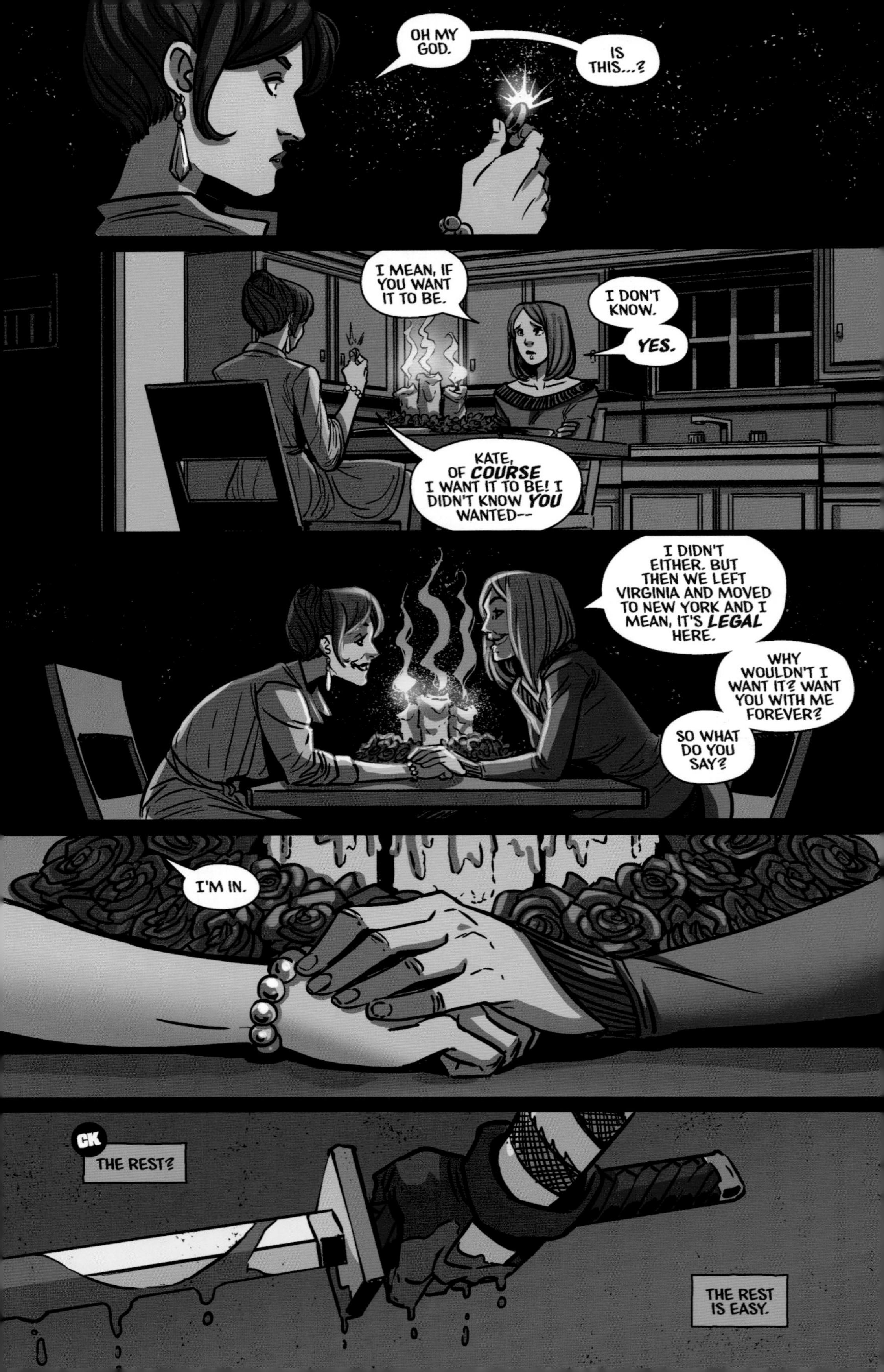
OH MY GOD.
IS THIS...?
I MEAN, IF YOU WANT IT TO BE.
I DON'T KNOW.
YES.
KATE, OF COURSE I WANT IT TO BE! I DIDN'T KNOW YOU WANTED--
I DIDN'T EITHER. BUT THEN WE LEFT VIRGINIA AND MOVED TO NEW YORK AND I MEAN, IT'S LEGAL HERE.
WHY WOULDN'T I WANT IT? WANT YOU WITH ME FOREVER?
SO WHAT DO YOU SAY?
I'M IN.
CK
THE REST?
THE REST IS EASY.

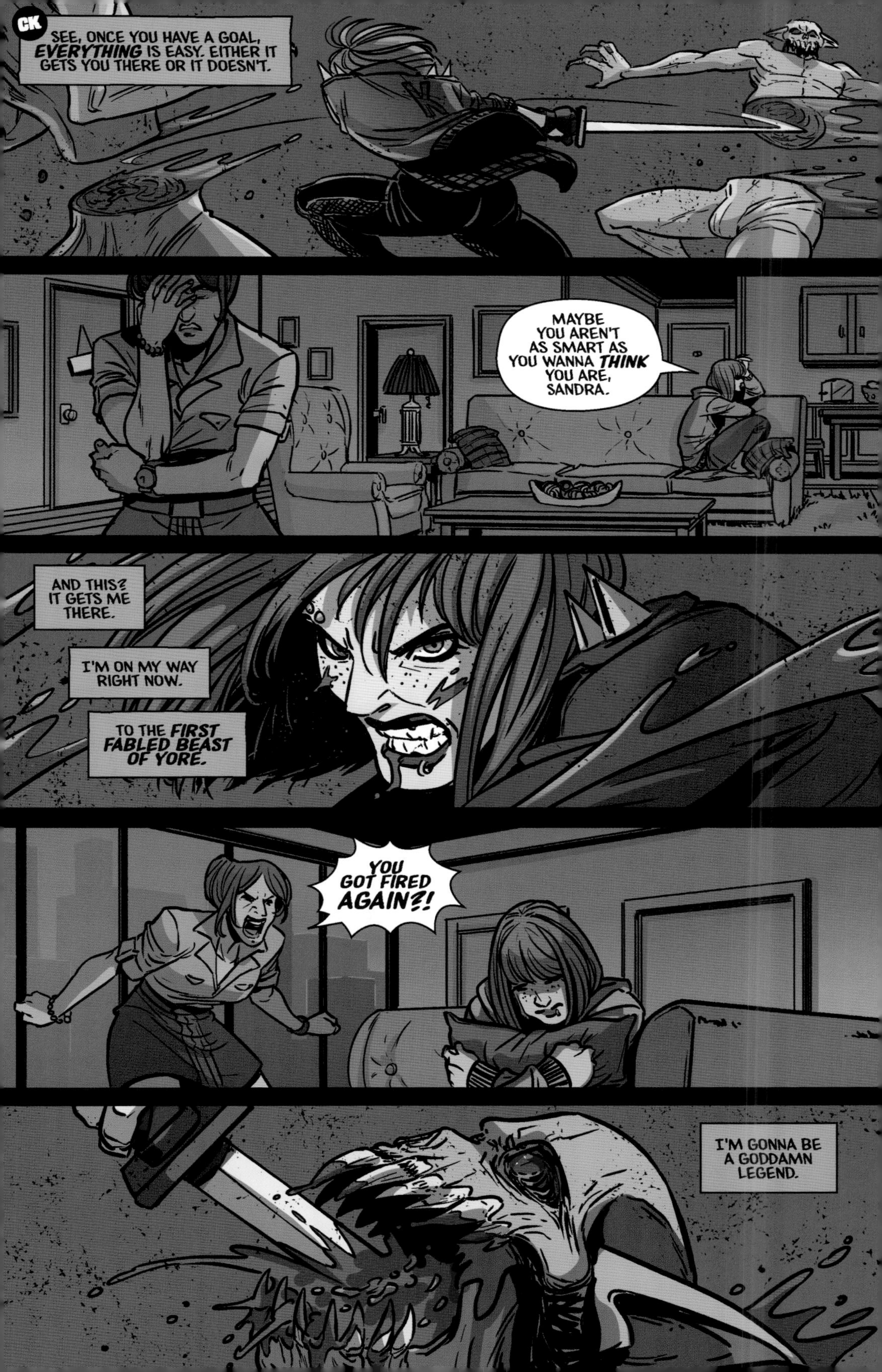
CK
SEE, ONCE YOU HAVE A GOAL, EVERYTHING IS EASY. EITHER IT GETS YOU THERE OR IT DOESN'T.
MAYBE YOU AREN'T AS SMART AS YOU WANNA THINK YOU ARE, SANDRA.
AND THIS? IT GETS ME THERE.
I'M ON MY WAY RIGHT NOW.
TO THE FIRST FABLED BEAST OF YORE.
YOU GOT FIRED AGAIN?!
I'M GONNA BE A GODDAMN LEGEND.

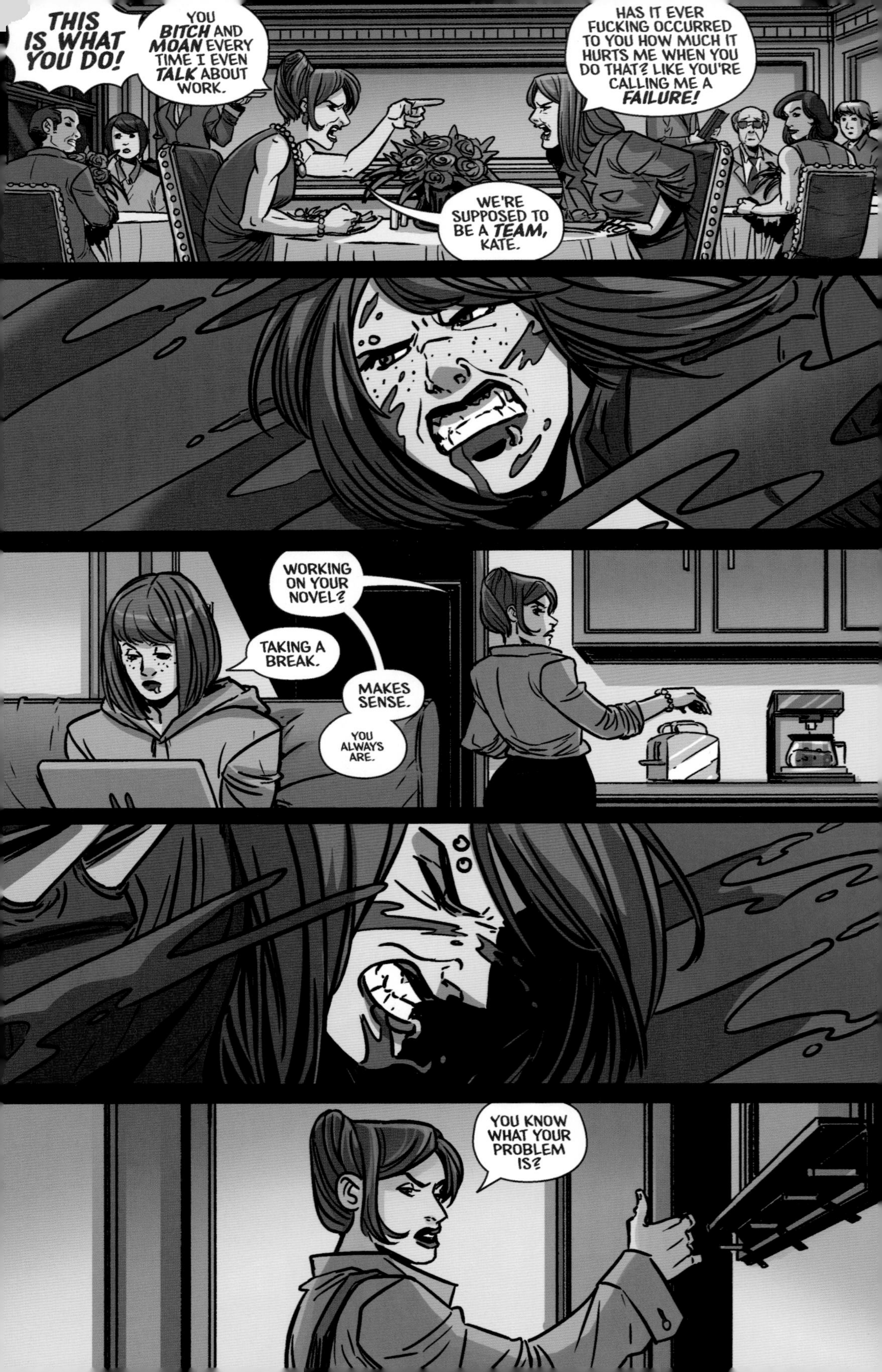
THIS IS WHAT YOU DO!
YOU BITCH AND MOAN EVERY TIME I EVEN TALK ABOUT WORK.
HAS IT EVER FUCKING OCCURRED TO YOU HOW MUCH IT HURTS ME WHEN YOU DO THAT? LIKE YOU'RE CALLING ME A FAILURE!
WE'RE SUPPOSED TO BE A TEAM, KATE.
WORKING ON YOUR NOVEL?
TAKING A BREAK.
MAKES SENSE.
YOU ALWAYS ARE.
YOU KNOW WHAT YOUR PROBLEM IS?

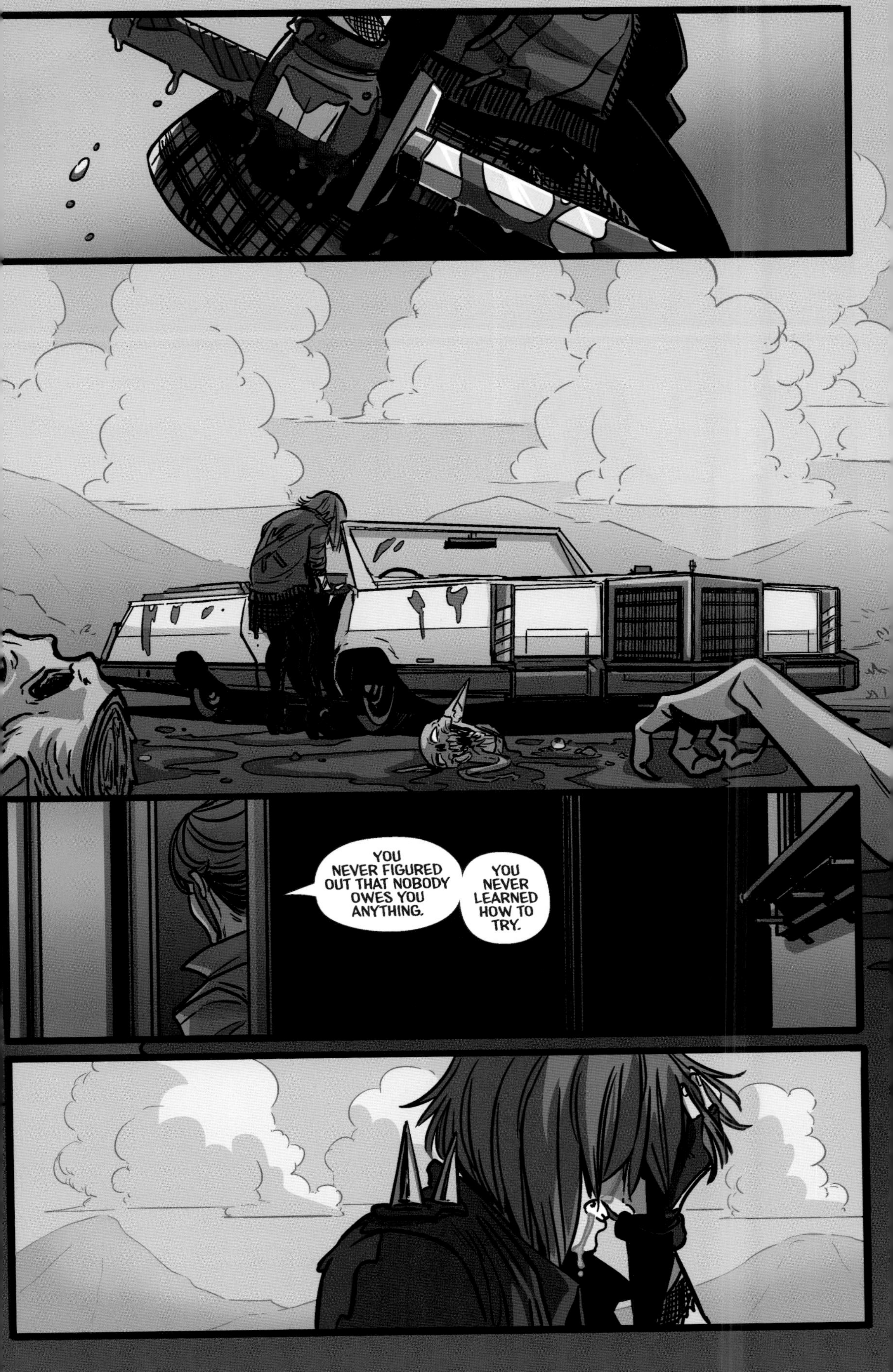
YOU NEVER FIGURED OUT THAT NOBODY OWES YOU ANYTHING.
YOU NEVER LEARNED HOW TO TRY.

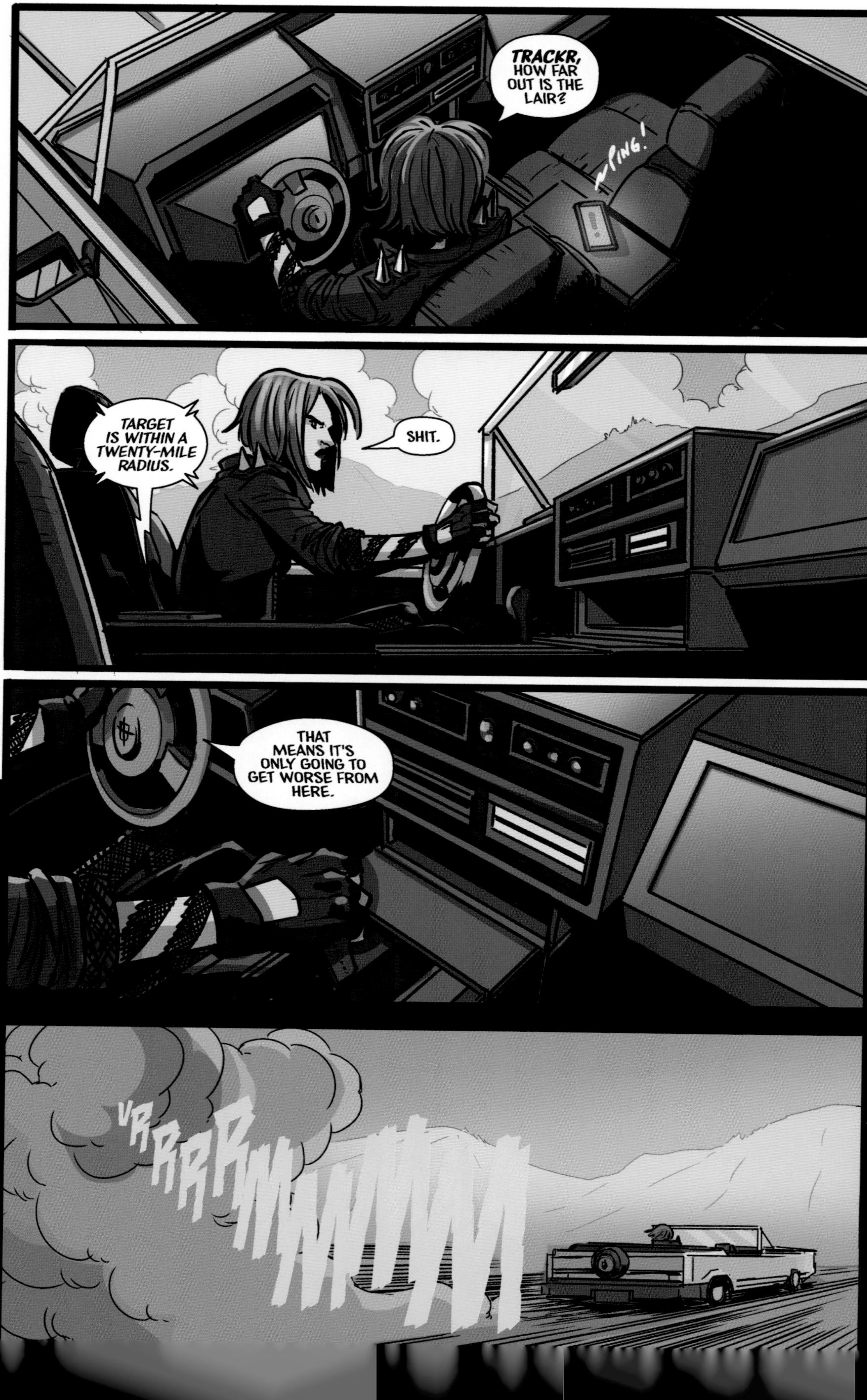
TRACKR, HOW FAR OUT IS THE LAIR?
PING!
TARGET IS WITHIN A TWENTY-MILE RADIUS.
SHIT.
THAT MEANS IT'S ONLY GOING TO GET WORSE FROM HERE.
VRRRRMMMMMMM

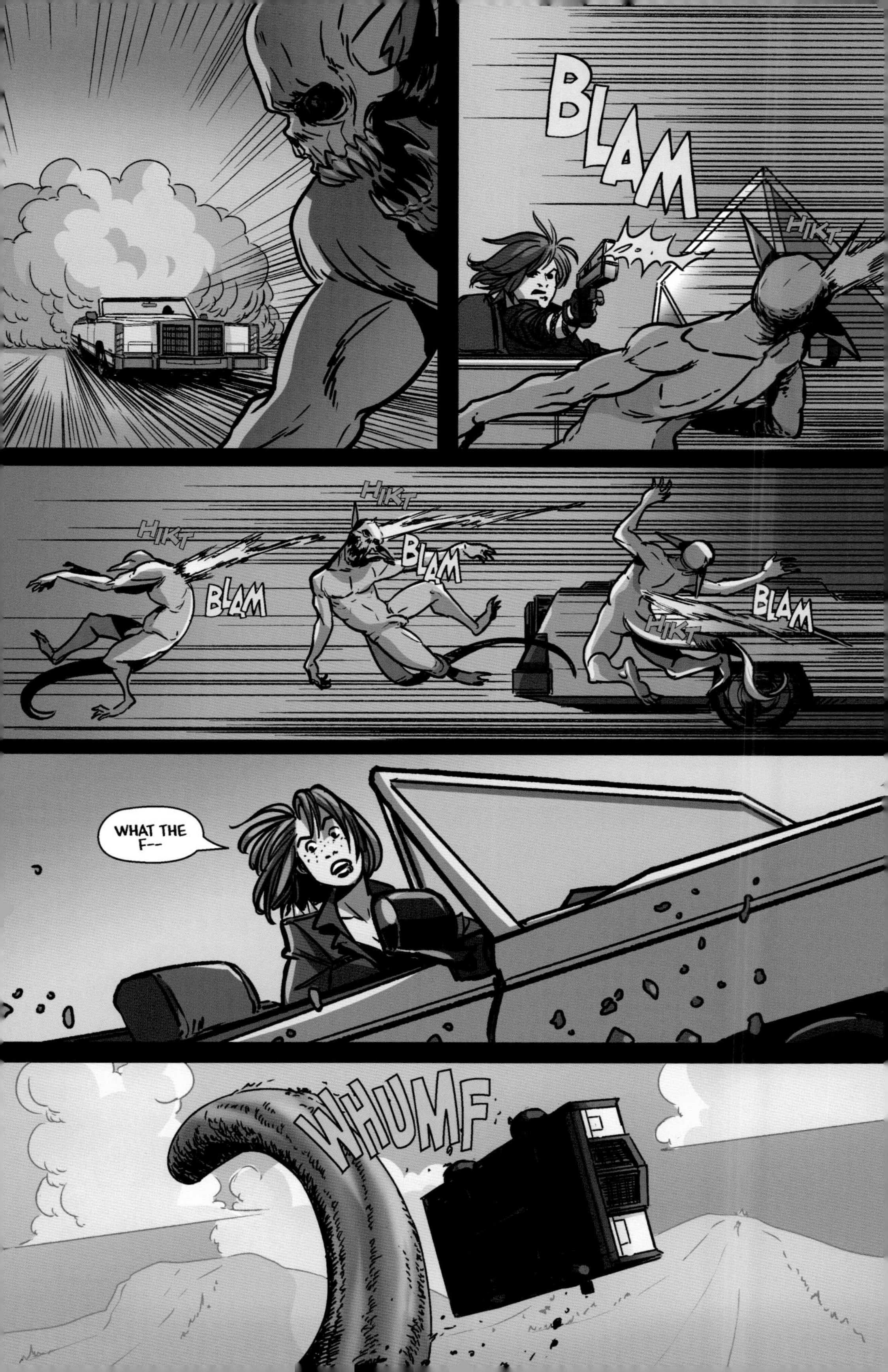
BLAM
HIKT
HIKT
BLAM
HIKT
BLAM
BLAM
HIKT
WHAT THE F--
WHUMF

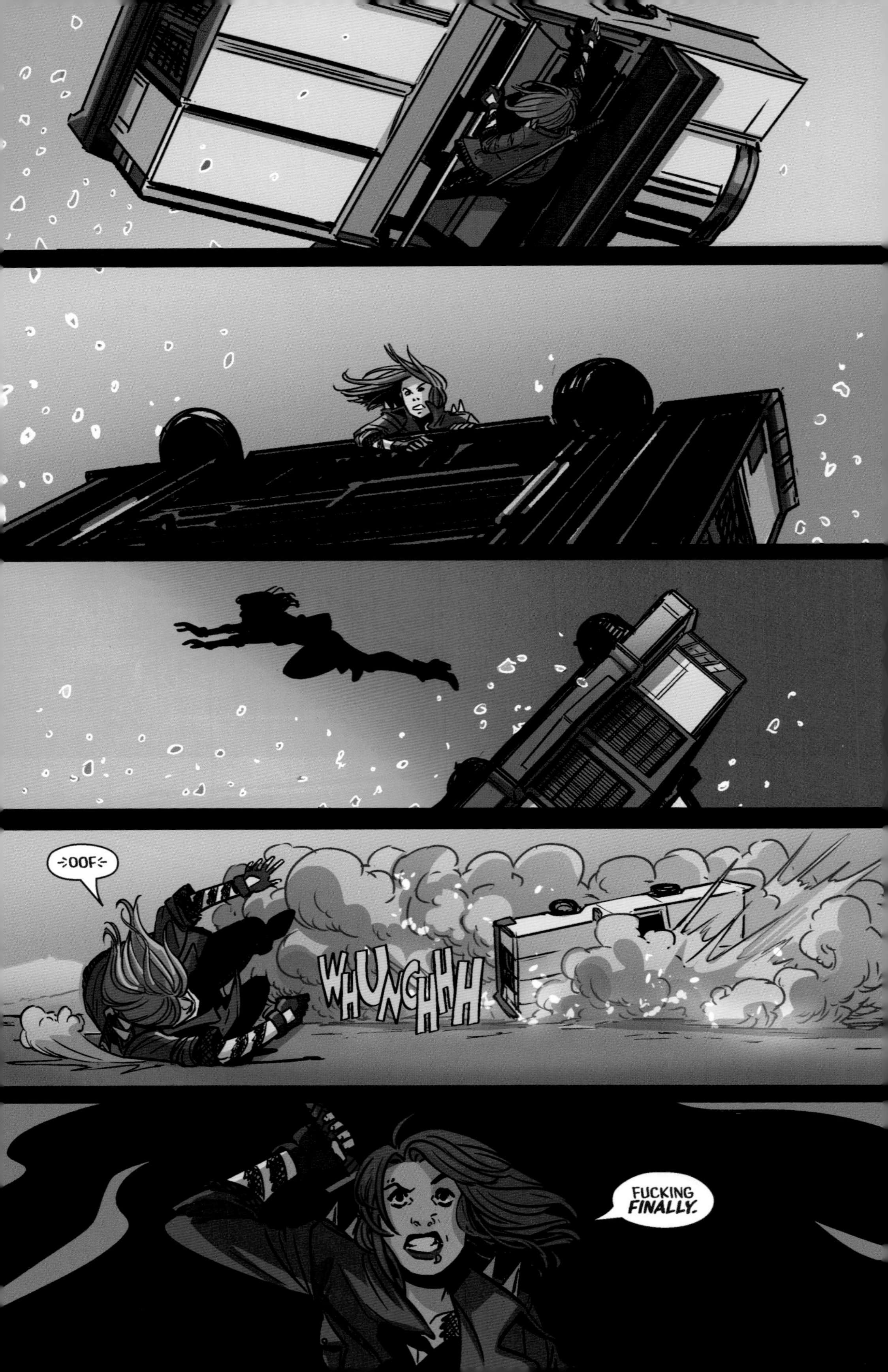
OOF
WHUNCHHH
FUCKING FINALLY.

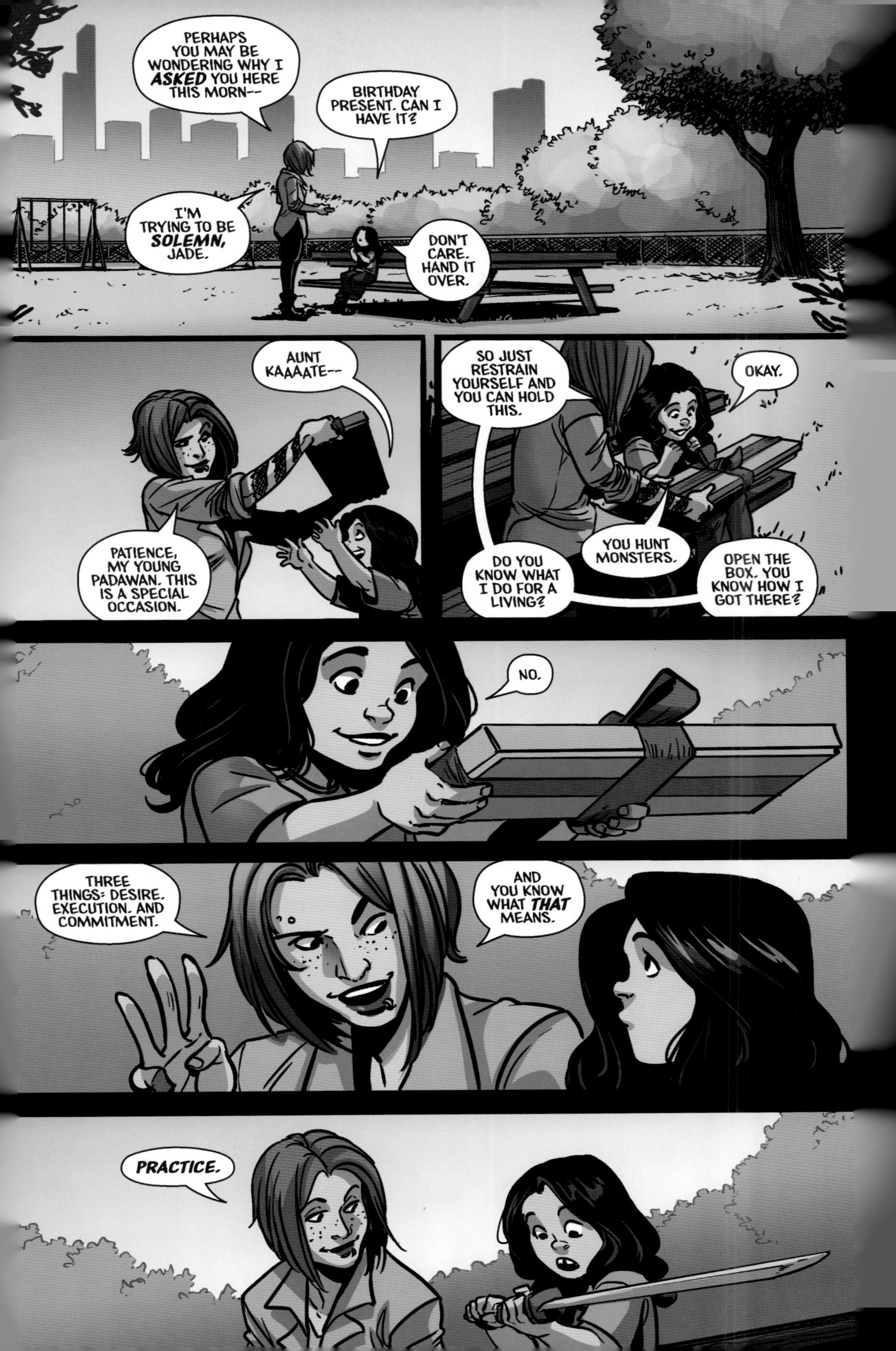
PERHAPS YOU MAY BE WONDERING WHY I *ASKED* YOU HERE THIS MORN--
BIRTHDAY PRESENT. CAN I HAVE IT?
I'M TRYING TO BE *SOLEMN,* JADE.
DON'T CARE. HAND IT OVER.
AUNT KAAAATE--
PATIENCE, MY YOUNG PADAWAN. THIS IS A SPECIAL OCCASION.
SO JUST RESTRAIN YOURSELF AND YOU CAN HOLD THIS.
OKAY.
DO YOU KNOW WHAT I DO FOR A LIVING?
YOU HUNT MONSTERS.
OPEN THE BOX. YOU KNOW HOW I GOT THERE?
NO.
THREE THINGS: DESIRE. EXECUTION. AND COMMITMENT.
AND YOU KNOW WHAT *THAT* MEANS.
PRACTICE.

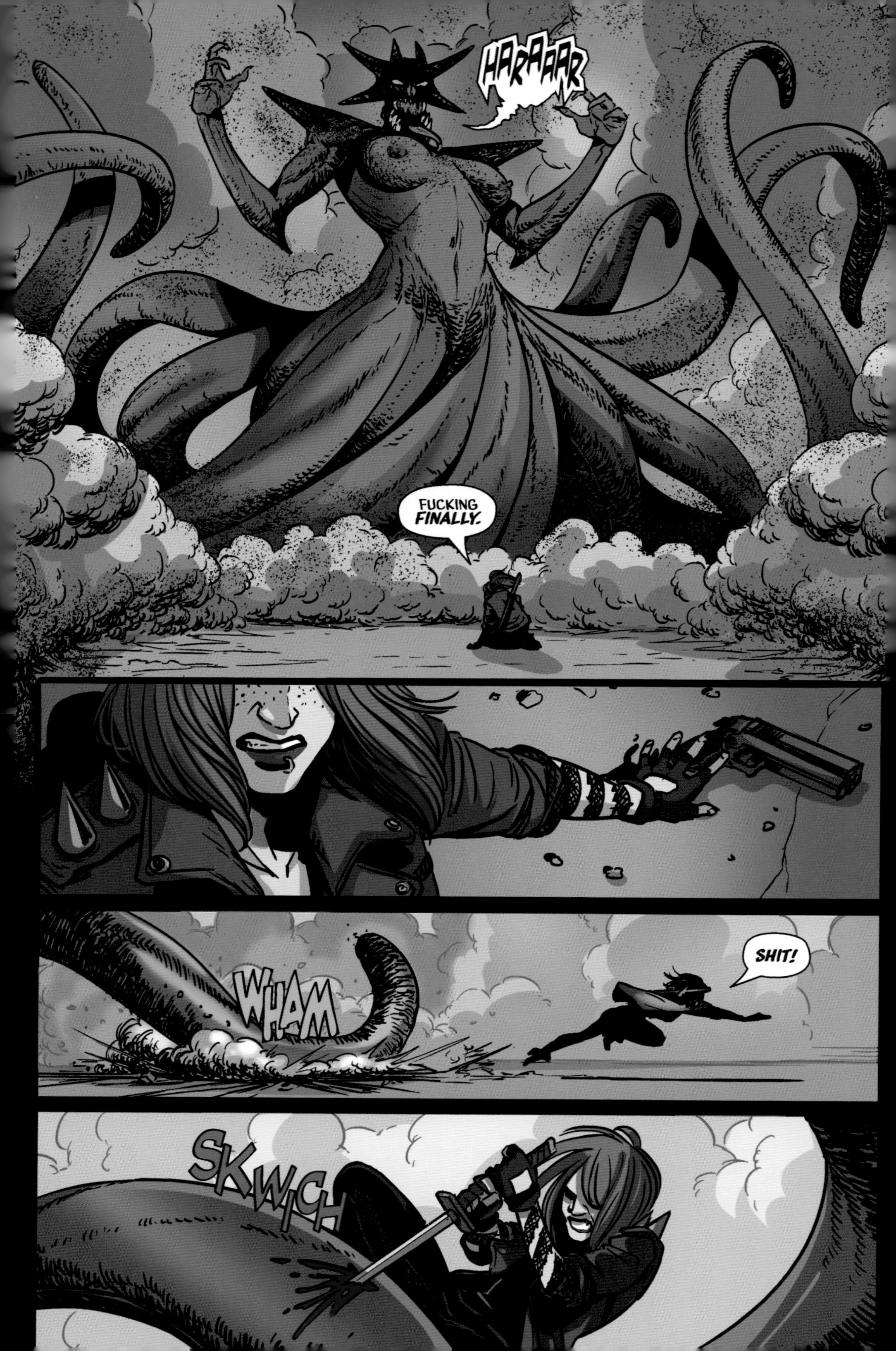
HARAAAR
FUCKING FINALLY.
WHAM
SHIT!
SKWICH

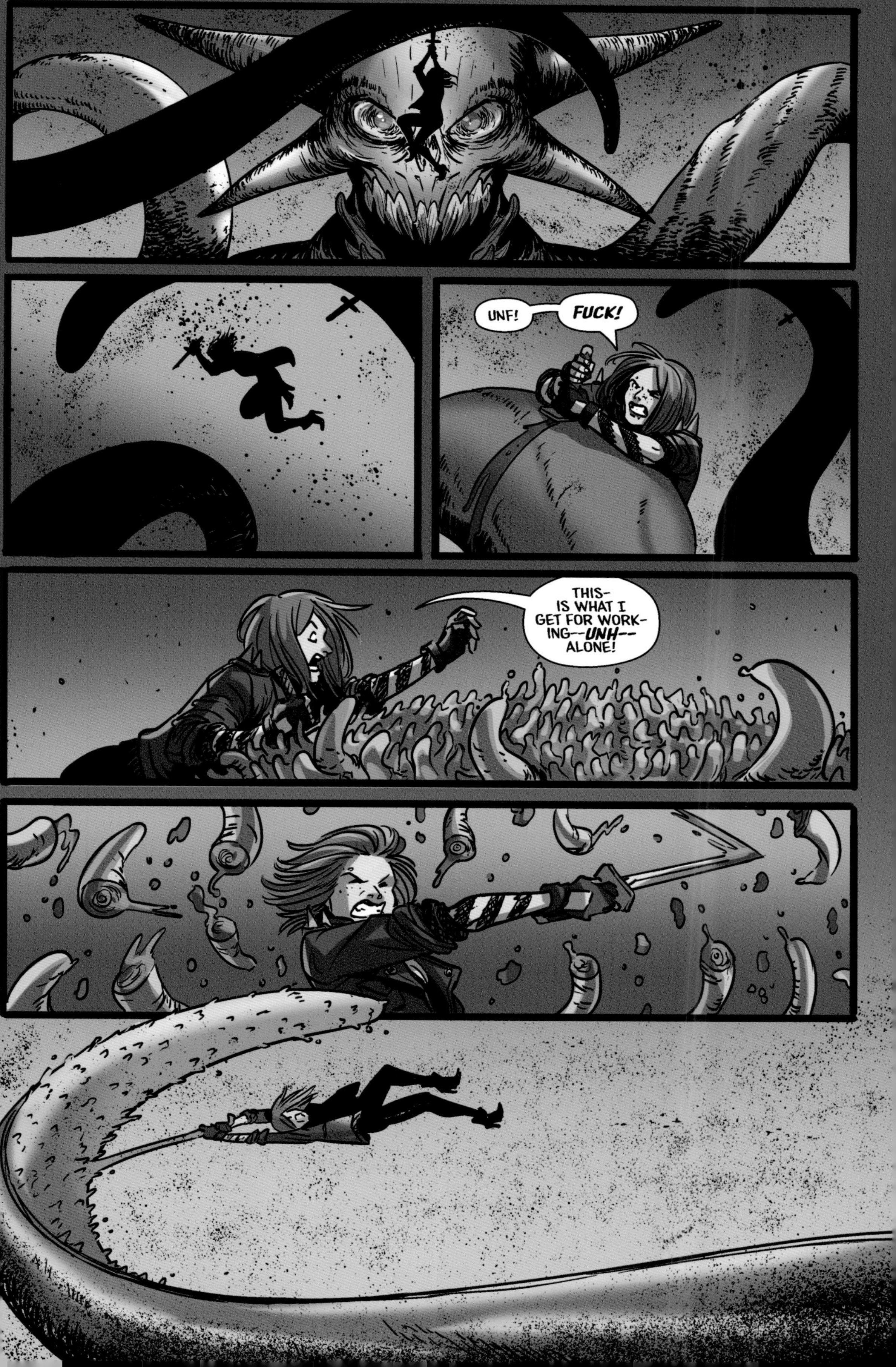
UNF!
FUCK!
THIS-
IS WHAT I
GET FOR WORK-
ING--UNH--
ALONE!

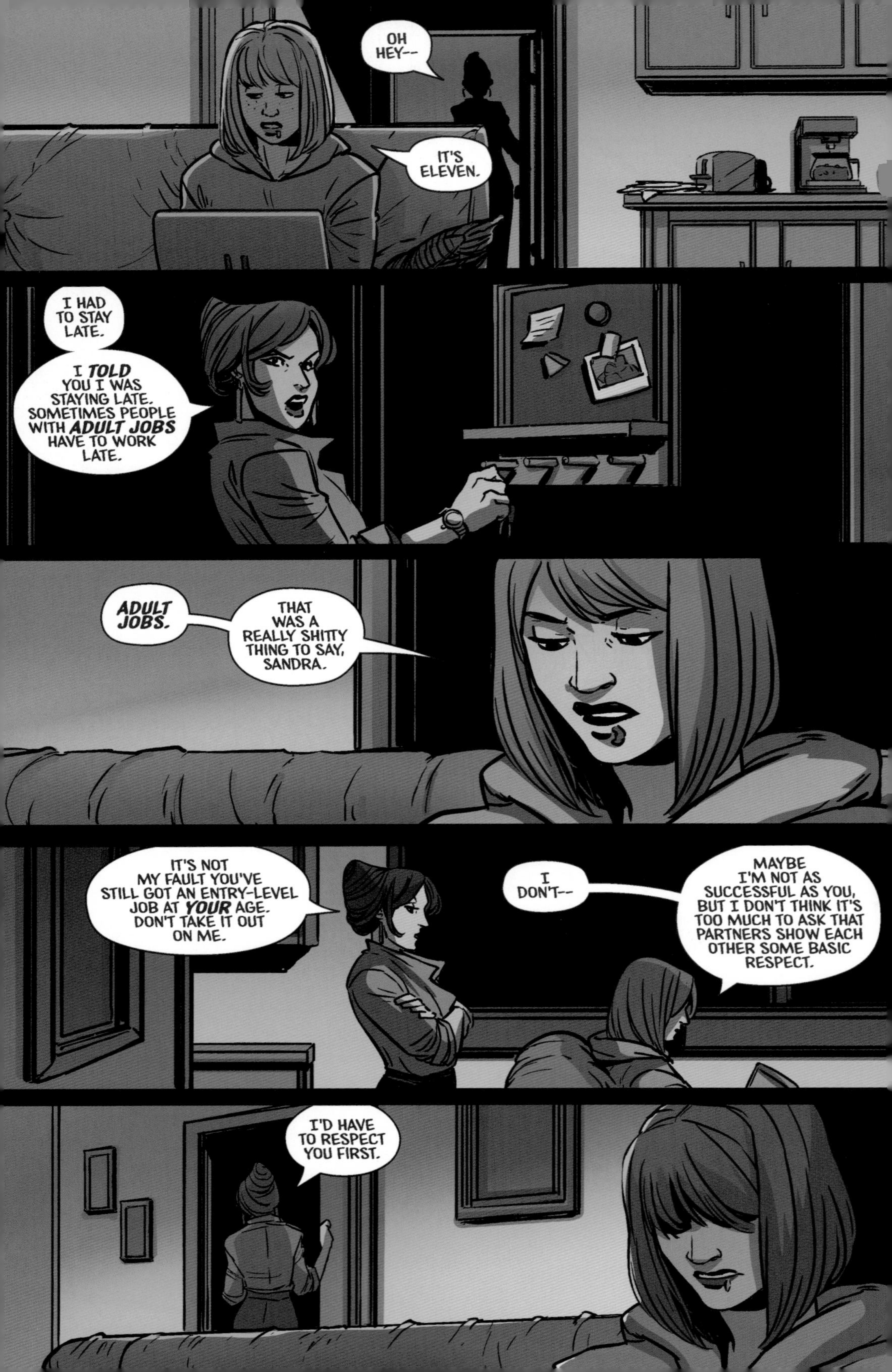
OH HEY--
IT'S ELEVEN.
I HAD TO STAY LATE.
I TOLD YOU I WAS STAYING LATE. SOMETIMES PEOPLE WITH ADULT JOBS HAVE TO WORK LATE.
ADULT JOBS.
THAT WAS A REALLY SHITTY THING TO SAY, SANDRA.
IT'S NOT MY FAULT YOU'VE STILL GOT AN ENTRY-LEVEL JOB AT YOUR AGE. DON'T TAKE IT OUT ON ME.
I DON'T--
MAYBE I'M NOT AS SUCCESSFUL AS YOU, BUT I DON'T THINK IT'S TOO MUCH TO ASK THAT PARTNERS SHOW EACH OTHER SOME BASIC RESPECT.
I'D HAVE TO RESPECT YOU FIRST.

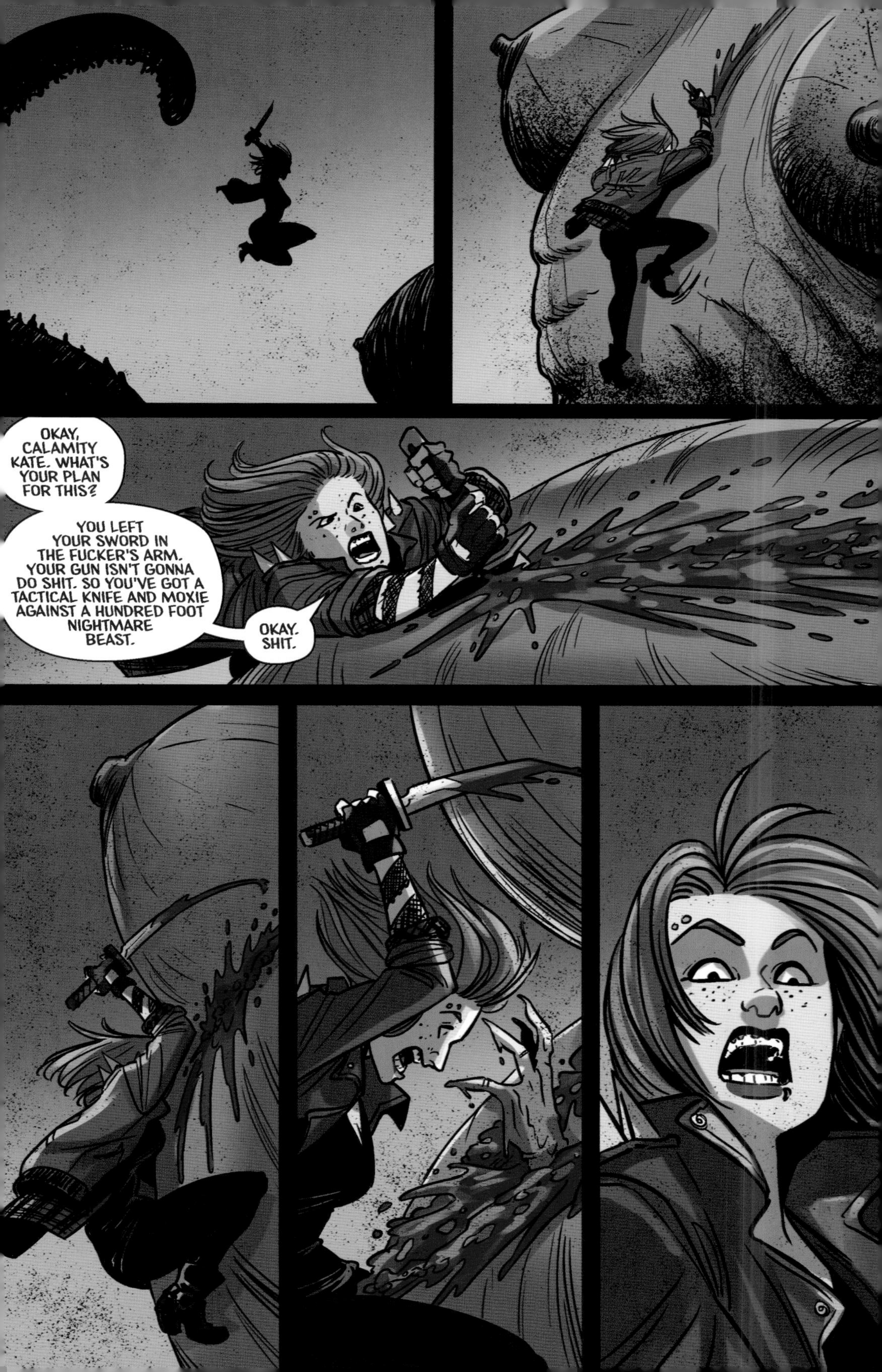
OKAY, CALAMITY KATE. WHAT'S YOUR PLAN FOR THIS?
YOU LEFT YOUR SWORD IN THE FUCKER'S ARM. YOUR GUN ISN'T GONNA DO SHIT. SO YOU'VE GOT A TACTICAL KNIFE AND MOXIE AGAINST A HUNDRED FOOT NIGHTMARE BEAST.
OKAY. SHIT.

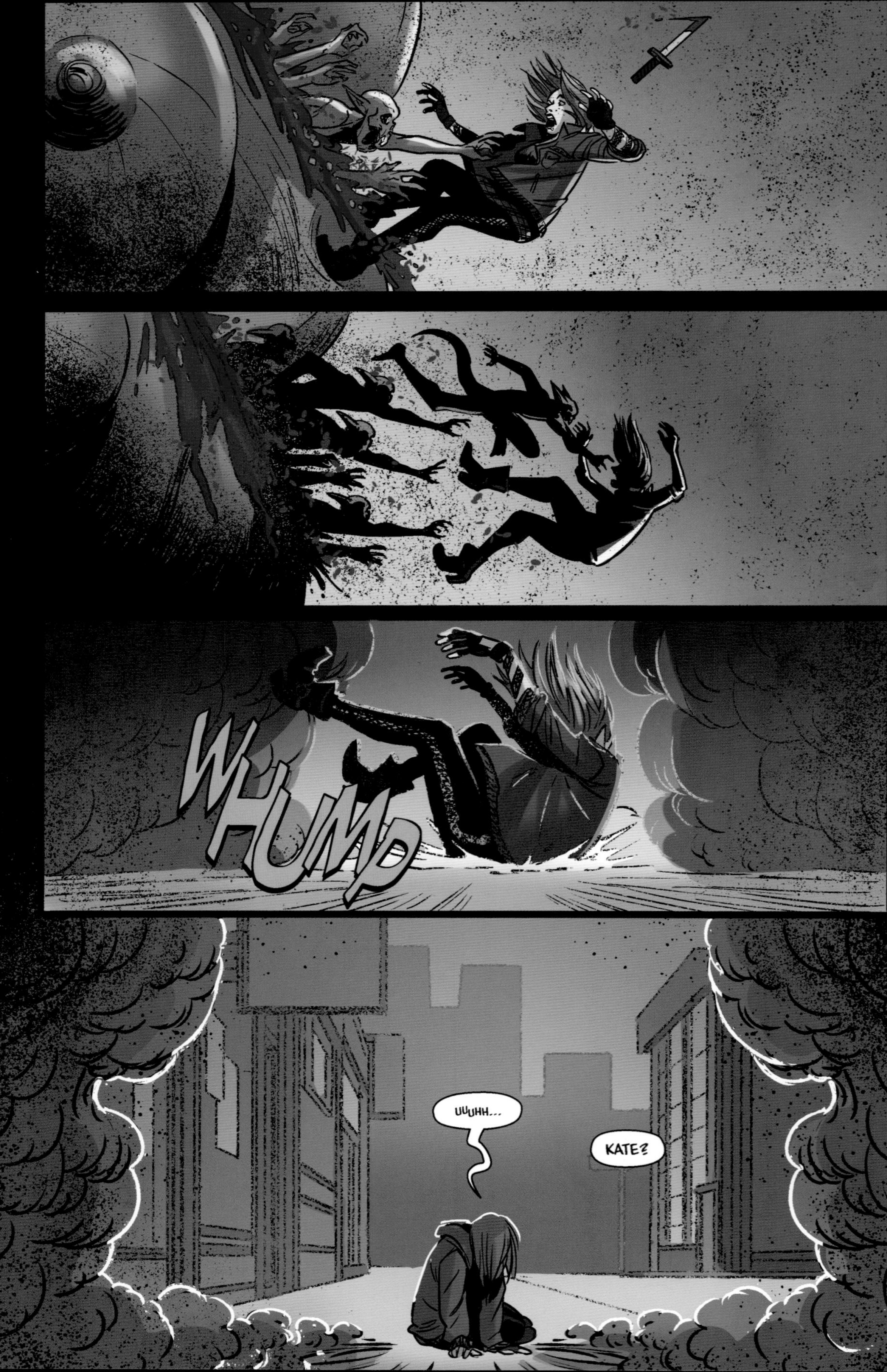
WHUMP
UUUHH...
KATE?

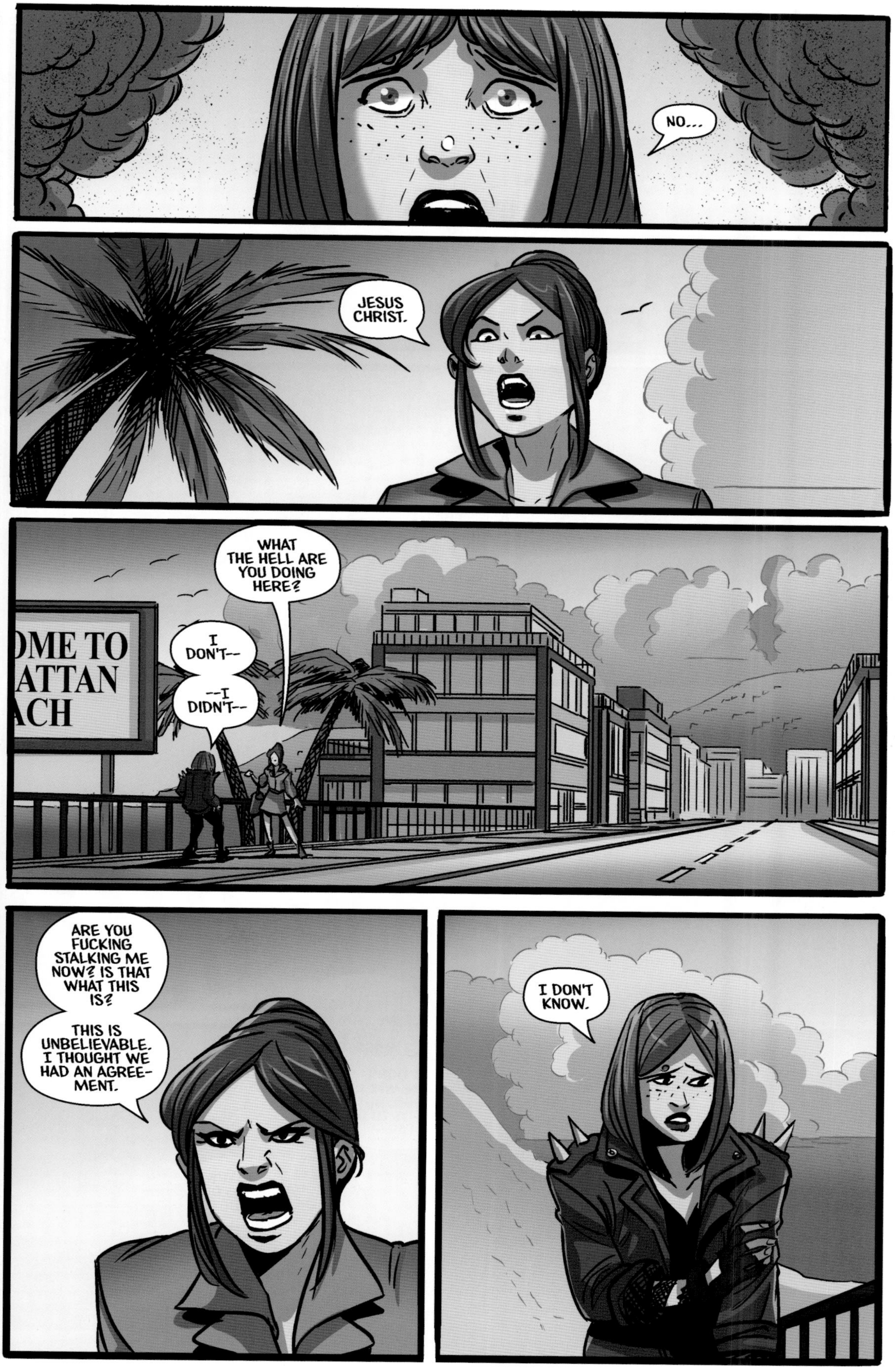
NO...
JESUS CHRIST.
WHAT THE HELL ARE YOU DOING HERE?
OME TO
ATTAN
ACH
I DON'T--
--I DIDN'T--
ARE YOU FUCKING STALKING ME NOW? IS THAT WHAT THIS IS?
THIS IS UNBELIEVABLE. I THOUGHT WE HAD AN AGREEMENT.
I DON'T KNOW.

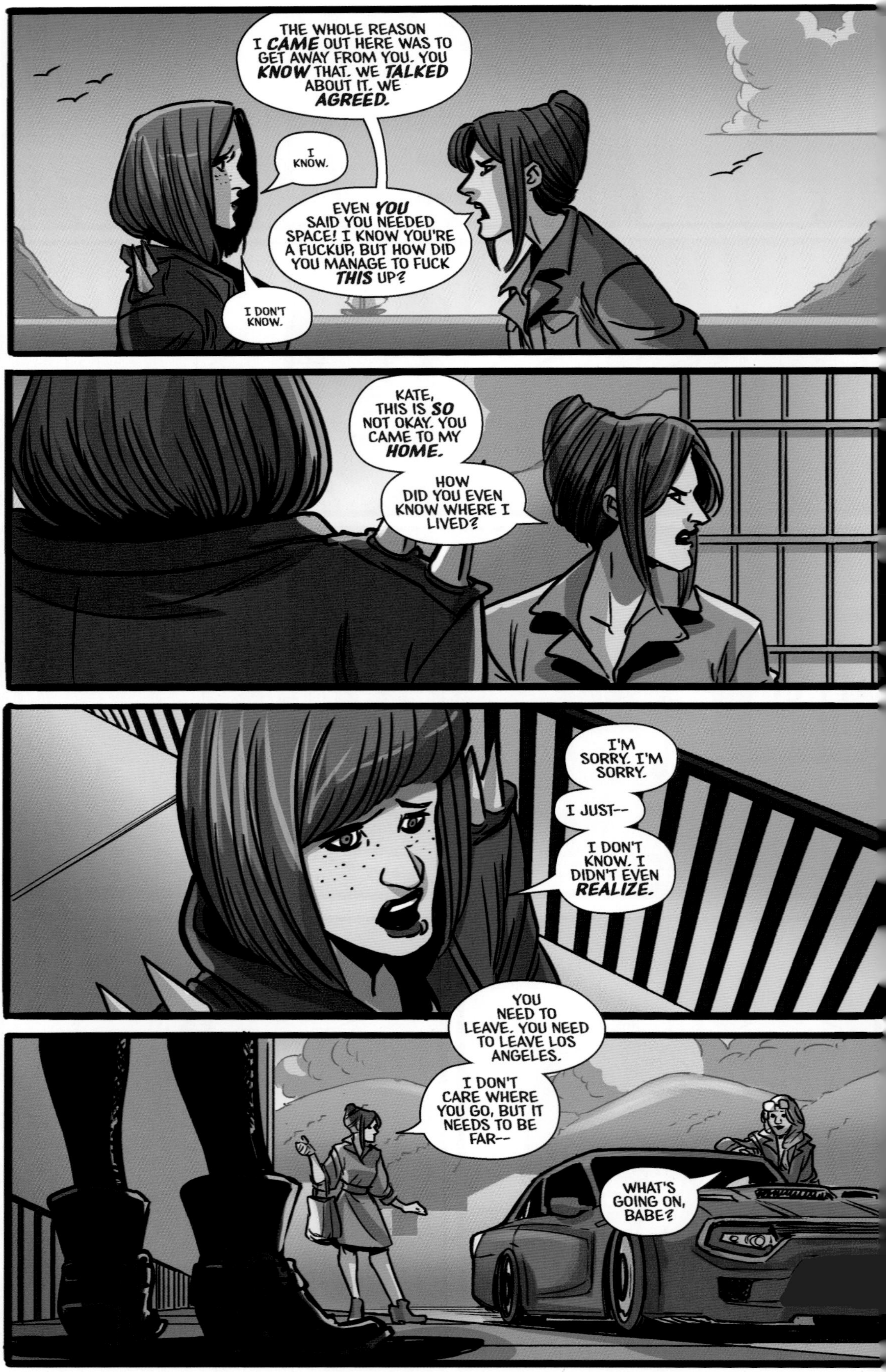
THE WHOLE REASON I CAME OUT HERE WAS TO GET AWAY FROM YOU. YOU KNOW THAT. WE TALKED ABOUT IT. WE AGREED.
I KNOW.
EVEN YOU SAID YOU NEEDED SPACE! I KNOW YOU'RE A FUCKUP, BUT HOW DID YOU MANAGE TO FUCK THIS UP?
I DON'T KNOW.
KATE, THIS IS SO NOT OKAY. YOU CAME TO MY HOME.
HOW DID YOU EVEN KNOW WHERE I LIVED?
I'M SORRY. I'M SORRY.
I JUST--
I DON'T KNOW. I DIDN'T EVEN REALIZE.
YOU NEED TO LEAVE. YOU NEED TO LEAVE LOS ANGELES.
I DON'T CARE WHERE YOU GO, BUT IT NEEDS TO BE FAR--
WHAT'S GOING ON, BABE?

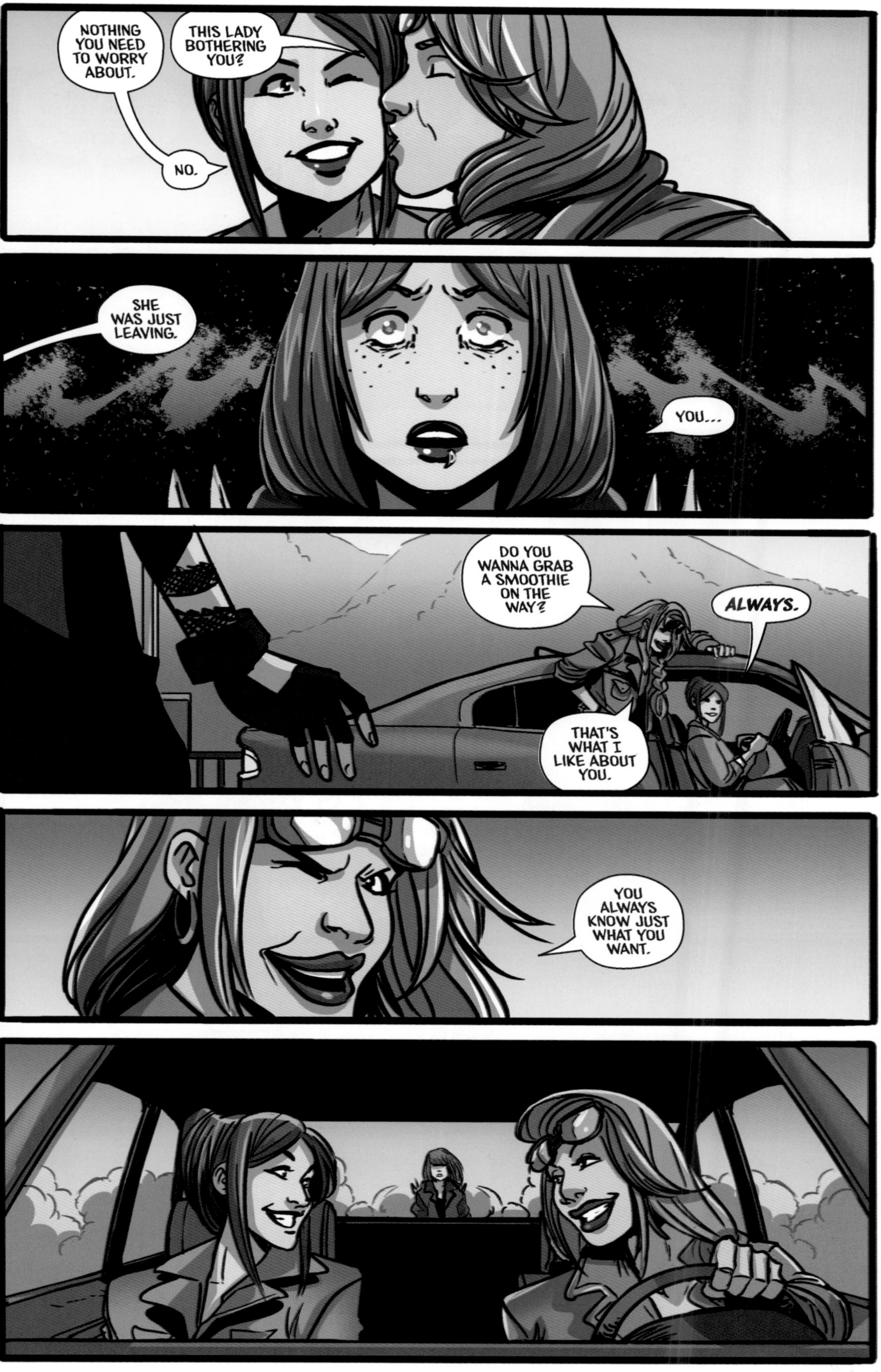

NOTHING YOU NEED TO WORRY ABOUT.
THIS LADY BOTHERING YOU?
NO.
SHE WAS JUST LEAVING.
YOU...
DO YOU WANNA GRAB A SMOOTHIE ON THE WAY?
ALWAYS.
THAT'S WHAT I LIKE ABOUT YOU.
YOU ALWAYS KNOW JUST WHAT YOU WANT.

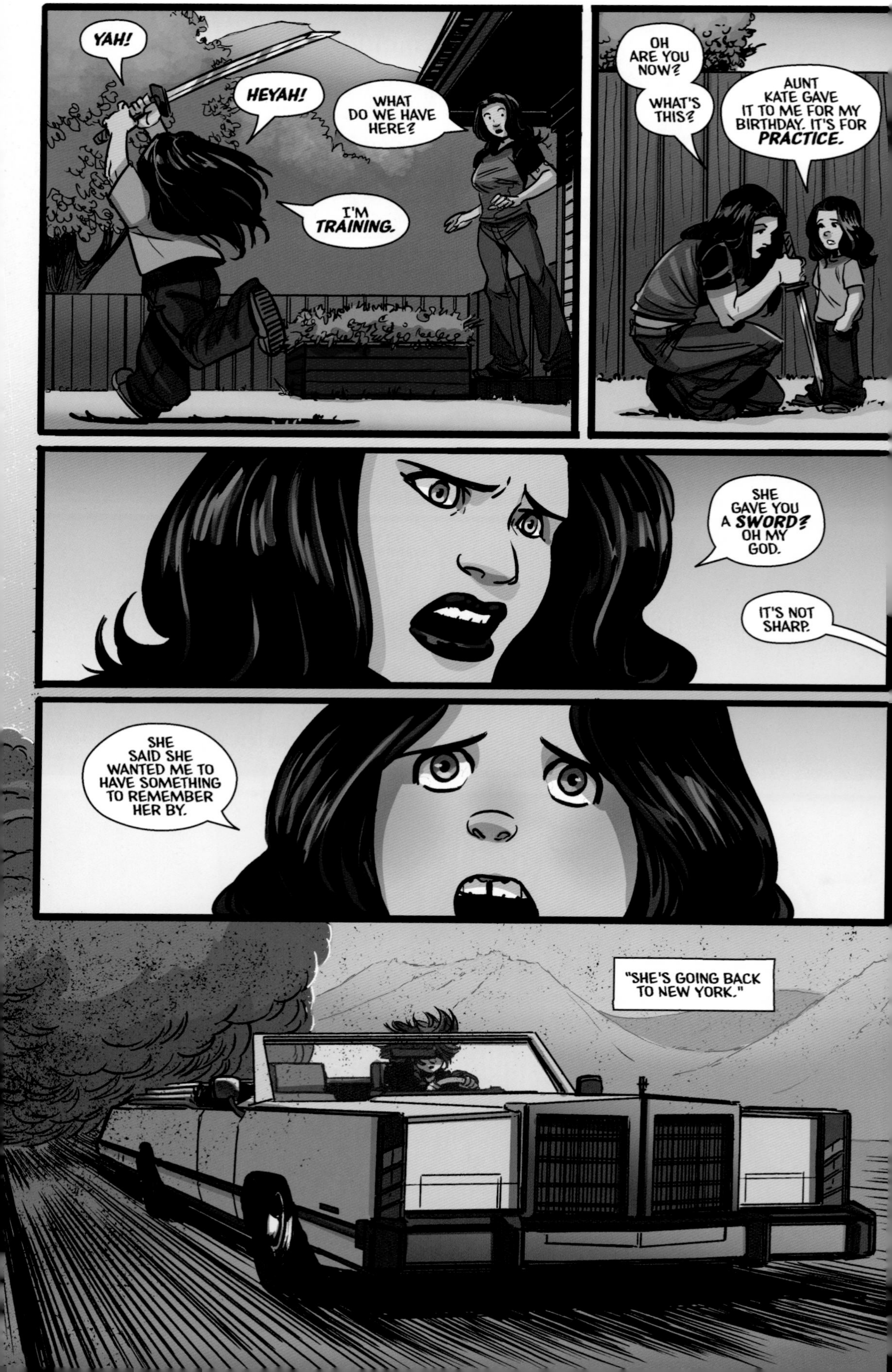
YAH!
HEYAH!
WHAT DO WE HAVE HERE?
I'M TRAINING.
OH ARE YOU NOW?
WHAT'S THIS?
AUNT KATE GAVE IT TO ME FOR MY BIRTHDAY. IT'S FOR PRACTICE.
SHE GAVE YOU A SWORD? OH MY GOD.
IT'S NOT SHARP.
SHE SAID SHE WANTED ME TO HAVE SOMETHING TO REMEMBER HER BY.
"SHE'S GOING BACK TO NEW YORK."

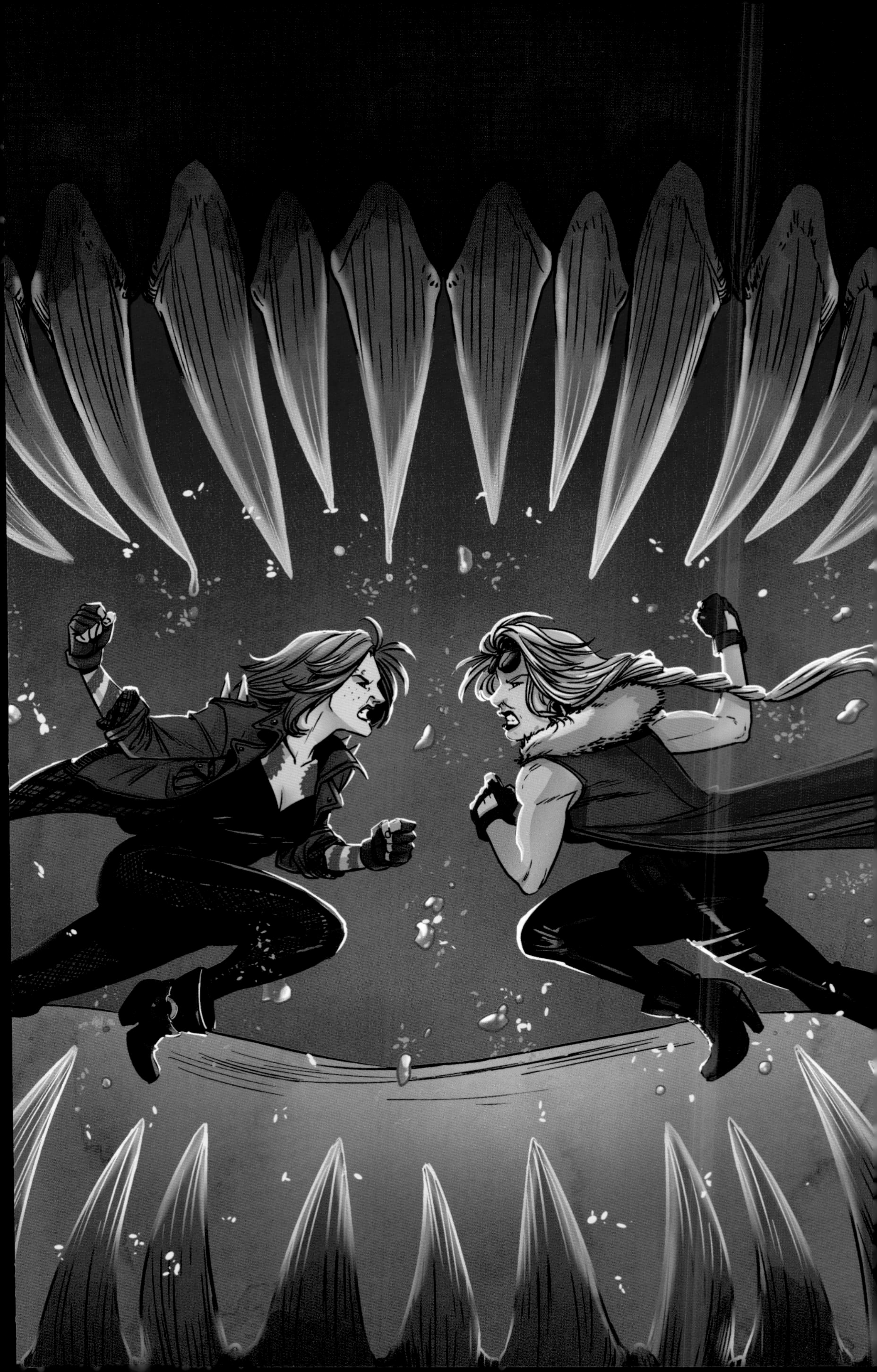

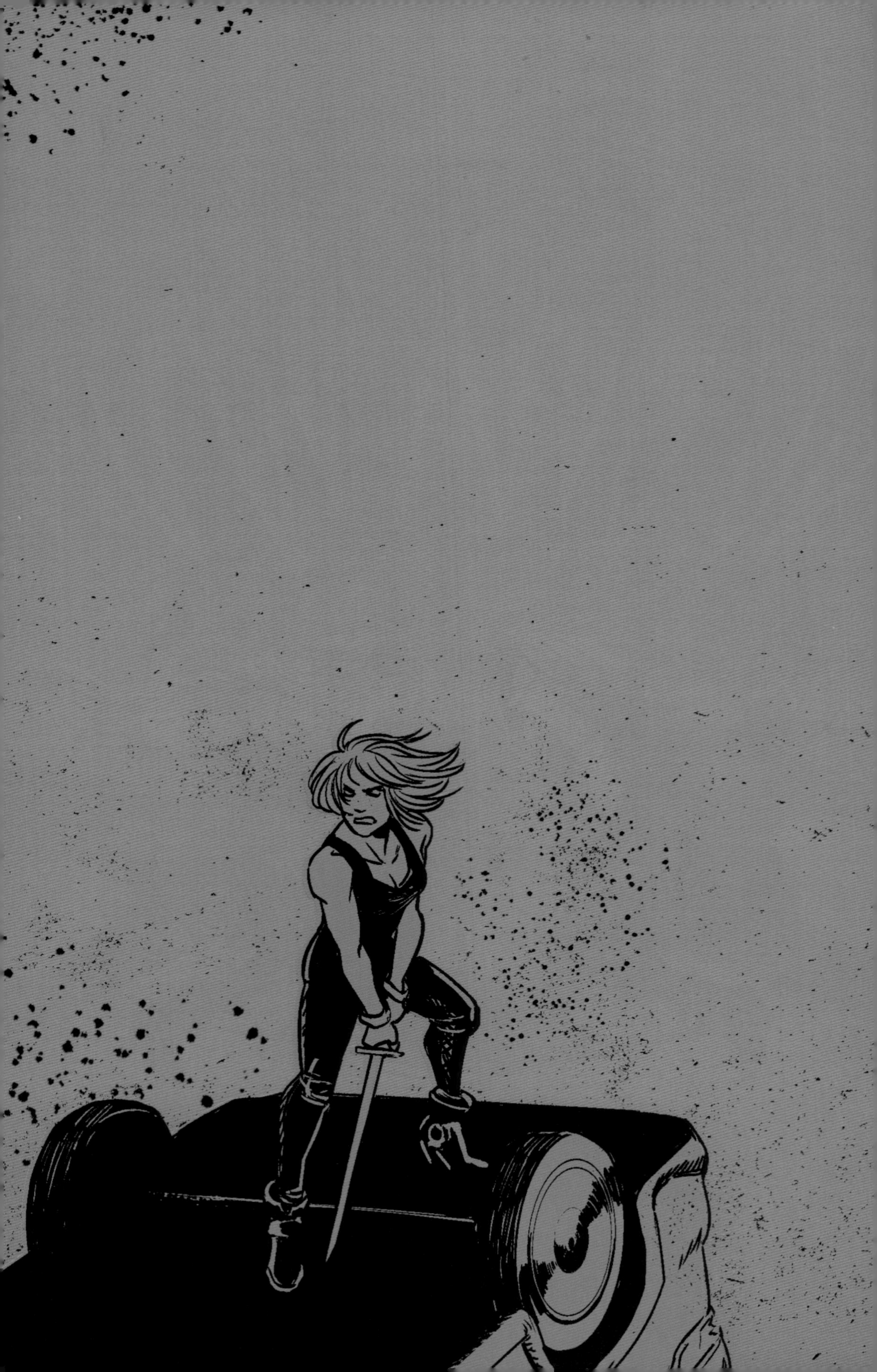

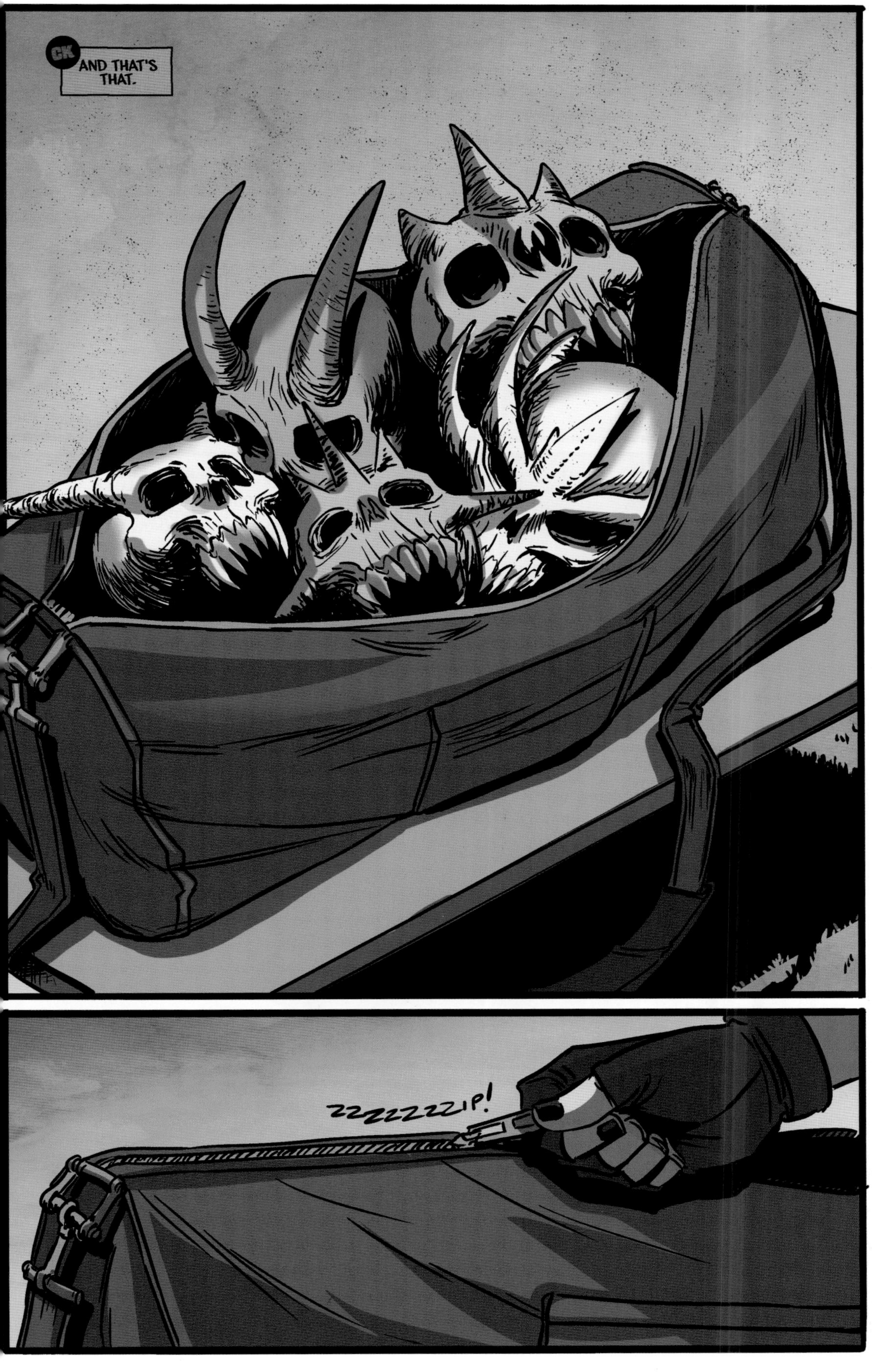
CK
AND THAT'S THAT.
ZZZZZZZZIP!

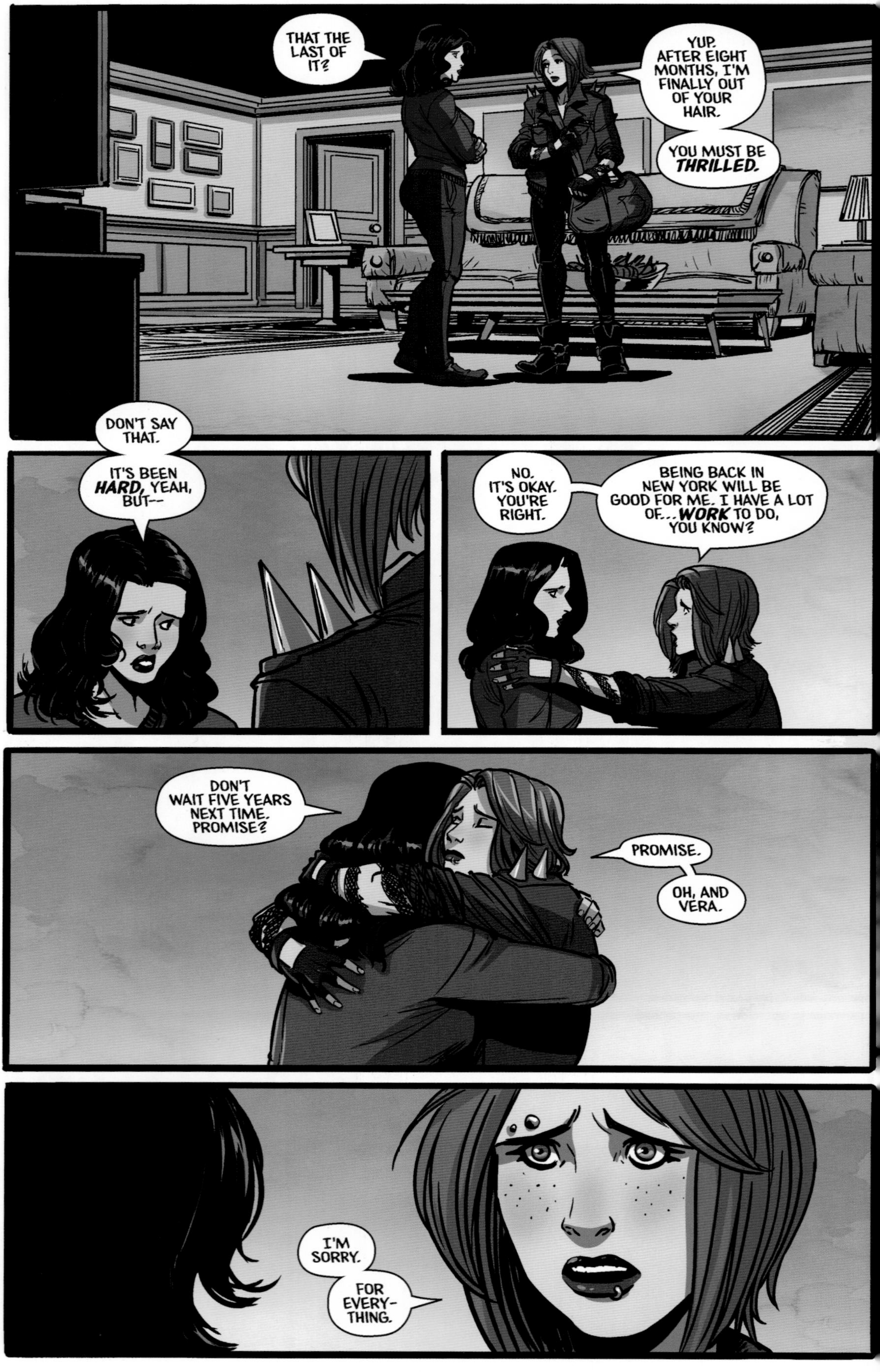
THAT THE LAST OF IT?
YUP. AFTER EIGHT MONTHS, I'M FINALLY OUT OF YOUR HAIR.
YOU MUST BE *THRILLED.*
DON'T SAY THAT.
IT'S BEEN *HARD,* YEAH, BUT--
NO. IT'S OKAY. YOU'RE RIGHT.
BEING BACK IN NEW YORK WILL BE GOOD FOR ME. I HAVE A LOT OF... *WORK* TO DO, YOU KNOW?
DON'T WAIT FIVE YEARS NEXT TIME. PROMISE?
PROMISE.
OH, AND VERA.
I'M SORRY.
FOR EVERY-THING.

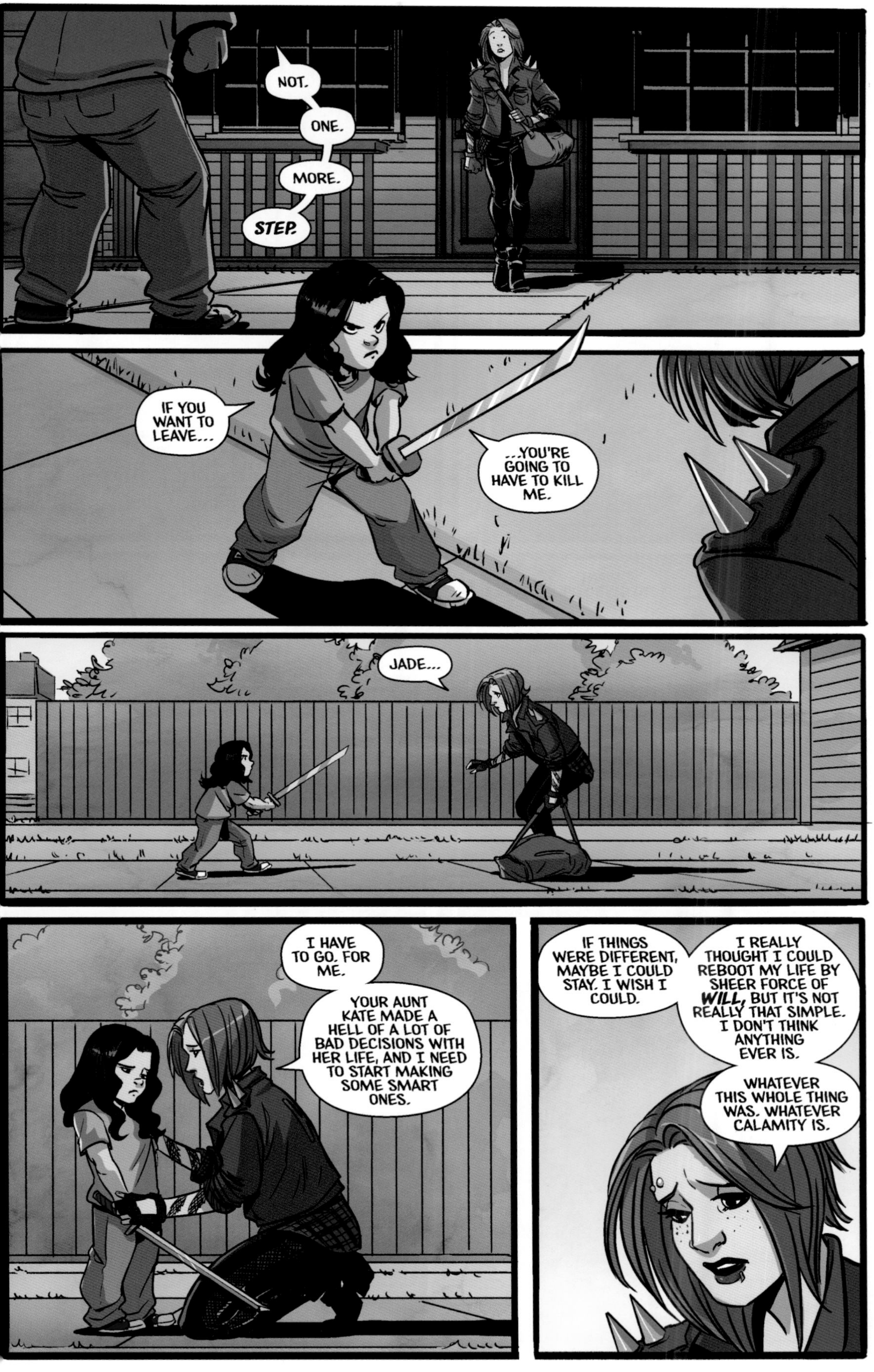
NOT.
ONE.
MORE.
STEP.
IF YOU WANT TO LEAVE...
...YOU'RE GOING TO HAVE TO KILL ME.
JADE...
I HAVE TO GO. FOR ME.
YOUR AUNT KATE MADE A HELL OF A LOT OF BAD DECISIONS WITH HER LIFE, AND I NEED TO START MAKING SOME SMART ONES.
IF THINGS WERE DIFFERENT, MAYBE I COULD STAY. I WISH I COULD.
I REALLY THOUGHT I COULD REBOOT MY LIFE BY SHEER FORCE OF WILL, BUT IT'S NOT REALLY THAT SIMPLE. I DON'T THINK ANYTHING EVER IS.
WHATEVER THIS WHOLE THING WAS. WHATEVER CALAMITY IS.

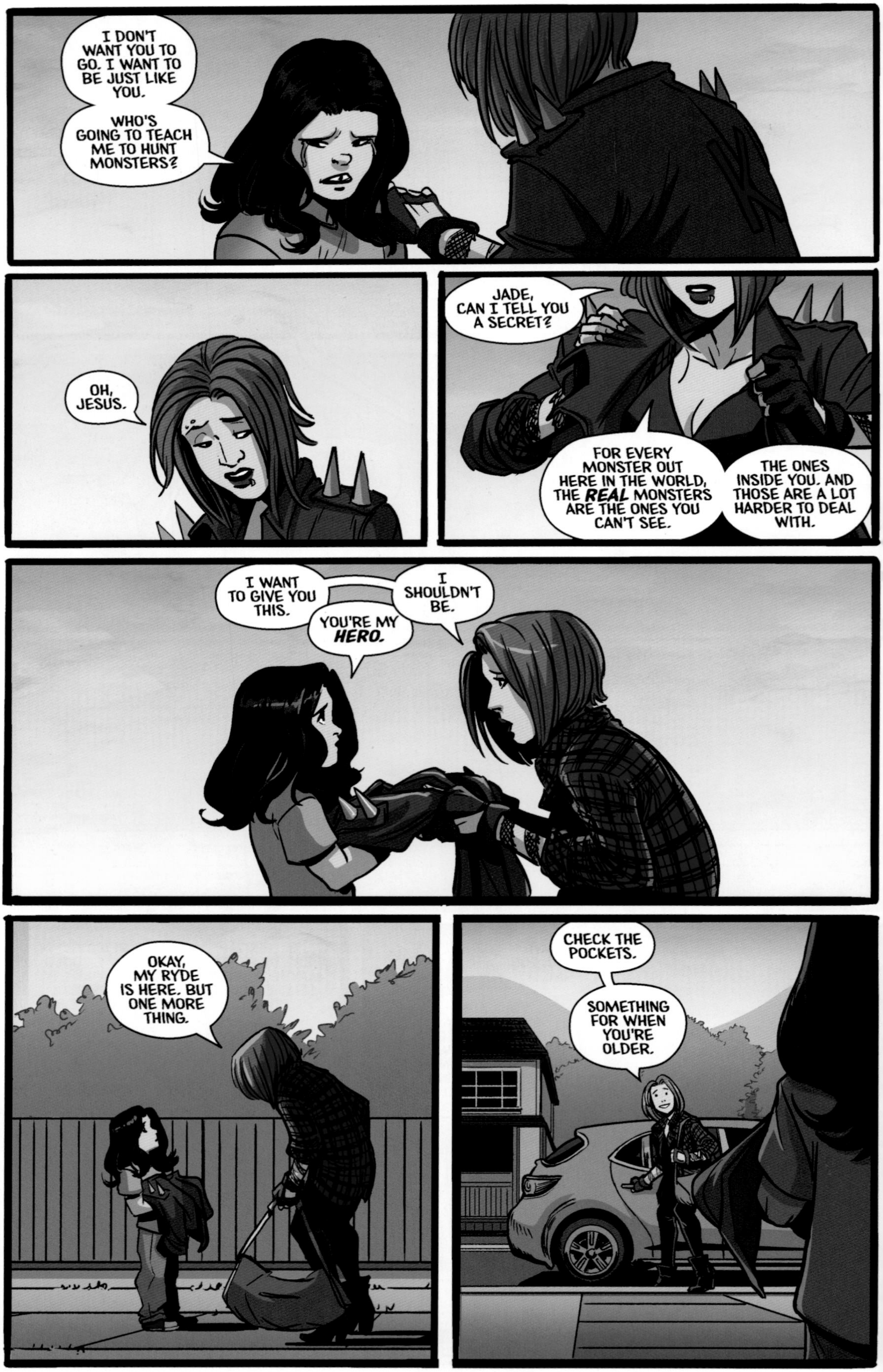
I DON'T WANT YOU TO GO. I WANT TO BE JUST LIKE YOU.
WHO'S GOING TO TEACH ME TO HUNT MONSTERS?
OH, JESUS.
JADE, CAN I TELL YOU A SECRET?
FOR EVERY MONSTER OUT HERE IN THE WORLD, THE REAL MONSTERS ARE THE ONES YOU CAN'T SEE.
THE ONES INSIDE YOU. AND THOSE ARE A LOT HARDER TO DEAL WITH.
I WANT TO GIVE YOU THIS.
YOU'RE MY HERO.
I SHOULDN'T BE.
OKAY, MY RYDE IS HERE. BUT ONE MORE THING.
CHECK THE POCKETS.
SOMETHING FOR WHEN YOU'RE OLDER.

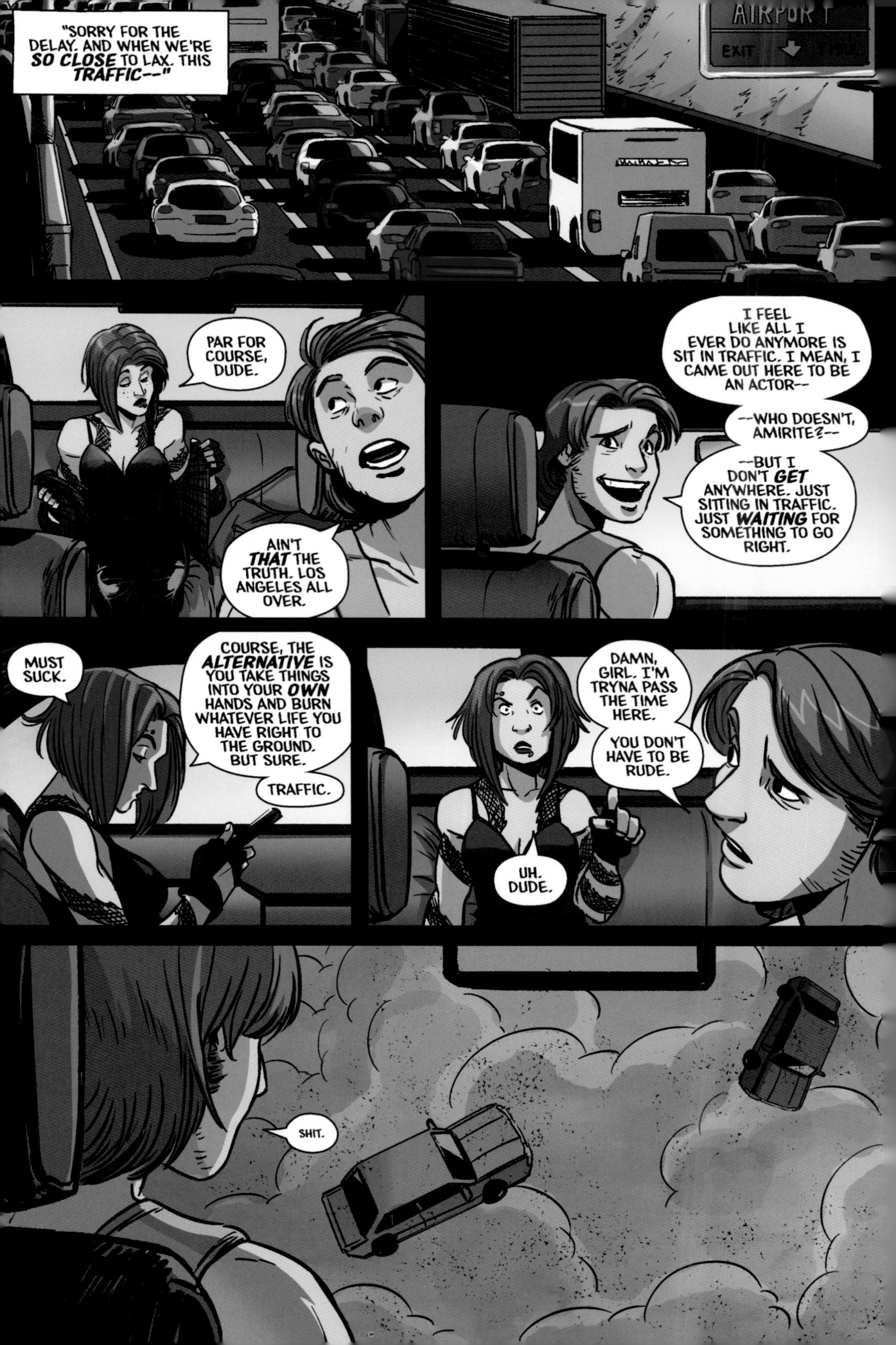
"SORRY FOR THE DELAY. AND WHEN WE'RE SO CLOSE TO LAX. THIS TRAFFIC--"
AIRPORT
EXIT
PAR FOR COURSE, DUDE.
AIN'T THAT THE TRUTH. LOS ANGELES ALL OVER.
I FEEL LIKE ALL I EVER DO ANYMORE IS SIT IN TRAFFIC. I MEAN, I CAME OUT HERE TO BE AN ACTOR--
--WHO DOESN'T, AMIRITE?--
--BUT I DON'T GET ANYWHERE. JUST SITTING IN TRAFFIC. JUST WAITING FOR SOMETHING TO GO RIGHT.
MUST SUCK.
COURSE, THE ALTERNATIVE IS YOU TAKE THINGS INTO YOUR OWN HANDS AND BURN WHATEVER LIFE YOU HAVE RIGHT TO THE GROUND. BUT SURE.
TRAFFIC.
DAMN, GIRL. I'M TRYNA PASS THE TIME HERE.
YOU DON'T HAVE TO BE RUDE.
UH. DUDE.
SHIT.

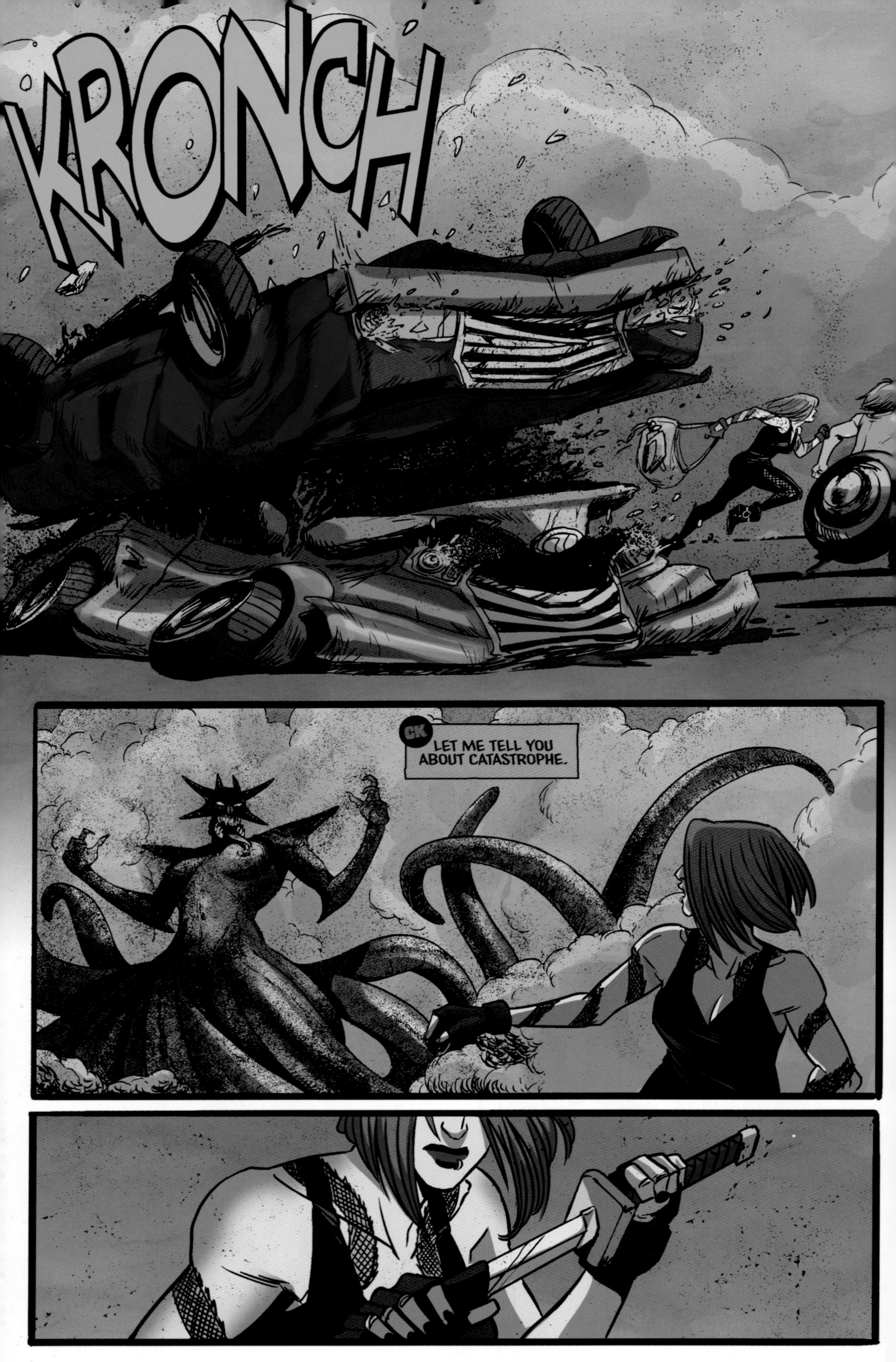
KRONCH
CK
LET ME TELL YOU ABOUT CATASTROPHE.

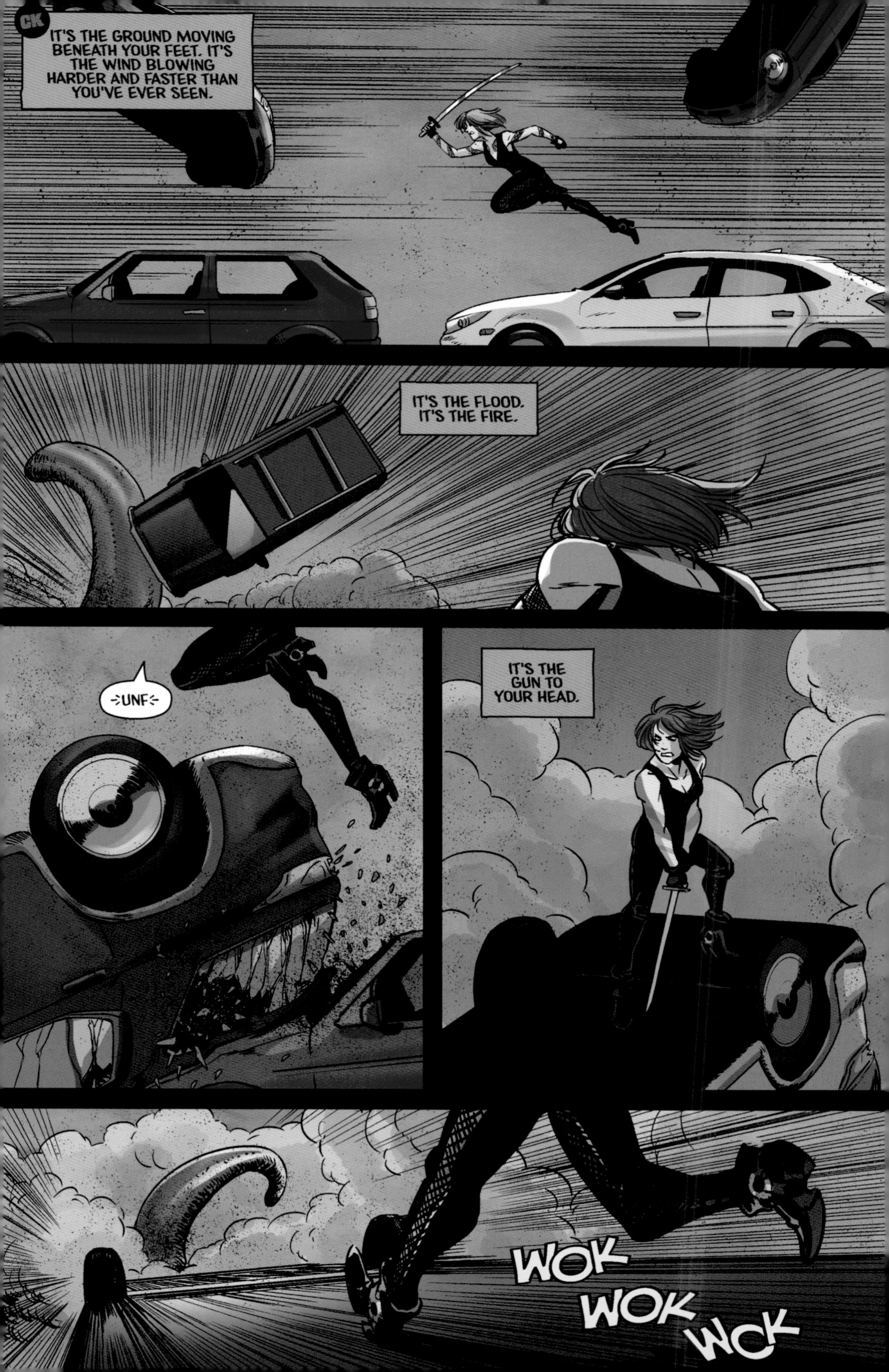
IT'S THE GROUND MOVING BENEATH YOUR FEET. IT'S THE WIND BLOWING HARDER AND FASTER THAN YOU'VE EVER SEEN.
IT'S THE FLOOD. IT'S THE FIRE.
UNF
IT'S THE GUN TO YOUR HEAD.
WOK
WOK
WOK

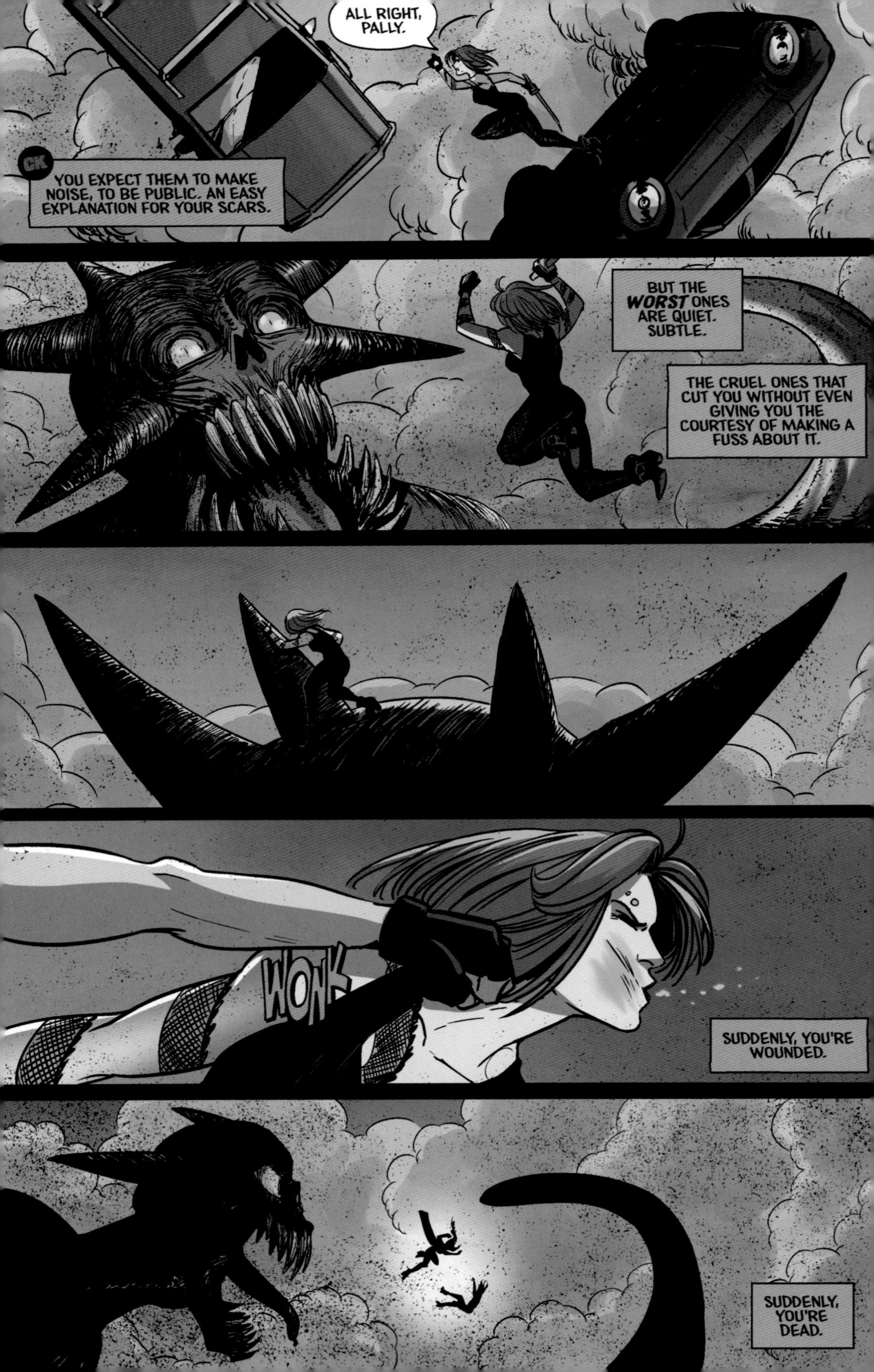
ALL RIGHT, PALLY.
CK
YOU EXPECT THEM TO MAKE NOISE, TO BE PUBLIC. AN EASY EXPLANATION FOR YOUR SCARS.
BUT THE WORST ONES ARE QUIET. SUBTLE.
THE CRUEL ONES THAT CUT YOU WITHOUT EVEN GIVING YOU THE COURTESY OF MAKING A FUSS ABOUT IT.
WONK
SUDDENLY, YOU'RE WOUNDED.
SUDDENLY, YOU'RE DEAD.

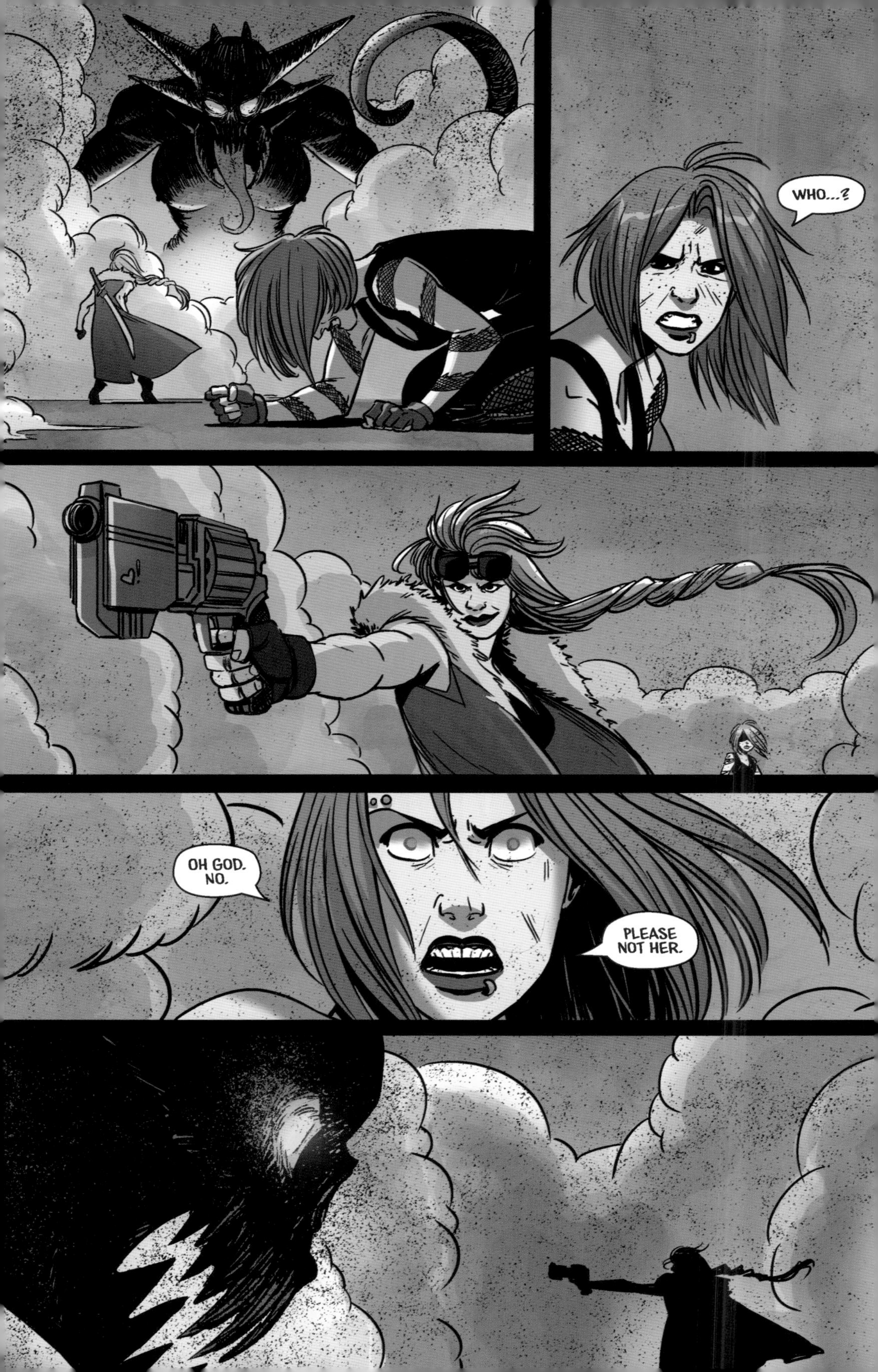
WHO...?
OH GOD. NO.
PLEASE NOT HER.

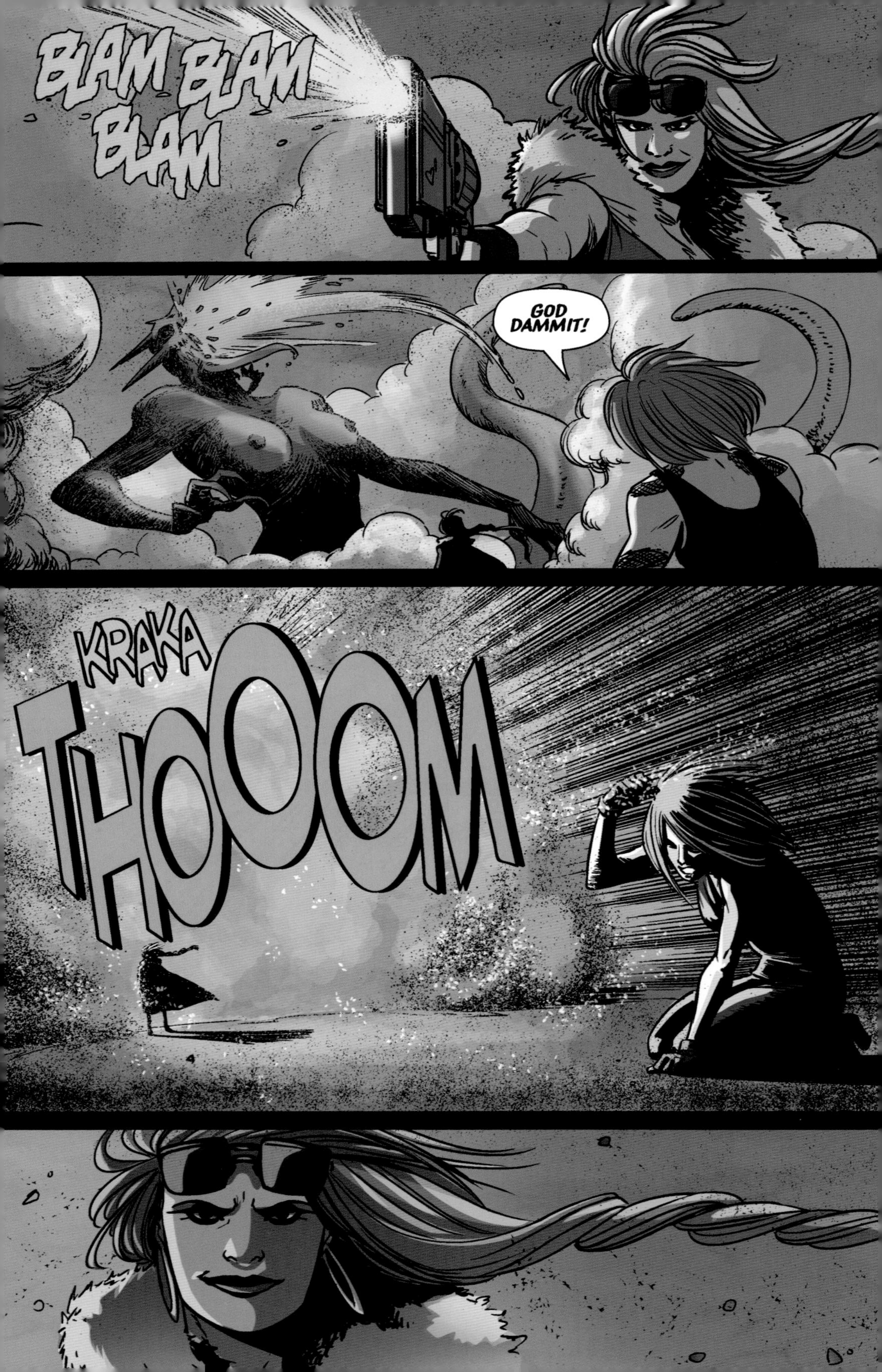
BLAM BLAM
BLAM
GOD DAMMIT!
KRAKA
THOOOM

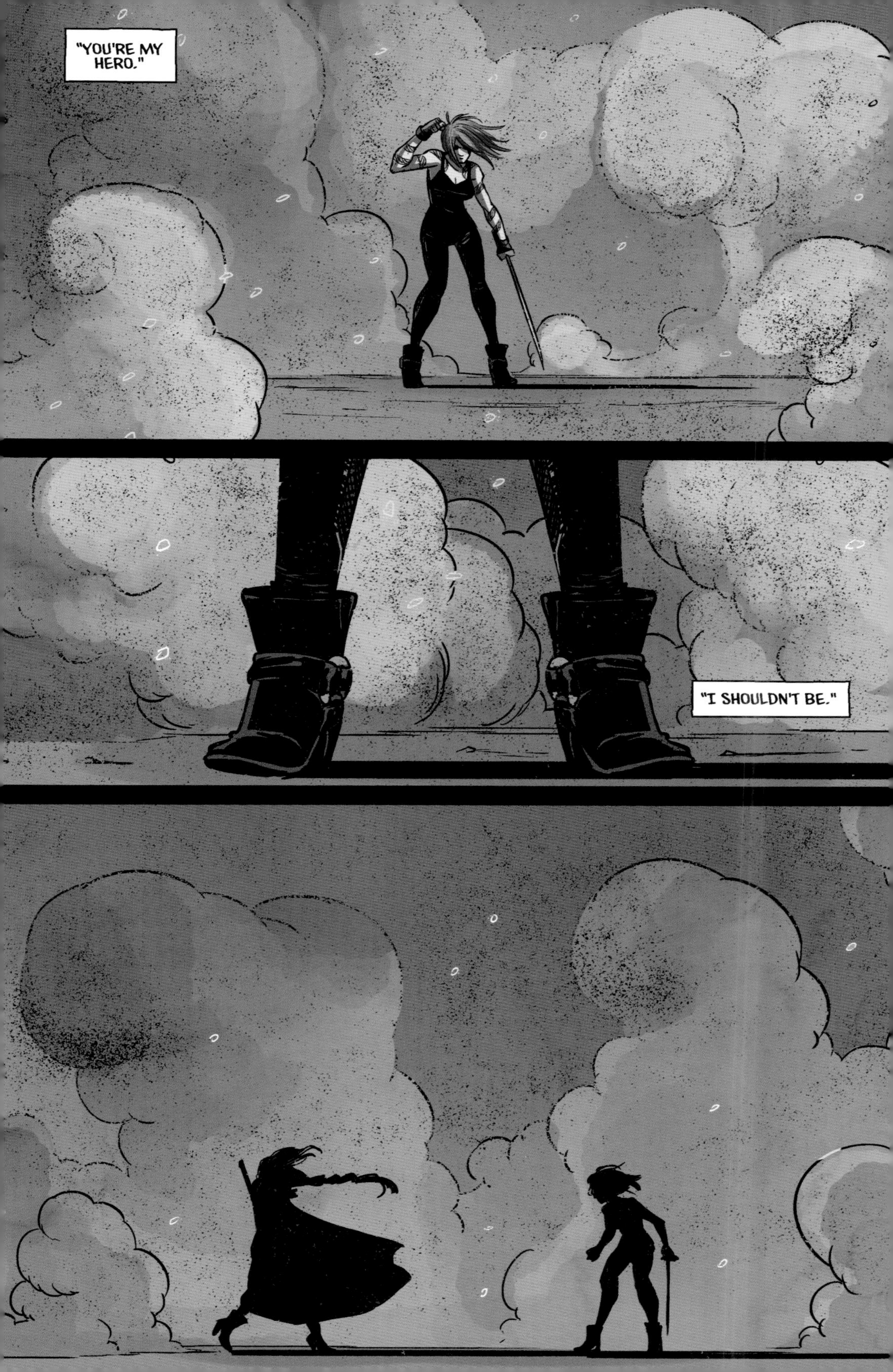
"YOU'RE MY HERO."
"I SHOULDN'T BE."

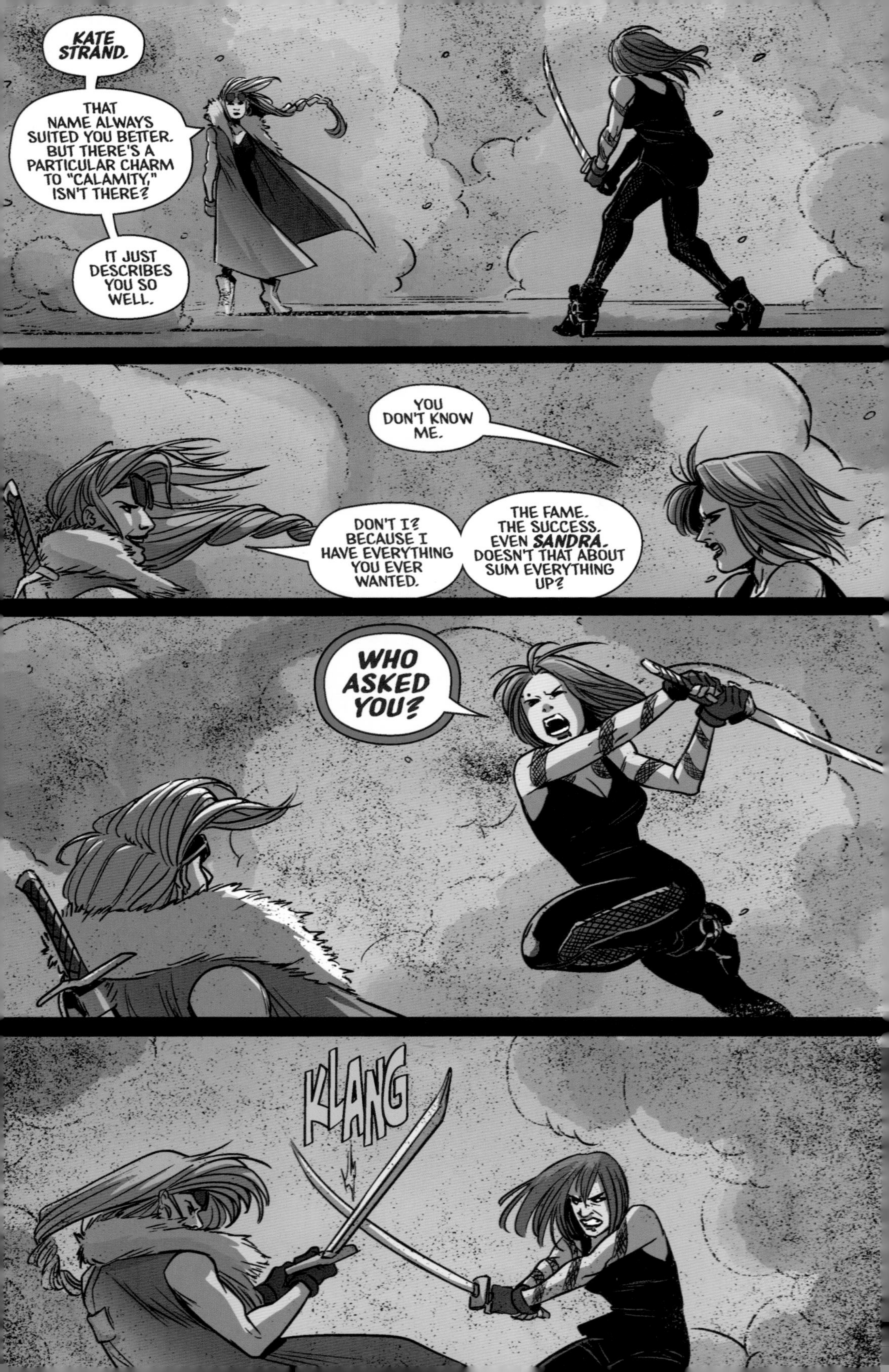
KATE STRAND.
THAT NAME ALWAYS SUITED YOU BETTER. BUT THERE'S A PARTICULAR CHARM TO "CALAMITY," ISN'T THERE?
IT JUST DESCRIBES YOU SO WELL.
YOU DON'T KNOW ME.
DON'T I? BECAUSE I HAVE EVERYTHING YOU EVER WANTED.
THE FAME. THE SUCCESS. EVEN SANDRA. DOESN'T THAT ABOUT SUM EVERYTHING UP?
WHO ASKED YOU?
KLANG

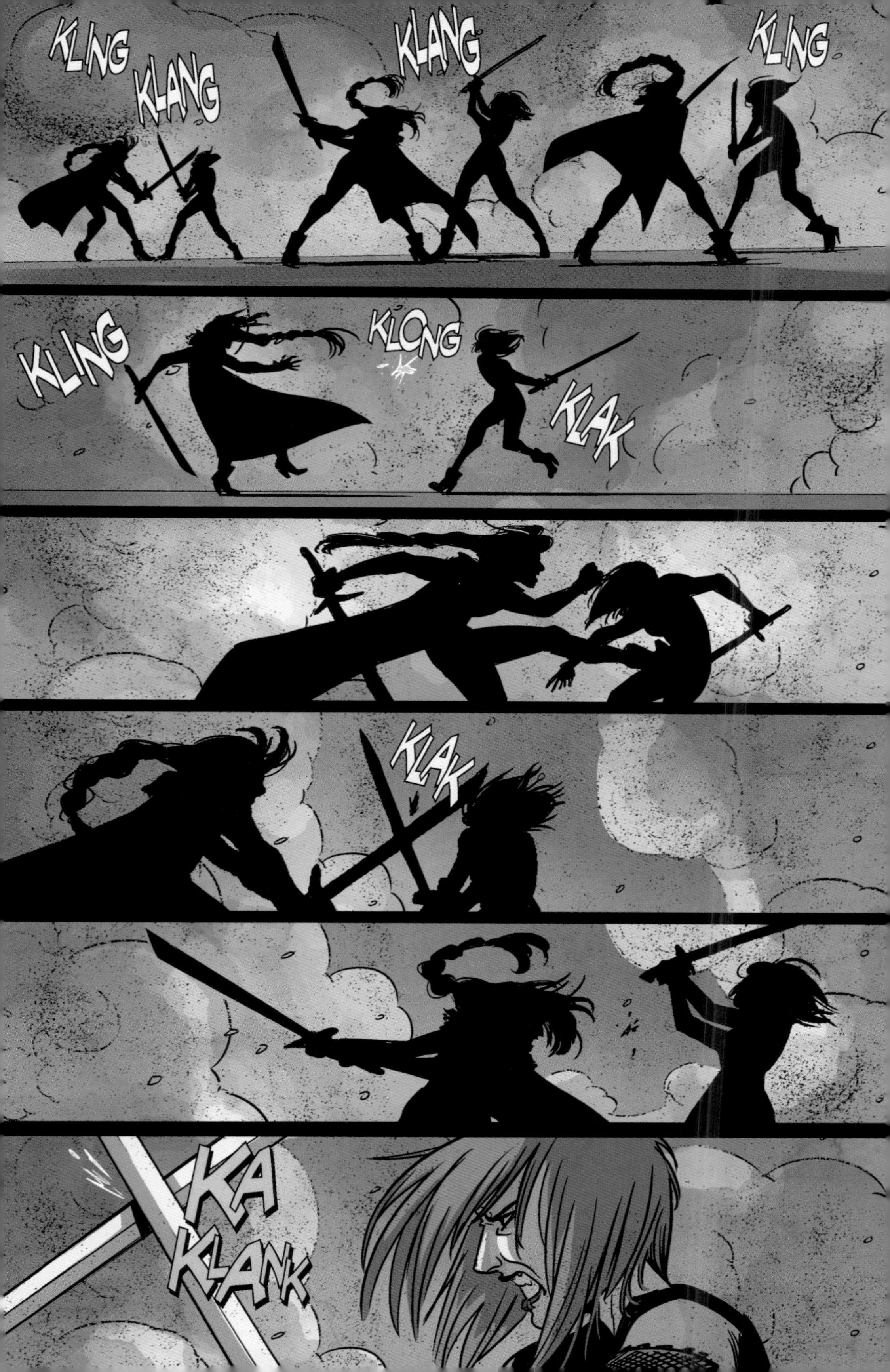
KLING
KLANG
KLANG
KLING
KLING
KLONG
KLAK
KLAK
KA KLANK

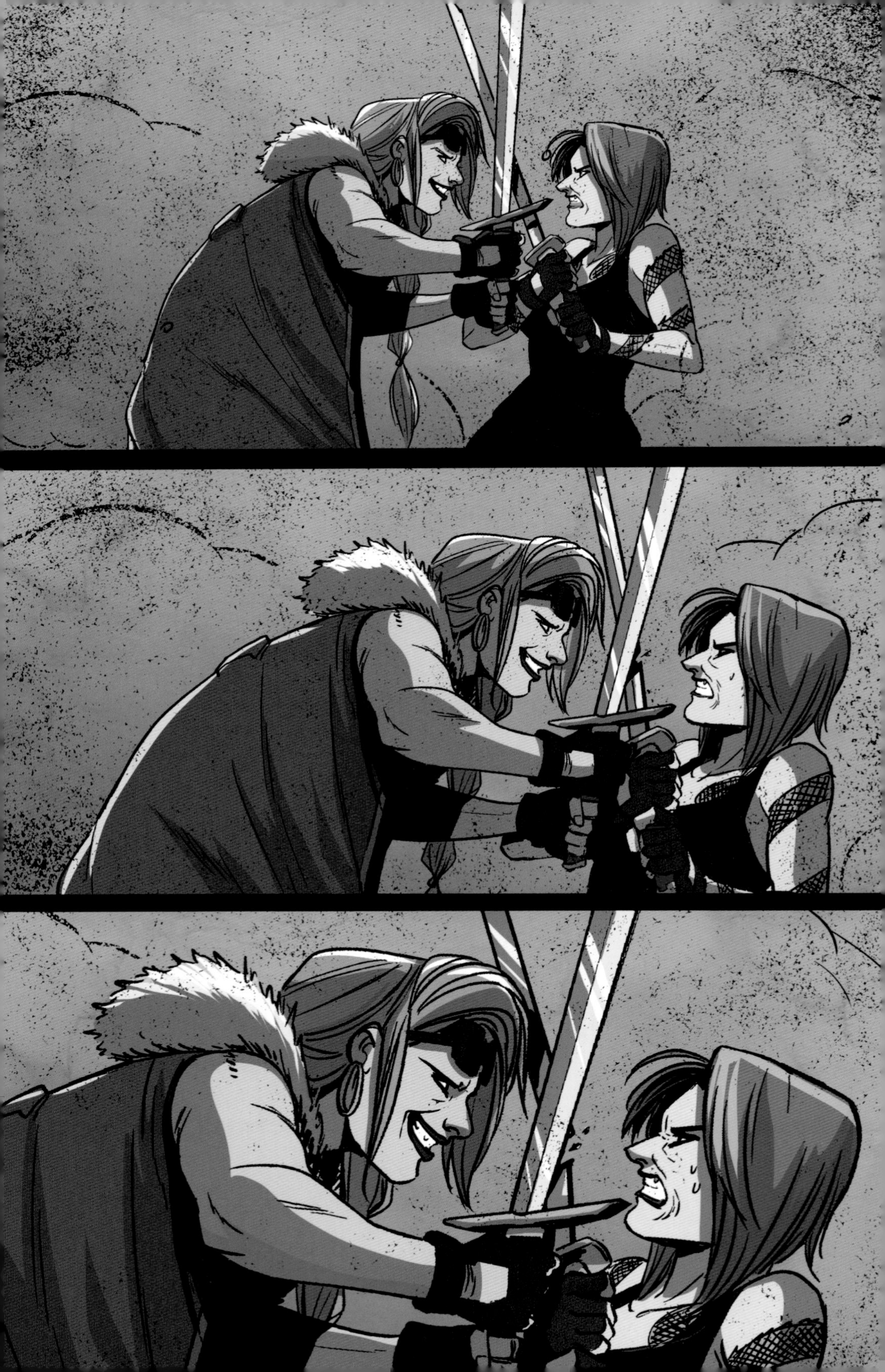

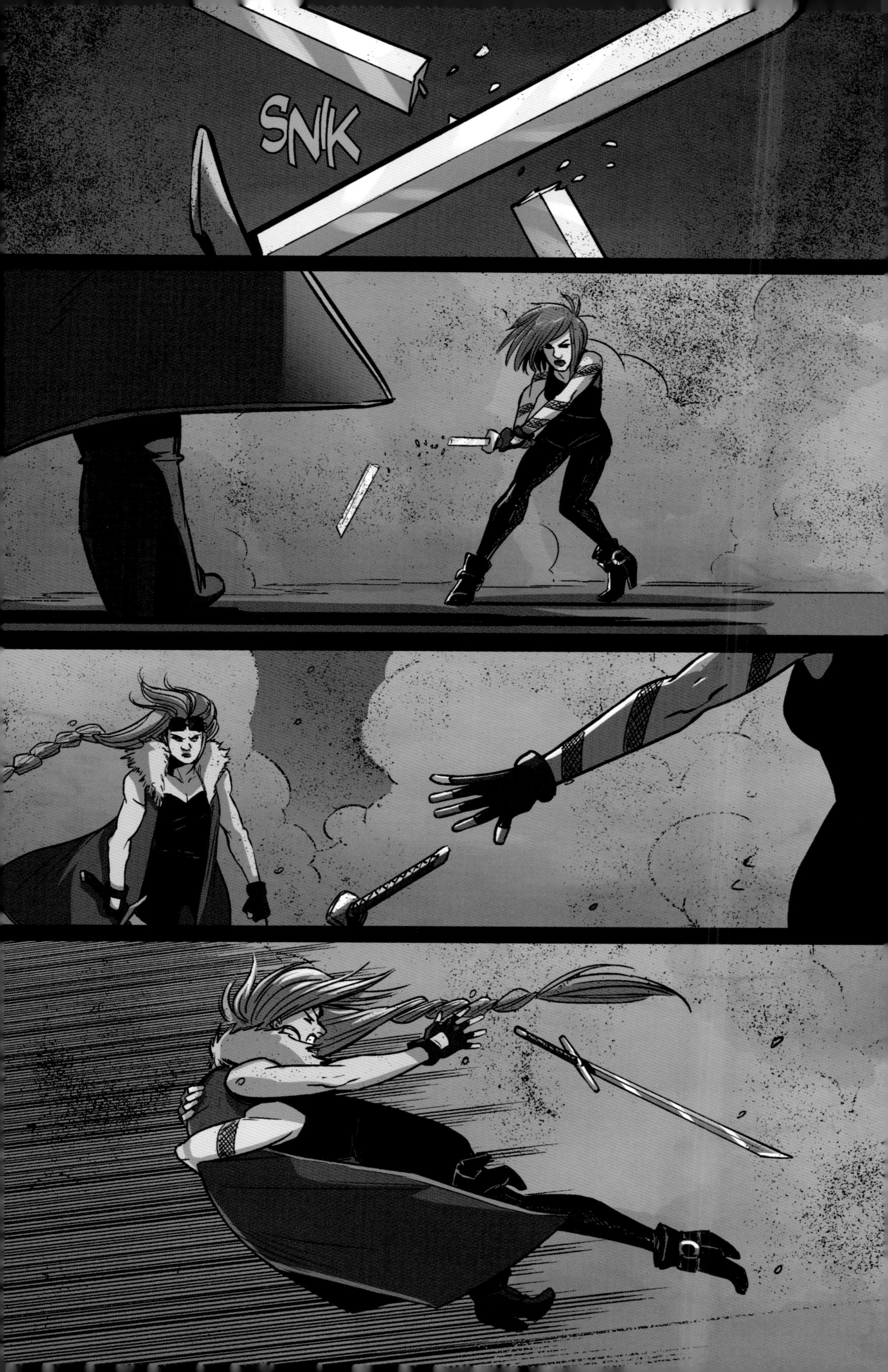
SNIK

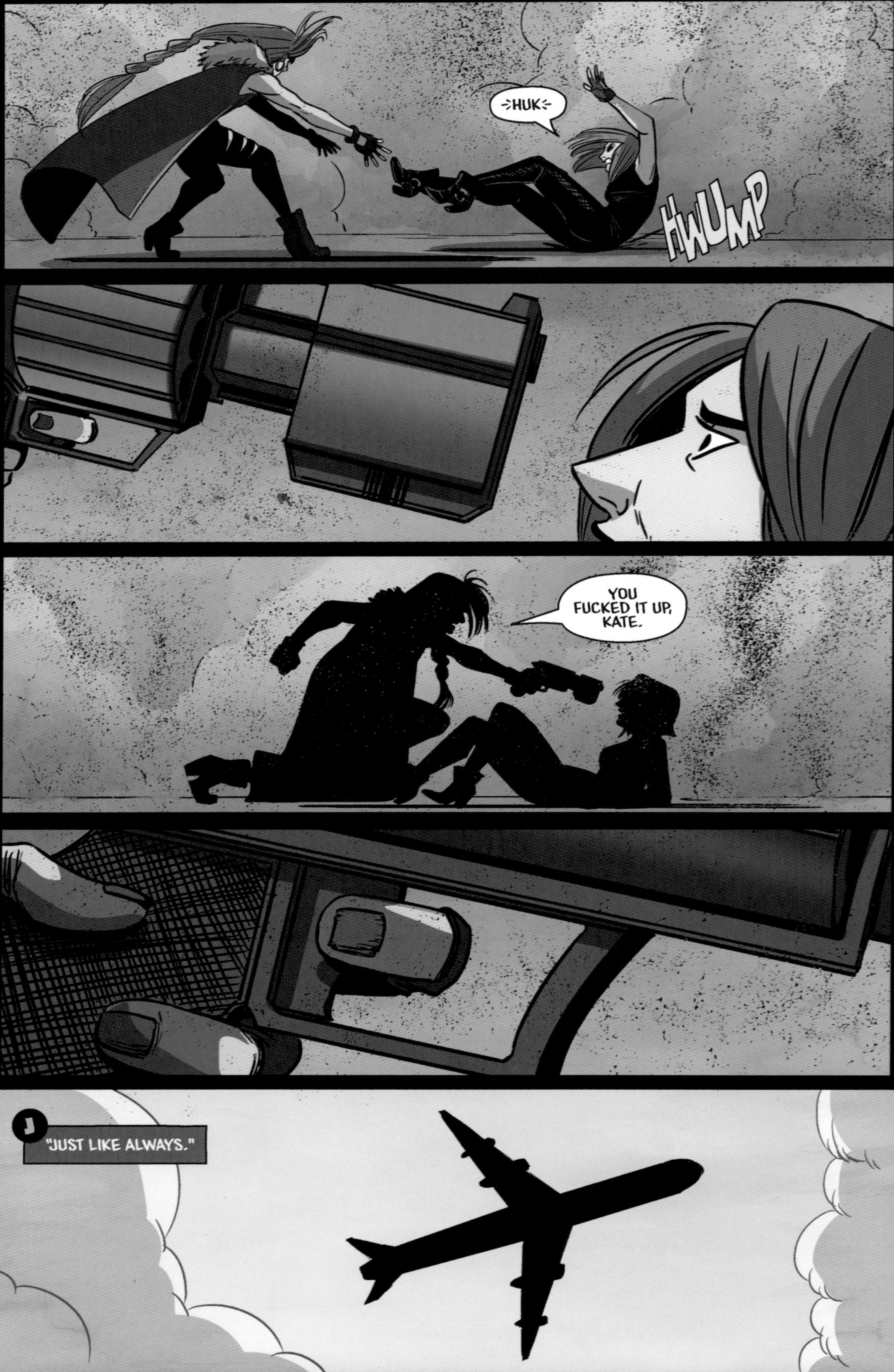
HUK
HWUMP
YOU FUCKED IT UP, KATE.
"JUST LIKE ALWAYS."

ALL RIGHT, THANKS FOR THE RIDE.

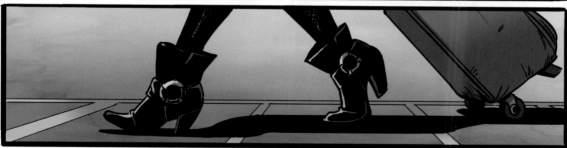

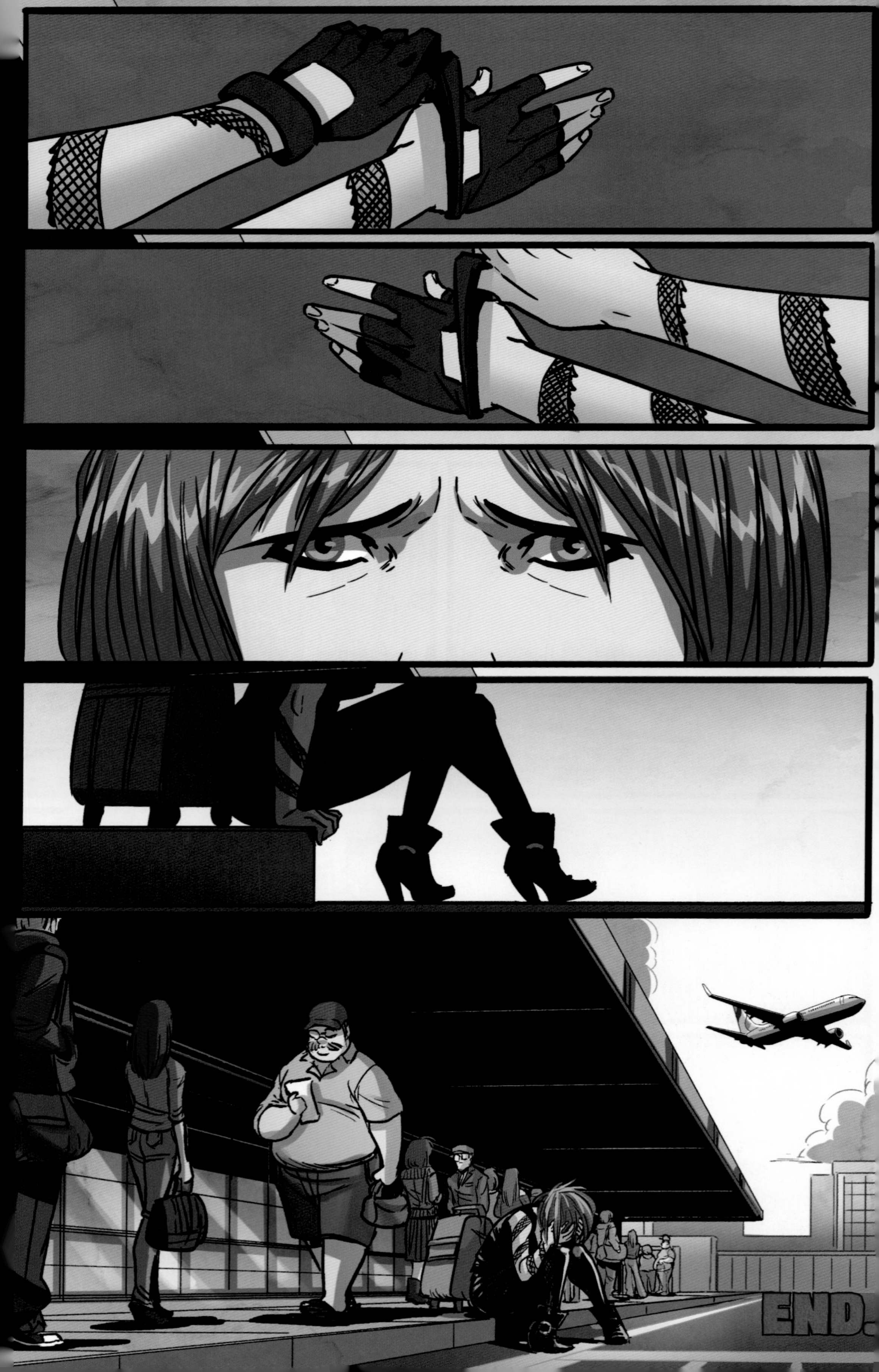
END.

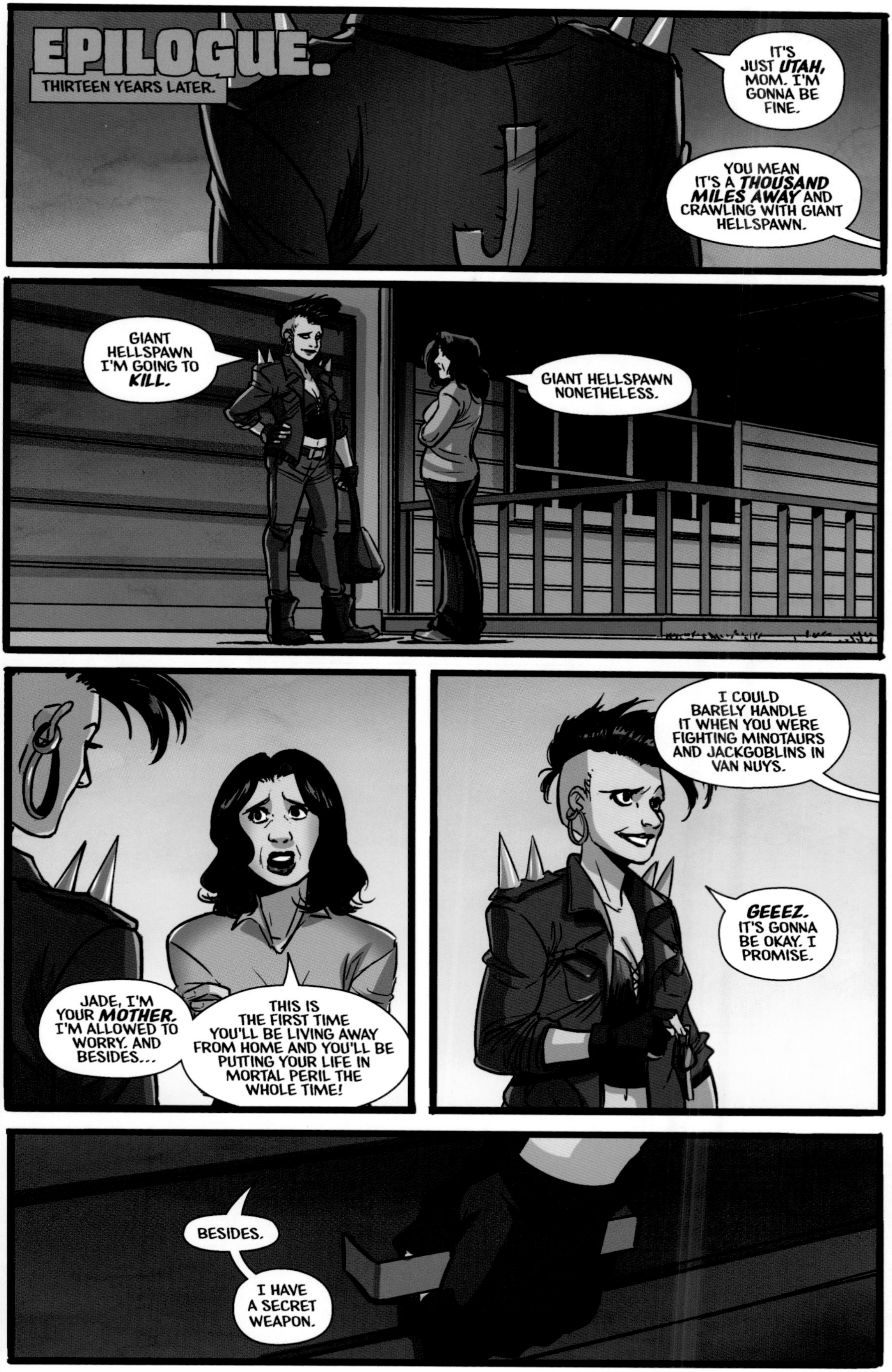
EPILOGUE.
THIRTEEN YEARS LATER.
IT'S JUST UTAH, MOM. I'M GONNA BE FINE.
YOU MEAN IT'S A THOUSAND MILES AWAY AND CRAWLING WITH GIANT HELLSPAWN.
GIANT HELLSPAWN I'M GOING TO KILL.
GIANT HELLSPAWN NONETHELESS.
JADE, I'M YOUR MOTHER. I'M ALLOWED TO WORRY. AND BESIDES...
THIS IS THE FIRST TIME YOU'LL BE LIVING AWAY FROM HOME AND YOU'LL BE PUTTING YOUR LIFE IN MORTAL PERIL THE WHOLE TIME!
I COULD BARELY HANDLE IT WHEN YOU WERE FIGHTING MINOTAURS AND JACKGOBLINS IN VAN NUYS.
GEEEZ. IT'S GONNA BE OKAY. I PROMISE.
BESIDES.
I HAVE A SECRET WEAPON.

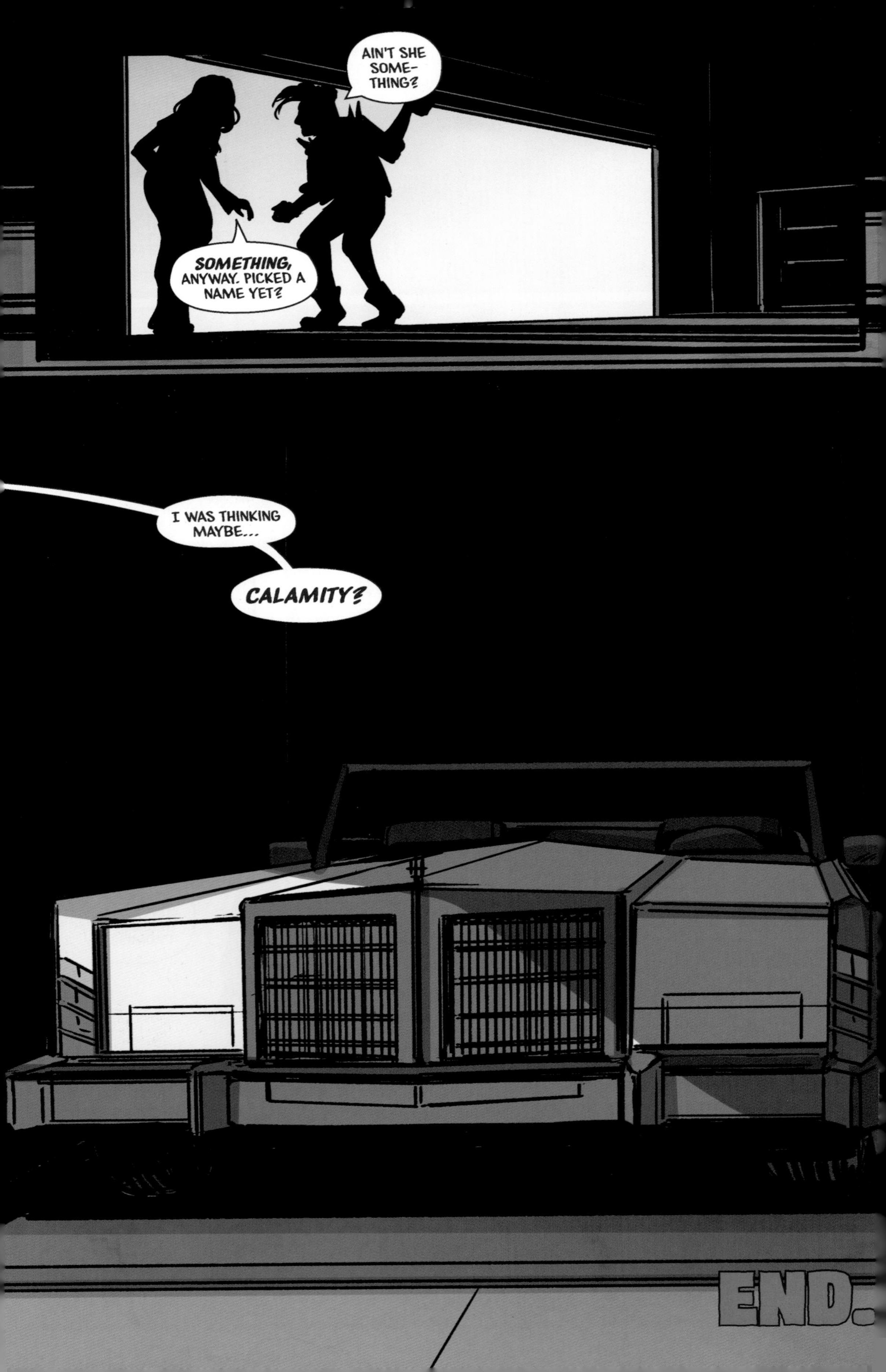
AIN'T SHE SOME-THING?
SOMETHING, ANYWAY. PICKED A NAME YET?
I WAS THINKING MAYBE...
CALAMITY?
END.

CALAMITY KATE™

SKETCHBOOK

NOTES BY **CORIN HOWELL**

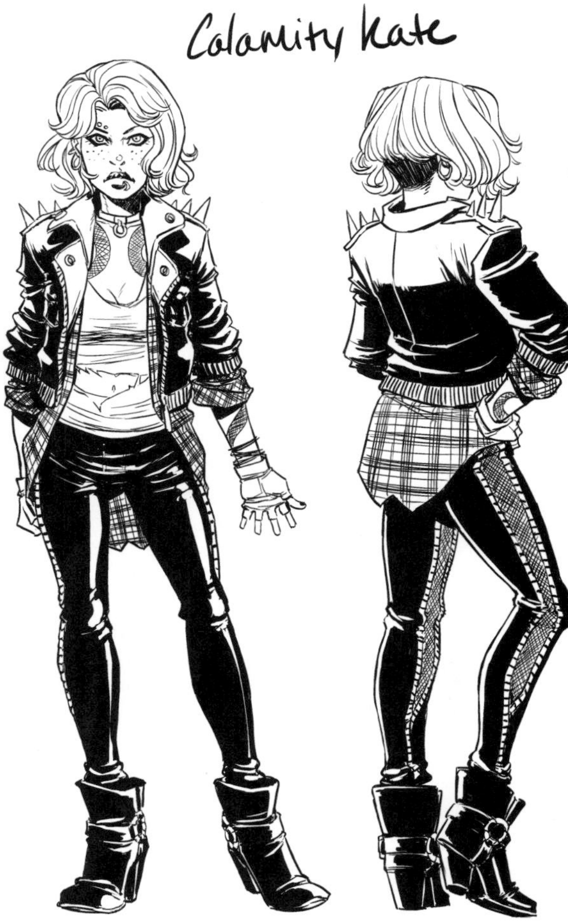
Calamity Kate

CALAMITY KATE: Balls to the wall and clearly stopped giving a fuck a long time ago. Going down a destructive path, that highway to hell scenario and there are no brakes to the car **whatsoever**.

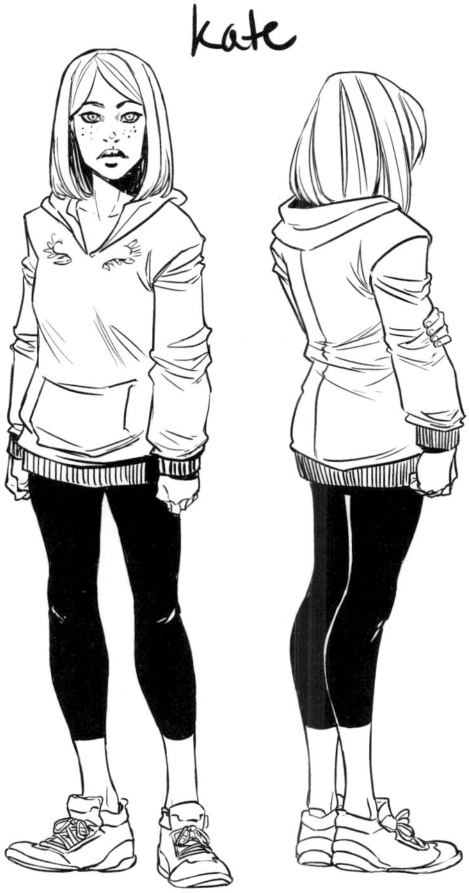
Kate

"PRE" CALAMITY KATE: Straightens her hair every morning, face full of freckles, probably wears big sweaters all the time, a little mousy. Very reserved, and possibly responsible to an extent.

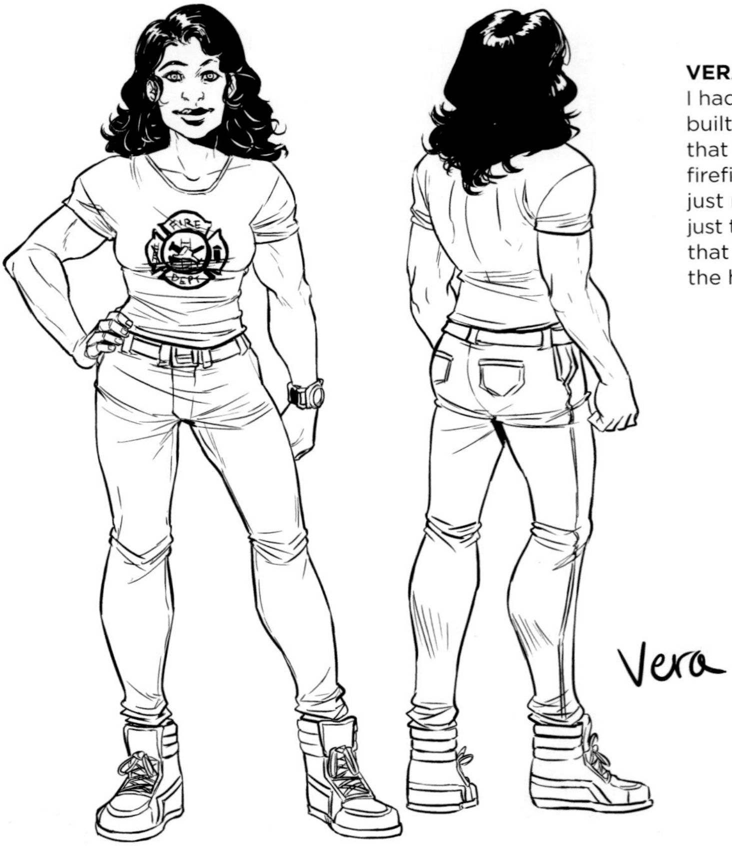
Vera

VERA: So this is the rough idea I had for Vera—hispanic, kind of built, possibly training for a job that requires a lot of activity like a firefighter or a cop. Or maybe she just really likes working out. Or is just the super badass-looking chick that works at the nurses station at the hospital down the street.

JAVELIN: Calm and cool, suave and skilled, she pretty much is the epitome of "that cool kid in school." Also I'm a fan of *The Hobbit* and I couldn't stop picturing her with Thorin Oakenshield's **majestic** fur coat, and possibly carried a sword. She's **majestic**.

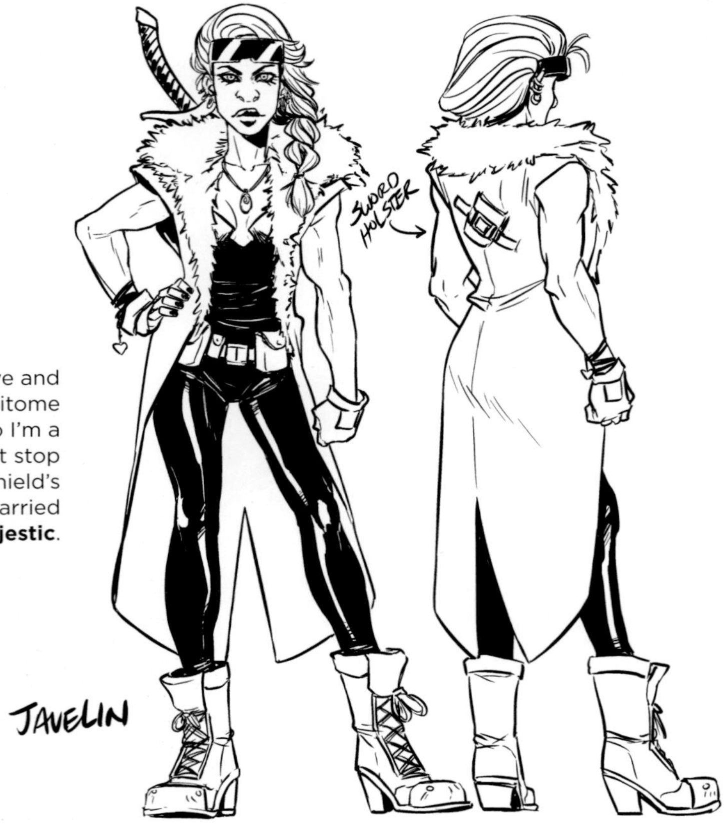
SWORD HOLSTER
JAVELIN

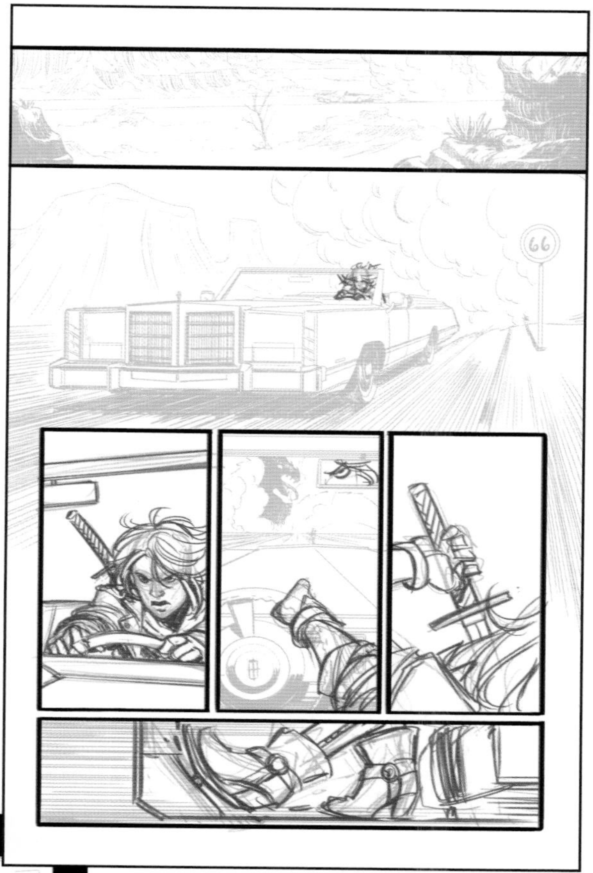
66

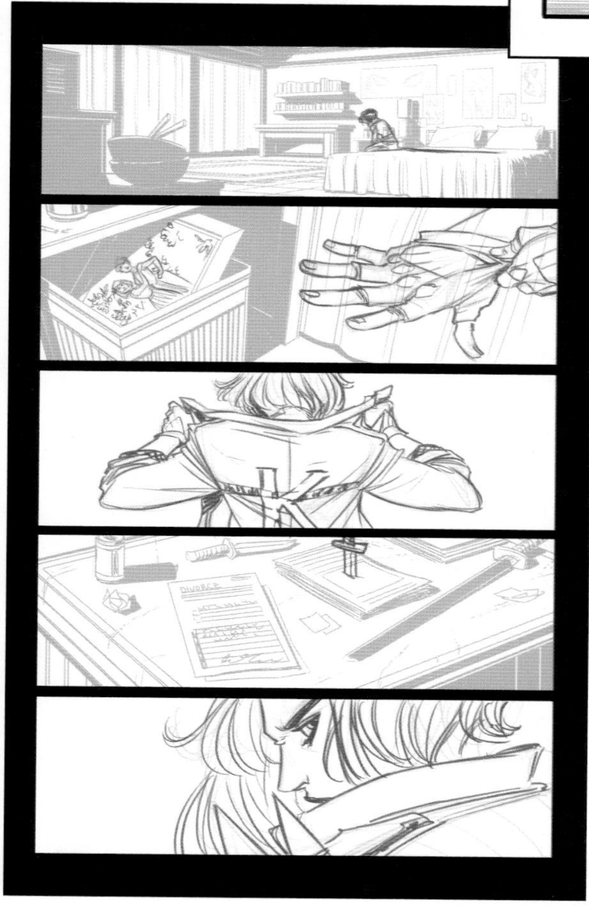
DIVORCE

VARIANT COVER FOR *CALAMITY KATE* #1
BY TANA FORD

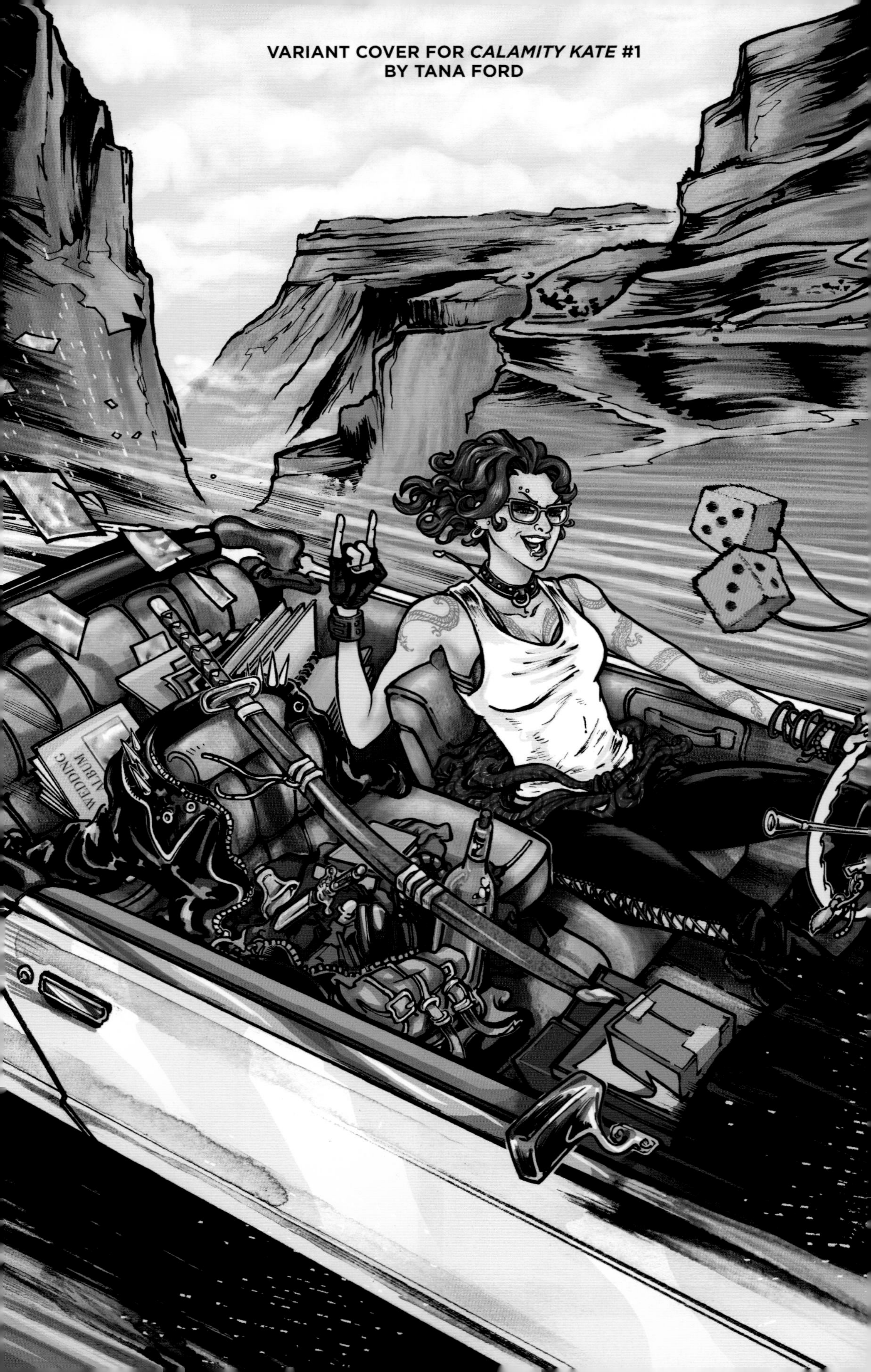
WEDDING
ALBUM

VARIANT COVER FOR *CALAMITY KATE* #2
BY JAMES STOKOE

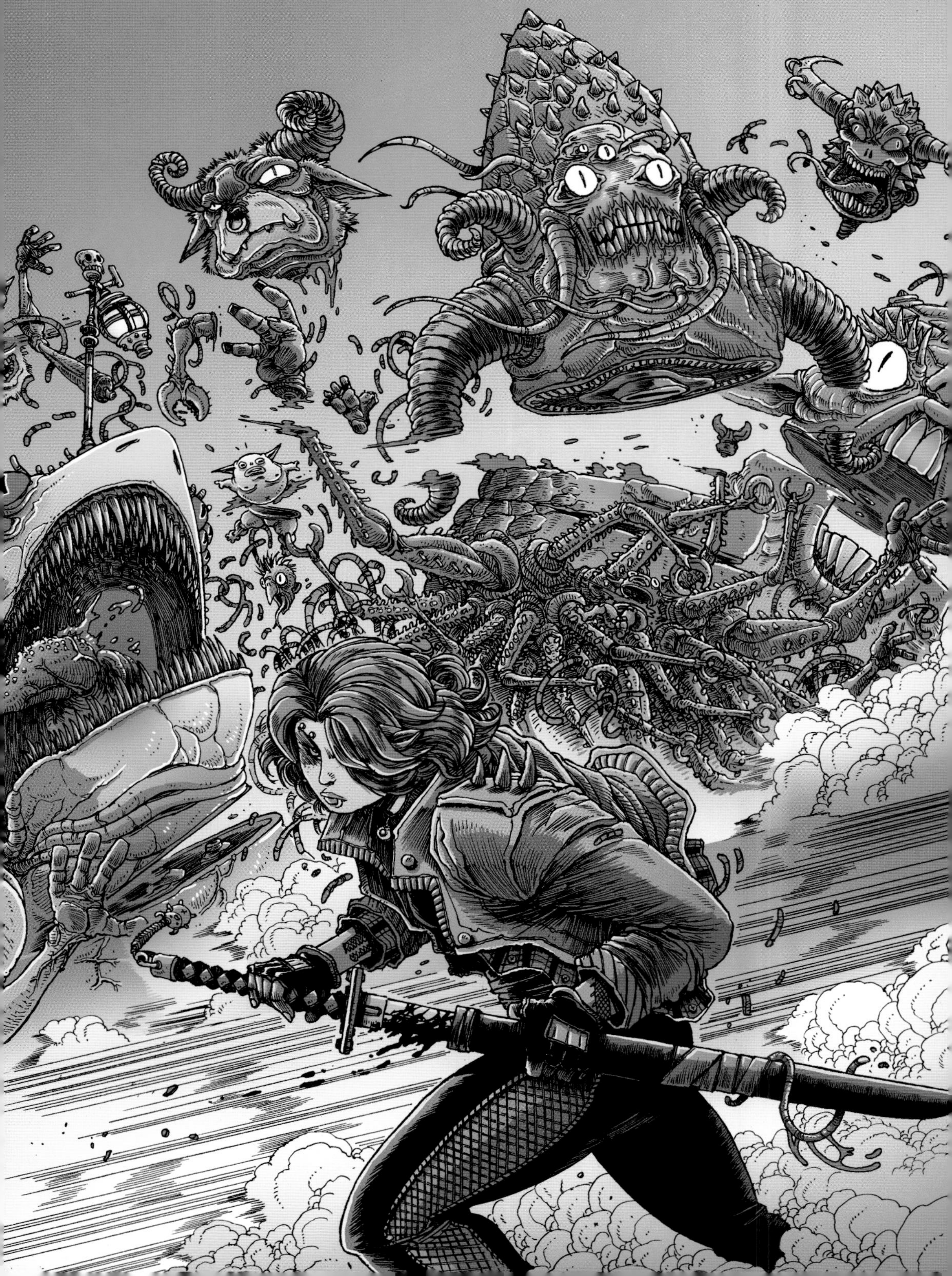

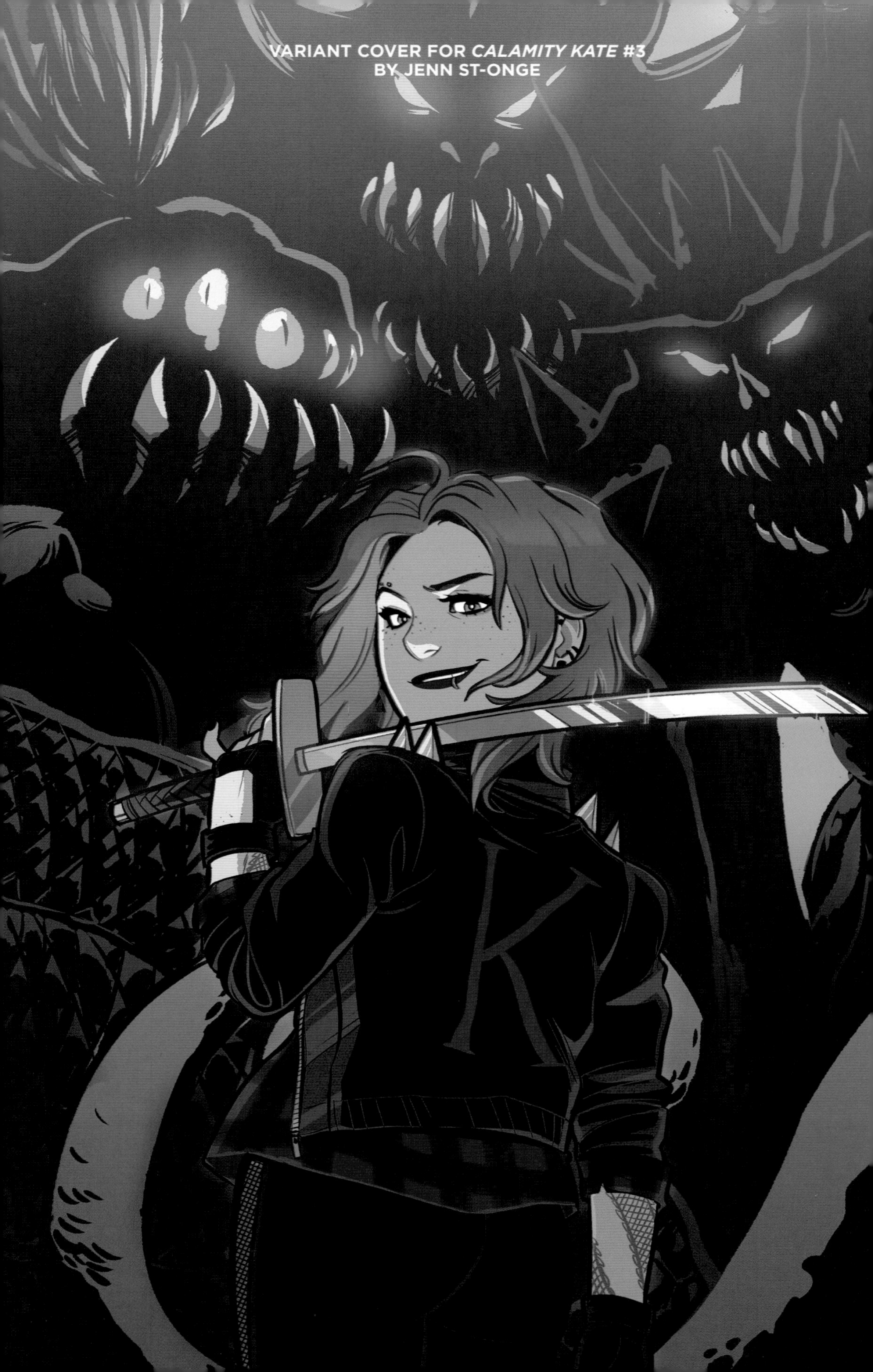

VARIANT COVER FOR *CALAMITY KATE* #3
BY JENN ST-ONGE

VARIANT COVER FOR *CALAMITY KATE* #4
BY BECKY CLOONAN

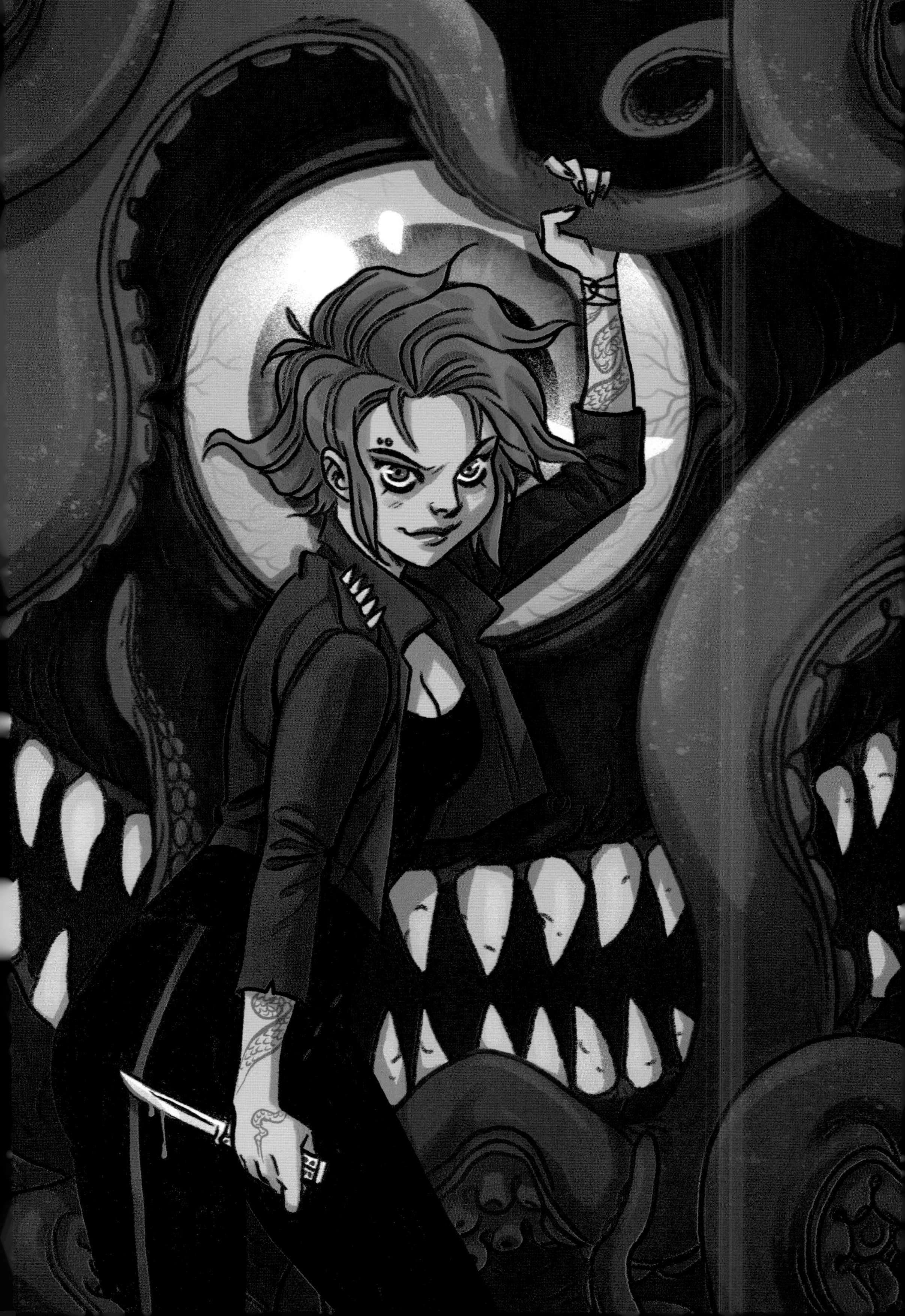

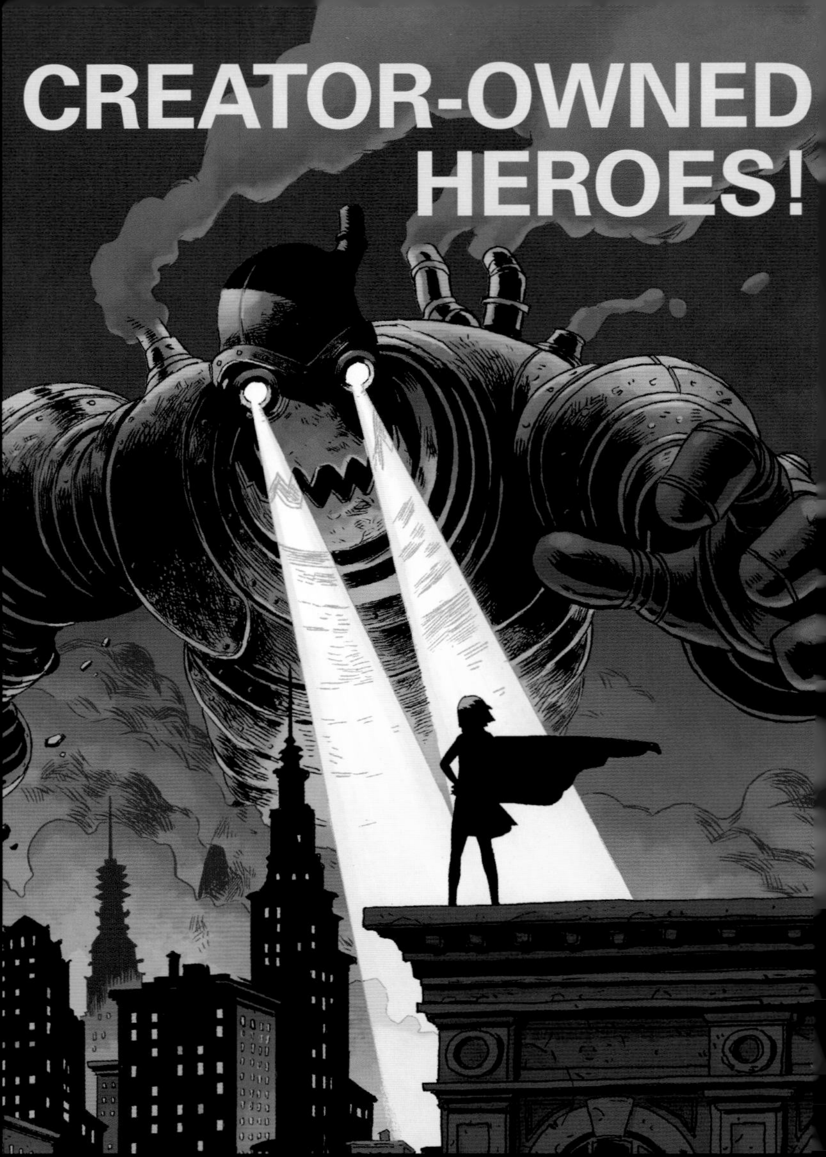
CREATOR-OWNED
HEROES!

BLACK HAMMER
eff Lemire and Dean Ormston
3LACK HAMMER LIBRARY
EDITION: VOLUME ONE
SBN 978-1-50671-073-0 | $49.99

VOLUME 1: SECRET ORIGINS
SBN 978-1-61655-786-7 | $14.99

VOLUME 2: THE EVENT
SBN 978-1-50670-198-1 | $19.99

SHERLOCK FRANKENSTEIN & THE LEGION OF EVIL: FROM THE WORLD OF BLACK HAMMER
eff Lemire and David Rubín
SBN 978-1-50670-526-2 | $17.99

EMPOWERED VOLUME 1
Adam Warren
SBN 978-1-59307-672-6 | $17.99

THE PAYBACKS COLLECTION
Donny Cates, Eliot Rahal and Geof Shaw
SBN 978-1-50670-482-1 | $24.99

THE BLACK BEETLE
Francesco Francavilla
NO WAY OUT
SBN 978-1-61655-202-2 | $19.99

KARA BOCEK
SBN 978-1-50670-537-8 | $12.99

THE COMPLETE ANGEL CATBIRD
Margaret Atwood and Johnnie Christmas
SBN 978-1-50670-456-2 | $24.99

MICHAEL AVON OEMING'S THE VICTORIES
Michael Avon Oeming
VOLUME 1: TOUCHED
SBN 978-1-61655-100-1 | $9.99

VOLUME 2: TRANSHUMAN
SBN 978-1-61655-214-5 | $17.99

VOLUME 3: POSTHUMAN
SBN 978-1-61655-445-3 | $17.99

VOLUME 4: METAHUMAN
SBN 978-1-61655-517-7 | $17.99

HELLBOY OMNIBUS
Mike Mignola and others
VOLUME 1: SEED OF DESTRUCTION
SBN 978-1-50670-666-5 | $24.99

VOLUME 2: STRANGE PLACES
SBN 978-1-50670-667-2 | $24.99

VOLUME 3: THE WILD HUNT
SBN 978-1-50670-668-9 | $24.99

HELLBOY IN HELL
SBN 978-1-50670-749-5 | $24.99

ORIGINAL VISIONS—THRILLING TALES!

"These superheroes ain't no boy scouts in spandex. They're a high-octane blend of the damaged, quixotic heroes of pulp and detective fiction and the do-gooders in capes from the Golden and Silver Ages."
—Duane Swierczynski

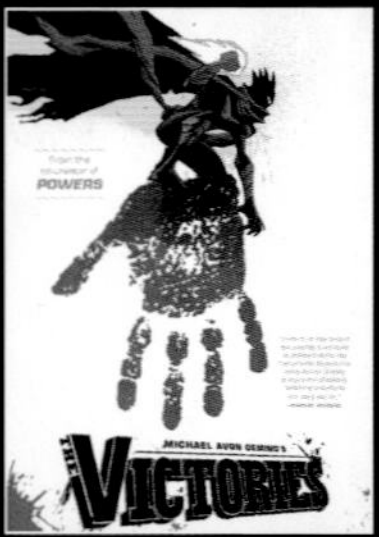
MICHAEL AVON OEMING'S
THE VICTORIES

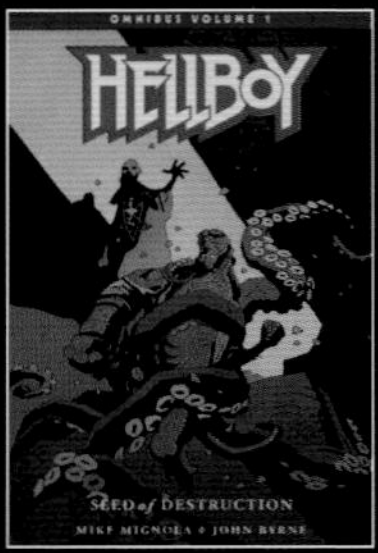
OMNIBUS VOLUME 1
HELLBOY
SEED of DESTRUCTION
MIKE MIGNOLA • JOHN BYRNE

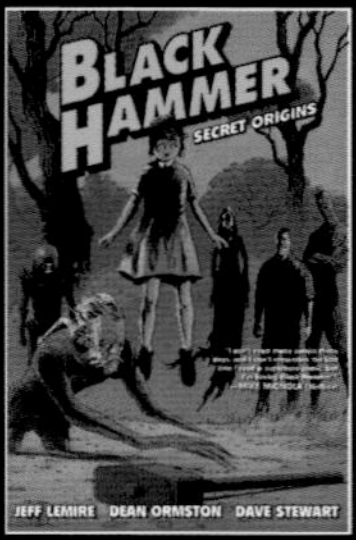
BLACK HAMMER
SECRET ORIGINS
JEFF LEMIRE DEAN ORMSTON DAVE STEWART

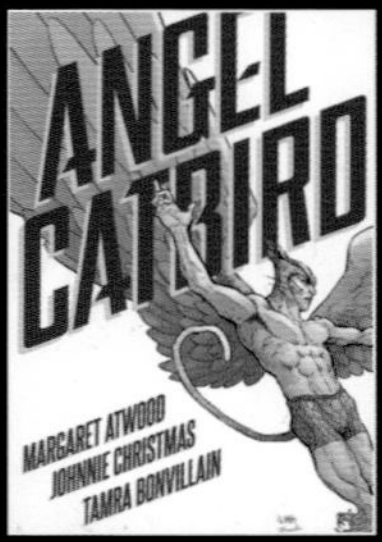
ANGEL CATBIRD
MARGARET ATWOOD
JOHNNIE CHRISTMAS
TAMRA BONVILLAIN

AVAILABLE AT YOUR LOCAL COMICS SHOP OR BOOKSTORE! • To find a comics shop in your area, visit comicshoplocator.com. For more information or to order direct visit DarkHorse.com or call 1-800-862-0052 Mon.–Fri. 9 a.m. to 5 p.m. Pacific Time. Prices and availability subject to change without notice.

BLACKSAD
DÍAZ CANALES GUARNIDO

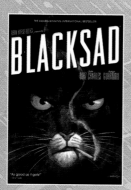

BLACKSAD

Juan Díaz Canales and Juanjo Guarnido

The *Blacksad* books first took Europe by storm in 2000 and sold over 200,000 copies in France alone. Now Dark Horse Comics presents the beautifully painted stories of private investigator John Blacksad, up to his feline ears in mystery, digging into the backstories behind murders, child abductions, and nuclear secrets.

Volume 1
978-1-59582-393-9 | $29.99
Volume 2: A Silent Hell
978-1-59582-931-3 | $19.99

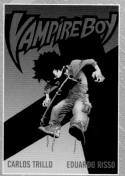

VAMPIRE BOY
CARLOS TRILLO
EDUARDO RISSO

VAMPIRE BOY

Carlos Trillo and Eduardo Risso

Left nameless by his father and sentenced to eternal life by a trick of fate and fortune, the protagonist of Carlos Trillo and Eduardo Risso's *Vampire Boy* has spent fifty centuries in a body that never ages, locked in an eternal struggle with a rival as immortal as he. Acclaimed writer Carlos Trillo teams with legendary artist Eduardo Risso (*100 Bullets*) to produce a poignantly engrossing twist on the classic vampire mythos, now presented in English for the first time!

978-1-59582-562-9 | $24.99

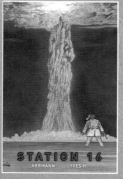

STATION 16
HERMANN
YVES H.

STATION 16

Hermann and Yves H.

May 1997, Russia, north of the Arctic Circle: A border patrol rookie receives a distress call from the long-abandoned Station 16, uninhabited since the heyday of massive nuclear testing more than thirty years ago. When he and his squad fly out to investigate the call, they find an injured man who claims that the rookie was his attacker—and suddenly a nuclear explosion blasts the sky!

978-1-61655-481-1 | $19.99

ENTER A WORLD OF MAGIC AND FANTASY!
DRAGONERO
Luca Enoch • Stefano Vietti • Giuseppe Matteoni

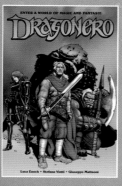

DRAGONERO

Luca Enoch, Stefano Vietti, and Giuseppe Matteoni

Beyond the civilized lands of Erondàr, the Stone Towers are crumbling. The great monoliths are falling one after another under the wild thrusts of an evil force. The Ancient Prohibition that binds the Abominables inside their dark world is soon to be broken. Alben the Wizard will send for Myrva, a young follower of the powerful Technocrats; he will choose Ecuba, the fighting nun, to protect him; and he will call back Ian Aranill, a former Empire officer—followed by Gmor the Orc, his loyal friend—to use his scouting experience. Together they will face the Painers, the evil beings who still live in the barren Dragonlands. Can Ian prevail against the last, horrible threat they will be facing?

978-1-59582-291-8 | $19.99

"If you think there's no r… another superhero comic, *Black Hammer* might just prove you wrong."—IGN

BLACK HAMMER

ONCE THEY WERE HEROES, but the age of heroes has long since passed. Banished from existence by a multiversal crisis, the old champions of Spiral City—Abraham Slam, Golden Gail, Colonel Weird, Madame Dragonfly, and Barbalien—now lead simple lives in an idyllic, timeless farming village from which there is no escape! And yet, the universe isn't done with them—it's time for one last grand adventure.

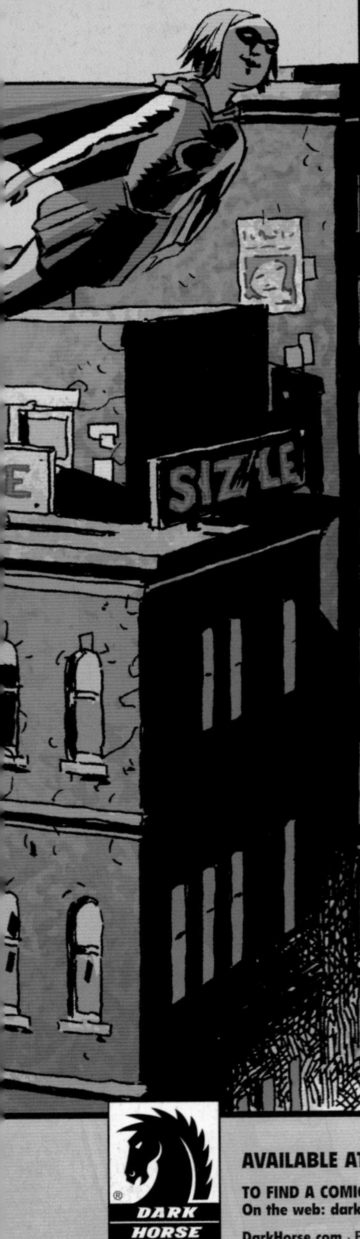
SIZ LE

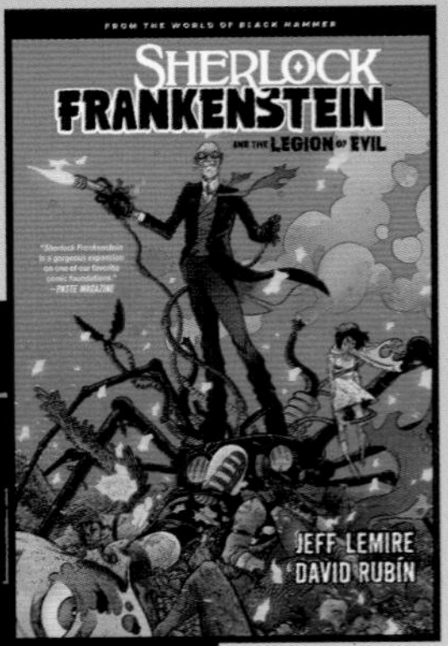
FROM THE WORLD OF BLACK HAMMER
SHERLOCK FRANKENSTEIN
AND THE LEGION OF EVIL
JEFF LEMIRE
DAVID RUBÍN

BLACK HAMMER
Written by Jeff Lemire
Art by Dean Ormston

VOLUME 1: SECRET ORIGINS
978-1-61655-786-7 • $14.99

VOLUME 2: THE EVENT
978-1-50670-198-1 • $19.99

VOLUME 3: AGE OF DOOM
978-1-50670-389-3 • $19.99

BLACK HAMMER LIBRARY EDITION VOLUME 1
978-1-50671-073-0 • $49.99

SHERLOCK FRANKENSTEIN & THE LEGION OF EVIL
Written by Jeff Lemire • Art by David Rubín
This mystery follows a reporter determined to find out what happened to her father, the Black Hammer. All answers seem to lie in Spiral City's infamous insane asylum, where some dangerous supervillain tenants reside, including Black Hammer's greatest foe—Sherlock Frankenstein!
978-1-50670-526-2 • $17.99

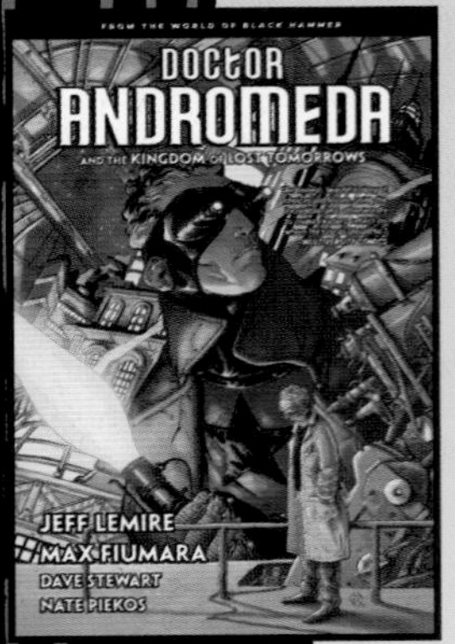
FROM THE WORLD OF BLACK HAMMER
DOCTOR ANDROMEDA
AND THE KINGDOM OF LOST TOMORROWS
JEFF LEMIRE
MAX FIUMARA
DAVE STEWART
NATE PIEKOS

DOCTOR ANDROMEDA & THE KINGDOM OF LOST TOMORROWS
Written by Jeff Lemire • Art by Max Fiumara
This dual-narrative story set in the world of *Black Hammer* chronicles the legacy of a Golden-Age superhero wishing to reconnect with his estranged son, whom he hoped would one day take the mantle of Doctor Andromeda.
978-1-50670-659-7 • $17.99

THE QUANTUM AGE: FROM THE WORLD OF BLACK HAMMER
Written by Jeff Lemire • Art by Wilfredo Torres
A thousand years in the future, a collection of superheroes, inspired by the legendary heroes of Black Hammer Farm, must band together to save the planet from an authoritarian regime, while a young Martian struggles to solve the riddle of what happened to the great heroes of the twentieth century.

VOLUME 1
978-1-50670-841-6 • $19.99

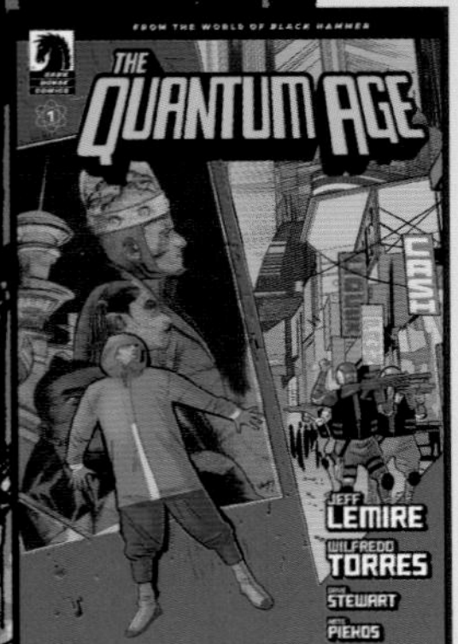
FROM THE WORLD OF BLACK HAMMER
THE QUANTUM AGE
JEFF LEMIRE
WILFREDO TORRES
STEWART
PIEKOS

BLACK HAMMER: STREETS OF SPIRAL
Jeff Lemire, Dean Ormston, Emi Lenox, and others
A Lovecraftian teen decides she will do anything to make herself "normal," a bizarre witch guides her guests through her house of horrors, and an all-star slate of guest artists illustrate a bizarre adventure with Colonial Weird on the farm. Also features a complete world guide to the *Black Hammer* universe and its characters!
978-1-50670-941-3 • $19.99

BLACK HAMMER '45: FROM THE WORLD OF BLACK HAMMER
With Jeff Lemire, Ray Fawkes, and Sharlene Kindt
During the Golden Age of superheroes, an elite Air Force crew called the Black Hammer Squadron bands together to combat the Nazis, a host of occult threats, and their ultimate aerial warrior the Ghost Hunter.
978-1-50670-850-8 • $17.99

DARK HORSE BOOKS

AVAILABLE AT YOUR LOCAL COMICS SHOP OR BOOKSTORE

TO FIND A COMICS SHOP IN YOUR AREA, VISIT COMICSHOPLOCATOR.COM. FOR MORE INFORMATION OR TO ORDER DIRECT:
On the web: darkhorse.com • E-mail: mailorder@darkhorse.com • Phone: 1-800-862-0052 Mon.–Fri. 9 a.m. to 5 p.m. Pacific Time.